SIR DOUGLAS HAIG'S
GREAT PUSH

THE BATTLE OF THE SOMME

A Popular, Pictorial and Authoritative Work on one of the
Great Battles in History, illustrated by about 700 wonderful
OFFICIAL PHOTOGRAPHS & CINEMATOGRAPH
FILMS and other authentic Pictures

BY ARRANGEMENT WITH THE WAR OFFICE

CONTAINING
597 BLACK AND WHITE ILLUSTRATIONS
AND 2 MAPS

LONDON: HUTCHINSON & CO., PATERNOSTER ROW

Printed and bound by Antony Rowe Ltd, Eastbourne

CONTENTS

LETTERPRESS

	PAGE
HISTORICAL INTRODUCTION: AUGUST, 1914—JUNE, 1916	3
CHAPTER I.	19
CHAPTER II.	42
CHAPTER III.	66
CHAPTER IV.	101
CHAPTER V.	136
CHAPTER VI.	174
CHAPTER VII.	209
CHAPTER VIII.	245
CHAPTER IX.	301
CHAPTER X.	333
CHAPTER XI.	361

MAPS AND PLANS

	PAGE
MAP TO ILLUSTRATE THE FIRST FEW DAYS OF THE GREAT PUSH	18
A GERMAN TUNNELLED DUG-OUT	183

ILLUSTRATIONS

	PAGE
General Sir Douglas Haig introducing General Joffre to Lieutenant-General Sir Pertab Singh	2
A sentry going up to his post	3
A view in Mametz after the bombardment	4
A view of the guns and mortars captured at the beginning of the Great Offensive	5
Searching German prisoners	5
Bringing in the wounded	6
A star shell bursting at night near our lines	7
Canadian infantry entrenches in a wood	8
An anti-aircraft gun firing at night	9
Red Cross men in the trenches attending to a wounded man	10
Australian pioneers at work behind the trenches in the Great Advance	11
German prisoners being brought in from Contalmaison	12
His Majesty the King on the battlefield looking at the grave of an unknown British soldier	13
A sentry in the trenches looking through an improvised periscope	14
The Great Assault of July 1st	15
Indian cavalry on the battlefield	15
German dead in a German first-line trench	16
The German trenches being blown up by a great mine before the assault	17
Two illustrations showing the British in preparation for the Great Advance in Picardy	19
Activities on the part of the Army Service Corps and artillery behind the British line between Fricourt-Mametz	19
A platoon of the Buffs (East Kents) answering roll-call at Bray prior to going forward to the front-line trenches	20
A platoon of the Bedfords moving up on the evening before the attack	20
While these great preparations were going on, industrious French peasants continued their daily work in the fields just outside the firing-line	20
A battalion of the Royal Welsh Fusiliers moving up on the evening before the attack	21
Evening before the attack	21
Stretcher-bearers marching by	21
Mules carrying baggage	21
More troops with a motor-cyclist rushing past at over thirty miles an hour	21
The whole battalion and its accompaniment passes	21
Unloading boxes of shells from transport wagons	22
There were vast stores of ammunition and dozens of empty limbers drawn up ready to be filled with shells	23
Horses being brought to water troughs specially set up	23
The mascot of the Royal Field Artillery caught in France	24
A transport wagon coming up to where the limbers are and bringing from the base hundreds of shells	24
Heavy bombardment of the German trenches	25
Re-filling limbers with 18-pounder shells after "dumping" the empty cases	26
Unpacking shells	27
A 4.7 gun being loaded	28
Here the same gun as shown on the previous page has been loaded and its sights adjusted ready to fire	29
The same gun is here shown immediately after being fired. Notice the recoil due to the force of the explosion	29
The men passing up the ammunition to the limbers hand to hand	30
The Hampshires moving up to the attack	31

Illustrations

	PAGE
One of our guns drawn up to a favourite position at the back of the firing-line	32
One of the many large "dumps" of empty cases, which could be seen over the entire front after the great artillery preparations previous to the attack	32
A 6-inch howitzer in action shelling the German first-line trenches at Mametz	33
The Lancashire Fusiliers being addressed by their Divisional Commander on the eve of the battle	34
Several 6-inch howitzers preparing to fire on the German first-line trenches at Mametz	35
East Yorks on the march to the front line	36
"Hot work at the guns." The gunners are busily engaged in putting over a curtain fire or barrage	37
One of the wonderful Canadian 60-pounders	38
A view of the same Canadian gun as shown on the previous page taken from within the gun-pit	39
Shrapnel bursting over the trenches keeps the Germans astir	39
The London Scottish starting for the trenches, led by their pipers and drummers	40
Officers and men of the London Scottish wearing steel helmets, which saved many a life during the Great Advance	40
A German shell bursting behind the British trenches	41
The Wiltshire Regiment on their way to the front	42
A wiring party going up to the trenches	43
The East Yorks marching to the trenches	44
This illustration and the one on the opposite page—	44
—show fine panoramic views of the Manchesters' church parade on the evening before the attack	45
Rank and file of the East Yorks	45
A huge "dump" of "plum-puddings"	46
Firing "plum-puddings" into the German trenches	47
A sergeant organizing the supply of bombs and an officer checking them	48
The men carrying up the bombs from the "dumps" under the direction of a non-commissioned officer	48
Men at work loading a 9.2-inch howitzer	49
Bombarding the Germans with 9.2-inch howitzers	49
High-explosive shells fired by the 12-inch howitzers	50
Preparing to load a heavy howitzer. Hoisting the shell	51
A complimentary message to Fritz	52
Ramming a shell into a 12-inch howitzer	53
Preparing the gun previous to firing	53
The gun in position after being fired	53
These high-explosive shells are fired by the 12-inch howitzers which have created such havoc in the enemy's lines	54
Royal Warwickshires in camp	55
The Royal Warwickshires waiting to receive their portion of stew	56
Men of the Royal Warwickshires having a meal in camp on the evening before the Great Advance	56
A view taken from the British trenches showing a shell bursting over Beaumont-Hamel	57
A further moving up of troops	57
A battalion of the Worcesters fixing wire-cutters to their rifles for forcing the German barbed-wire entanglements	58
A new battalion of the Royal Warwickshires resting on their way to the trenches	58
Royal Warwickshires resting in reserve	59
The Royal Warwickshires resting	60

	PAGE
A field battery brought up across the captured German trenches, in action within two hours of the Germans retiring	61
Two dumb victims—horses killed in bringing the battery up	61
The catch of a 9.45-inch trench mortar being released to enable it to be revolved on its base	62
The gun is being pushed round for the gunners to load with a "flying pig," as the ammunition is called	62
Here the gun is shown being lowered and loaded	62
It is then raised again—	63
—and revolved back to its former position and prepared for firing	63
—The men then retire, and the bomb is fired into the German trenches	63
A huge shell, weighing 1,400 lbs., ready to be fired by the 15-inch howitzer, or "Grandmother," as it is called	64
These shells tore up the ground and made great craters, which would be large enough in many cases to hold a motor-'bus	65
Over twenty shells, each weighing 1,400 lbs., before they were fired by "Grandmother" on the German lines	65
Operating the 15-inch howitzer, or "Grandmother," manned by the Royal Marine Artillery	66
Loading a 15-inch howitzer, or "Grandmother"	67
A 15-inch howitzer, or "Grandmother," firing its 1,400 lbs. shell	68
The morning of the attack, July 1st, 1916	69
Terrific bombardment of the German trenches	69
A Lancashire battalion awaiting instructions	70
Anzacs resting for a few minutes on their way to the trenches	70
Troops moving up a communication-trench into the front line	71
The Loyal North Lancashire Regiment parading for the trenches	72
A big railway gun firing	73
Setting a machine-gun on the top of the parapet	74
A machine-gun being adjusted	74
Just before the attack. Blowing up the enemy trenches by a huge mine. Successive stages in the explosion	75
Troops coming through a wood	76
An officer in our front-line trenches watching the explosion of the mine shown on page 75	77
Engineers rushing off to wire the crater for occupation by the advance troops	77
At a signal along the entire sixteen-mile front the British troops leaped over the trench parapet and advanced towards the German trenches under heavy rifle and machine-gun fire	78 & 79
A panorama of a part of our line showing on the—	80
—extreme left of the picture a machine-gun in action	81
A panoramic view of the assault on La Boiselle on July 1st, showing—	80
—our troops rushing to occupy the trenches after our artillery bombardment	81
Here our troops are shown advancing over the barbed-wire entanglement	82
A sunken road in "No Man's Land" occupied by the Lancashire Fusiliers	82
Warwickshires advancing up a captured trench to relieve the Queen's in the front line	82
A long white line. A common sight in France	83

Illustrations

	PAGE
British troops attacking German trenches at Mametz	84
A scene in the trenches at night on July 1st, after the first day of the battle	85
British Tommies rescuing a comrade under shell fire	86
Stretcher-bearers bringing in the wounded on wheeled-stretchers	86
A captured German trench. A view of an old German trench. Ovillers can be seen in the background. The white chalk trench can be followed for miles	87
A captured German trench after our bombardment	88
These four pictures show one of our Tommies bringing a seriously wounded man along a trench to a dressing-station	89
Bringing in the wounded during the battle	90
Miners in a mine-chamber laying a charge	90
Bringing in a wounded German prisoner and placing him in one of our dug-outs	91
The first batch of German prisoners to come in after the successful assault on July 1st	92
Bringing in the wounded on stretchers through the trenches during the height of the battle	93
Helping along a wounded German prisoner	94
Stretcher-bearers bringing in a wounded man	94
Placing the wounded man under the charge of a R.A.M.C. man	94
Bringing in German prisoners	95
German prisoners—wounded and unwounded—being brought in near Carnoy	96
A captured mine-crater	97
Signallers operating during the British advance	98
Bombardment of Fricourt on the 2nd of July	99
One of the captured mine-craters	99
Samples of captured machine-guns, etc., German trench-mortar, German machine-gun, Russian machine-gun, and automatic rifle	100
Captures made during the first days of the advance: two periscopes with cases, one telephone, one gas-helmet, and one first aid for gas-poisoning (Selbstretter) are shown	100
A view of a trench, Ovillers	101
An aeroplane going out to reconnoitre	102
A kite-balloon ascending during the advance	103
Two photographs showing an interior of a signal exchange during the battle	104
Bringing in a wounded soldier	105
Royal Engineers moving their home	105
The Royal Field Artillery moving up during the battle over ground where the Gordons' and Devons' dead are lying	106
Another photograph showing the Royal Field Artillery moving up	106
A view of Fricourt, captured on the 2nd of July by the British	107
Anti-aircraft guns about to fire on hostile aircraft	108
Canadian infantry in the trenches, wearing the new steel helmets	109
Men of a West Indian regiment watching a German aeroplane being chased by our planes	110
Artillerymen examining a German gun captured by the Royal Irish, prior to firing into the German lines with it	111
Activity at Minden Post	112–113
Scenes in "Dantzig Alley," captured and held by a battalion of the Manchesters	112–113
A captured trench mortar	114
One of the five unsuccessful German counter-attacks at La Boiselle	114
Australian machine-gunners returning from the trenches	115
Labour battalion making a road over ground recently captured	116
Stretcher cases for the ambulance	117
The wounded waiting their turn for treatment	117
A wounded soldier being handed a cigarette after his wounds have been dressed	118
Scenes at the dressing-station for slightly wounded at Minden Post. The soldier shown in the above four illustrations has been wounded in both arms, and is having his wounds temporarily dressed	119
Further scenes at Minden Post dressing-station	120
More German prisoners being rounded up and brought in by battle-police from No Man's Land	120
Wounded soldiers leaving the dressing-station after having their wounds attended to	120
Prisoners in compound awaiting transportation	121
A 75-mm. field-gun captured near Montauban	122
A captured German field-gun	123
A German machine-gun and an automatic rifle captured	124
A captured German trench-gun	124
A view of another captured German trench-mortar	125
A captured German 10-cm. field-gun	126
A captured German trench-mortar	127
A captured German field-gun	127
Some machine-guns captured by our troops on the 1st of July	128
The mascot of the Anzacs	129
A view of Ovillers	130
A little music by the Black Watch after coming back from the capture of Longueval	131
Scenes behind the Anzac trenches	132
A night scene within the Australian lines	133
A view in Mametz Wood	134
A German look-out post in Mametz Wood	135
A monster gun in action	136
Two pictures showing our men clearing the battlefield of snipers and hidden machine-guns	137
Routing Germans from dug-outs	137
Handing out letters	138
The post reaches the Devonshires during battle	139
A big howitzer in action	139
Royal Fusiliers resting after the storming of La Boiselle	140
Effect of British shell fire on German trenches between Fricourt and Mametz	141
Scenes on the battlefield	141
The Manchesters' pet dog fell with his master, charging Dantzig Alley	142
Wrecked dug-outs, twenty to thirty feet under level of field	142
Scenes on the battlefield	143
The battered German stronghold at Fricourt	144
A view of the battlefield showing a mine-crater on the right-hand side	145
A mine-crater forty feet deep	145
A view of the shell-shattered village of Mametz	146
A distant view of the shell-shattered village of Mametz	146
A view of the wrecked main street of Mametz	147
Wrecked German village of Mametz	147
The battered German stronghold at Fricourt. On the left our men can be seen repairing the road	148

Illustrations

	PAGE
Wrecked German dug-outs	148
A few of the captured trench-mortars near La Boiselle	149
Some of the captured guns near La Boiselle	150
A welcome rest: Lancashire Fusiliers after the battle	151
Tired out: Lancashire Fusiliers having a well-earned rest after the battle	151
Lancashire Fusiliers resting after the battle	152
Royal Fusiliers cleaning up after the successful advance	152
Essex Regiment washing up at a wayside pool	153
Roll-call of the Seaforth Highlanders	153
Another view of the Royal Fusiliers cleaning up after the successful advance	153
Examining the ammunition for machine-guns after the battle	154
Cleaning up machine-guns	154
A cheery group of gunners	154
A heavy howitzer	155
Some of our giant howitzers in hiding, and their shells	156
German wounded prisoners being put on board an ambulance after treatment at the special field-hospital for wounded prisoners	157
Conducting German prisoners to rail-head for transport to England	158
Effect of one high-explosive shell on barbed-wire entanglement	159
Bringing up an 8-inch howitzer and placing it in an advanced position in the next bombardment	160
Bringing up an 8-inch howitzer	161
Seeking further laurels: The Worcesters off to continue the Great Advance	162
A view in Trônes Wood	162
A German observation-post in Trônes Wood	163
Troops resting in German trenches	164
A crater made by a German aerial torpedo	165
Some of the German prisoners at Carnoy just after they were captured on the 14th of July	165
On the horizon of this picture once stood a flourishing village, La Boiselle	166
Further view of wrecked German dug-outs	166
Another view of German ammunition wagons destroyed by our bombardment	167
German ammunition wagons near Mametz Wood destroyed by our artillery fire	169
Trophies captured by the Sherwood Foresters. The dog was found in a German dug-out	169
An armoured car in France	170
Our men are very comfortable in the old German dug-outs	171
British shells bursting on the German trenches	172
Australians parading for the trenches	173
Bringing up water-pipes to supply the men in the front line with water	174
Germans cleaning some of the captured guns and trench-mortars	175
Some shells and men who know how to use them	176
Tired out: A gunner asleep on live shells	176
Cat-o'-nine-tails found in the German trenches	177
The connecting passage of a dug-out	177
Petrol cans filled up with water ready to be taken up to the men in the trenches	178
German barbed-wire entanglements	179
Allies' barbed-wire entanglements	179
This shows a tunnelled corridor which runs straight forward for anything up to fifty yards, out of which open various rooms and passages on each side	180

	PAGE
A view in the officers' quarters of the dug-outs	180
This illustration shows the main entrance, through a steel door, to one of the German trench houses	180
These staircases, passages and rooms are lined throughout with wood, and are as fully strengthened with it as the entrance staircase	181
A section of the mine which the Germans blew up under the base of the old crater at the moment of the advance in July	181
The nights begin to get cold, so the men don their winter clothes	182
Bombardment by heavy trench-mortars	184
A huge mine going up	184
A peep into a casualty clearing-station just behind the line	185
The river hospital	186
Patients being taken on board a hospital barge	187
Motor-'buses taking the Takers of Guillemont away to rest	188
View of a mine-crater being consolidated	189
Trench-mortar bombs in a reserve trench ready for use	190
Indian cavalry waiting to advance on July 14th	191
Indian cavalry on the move, July 15th	192
Working behind a smoke attack	193
The centre, or High Street, of Guillemont after it was taken	194
A smashed Boche trench at Morval	195
Australians returning from the trenches with their mascot	196
Irish Brigade returning from Guillemont	197
An old British trench near Fricourt. This gives an idea of the number of sandbags used in trench construction	198
Mr. Asquith watching men adjusting fuses	199
General Birdwood meets some of the Australians in a wood after the battle	200
King Albert of Belgium introducing his Generals to King George	201
German prisoners arriving at a divisional cage in motor-lorries	202
THE KING IN FRANCE: The illustration, from left to right, shows General Joffre, President Poincaré, King George, General Foch and General Haig	203
Australian troops cheering the King	204
The King is carrying a bouquet which was presented to him by a little girl	205
The King in a gun-pit	206
The King passing between two mine craters near Mametz	207
The King on the battlefield with Sir Henry Rawlinson and General Congreve	208
The King meets the matron of a hospital	209
The King outside a German dug-out	210
The King attends church service among his troops	211
The King conversing with wounded officers	212
The King in a captured German trench	213
Sorting the packs of dead and wounded for letters, etc., to send to relations	214
A German machine-gun emplacement smashed up by our artillery	215
Royal Engineers on the march	216
Gun captured in Mametz Wood	217
Captured German howitzer photographed on the battlefield	218
Tommy's cookhouse near Thiépval	219

Illustrations

	PAGE
Scene at the burial of some of our men behind the line.	220
View in Pozières	221
Scene at an aerodrome	222
Everything is so well arranged in this advance that Tommies can get their water from the main just behind the front line	223
Putting up a water-trough for the cavalry	223
A view of Mametz	224
Preparing for winter in the trenches	225
Making a road through captured ground	226
An observation balloon and its nurse in a pit	227
Men of the R.F.C. bringing up a nurse balloon	228
How a German trench between Cuinchy and Guillemont looked after our infantry had taken it	229
A view of what was once the railway station of Guillemont	230
Stretcher-bearers and dressing-station at Guillemont	231
Respirator drill for the Guards near the Somme	232
Drawing water for the guns' crews. Working a heavy gun is thirsty work	233
Once the main road of Guillemont	234
An advanced dressing-station. A Red Cross flag is affixed to the tree	235
Cavalry on the march	236
Ammunition pack-horses going up to the front during the battle of the 15th of September	237
Cavalry on the march near the Somme	238
A British graveyard, a smashed railway track, German ammunition left in their retreat, and a transport wagon going up to the front line	239
Battlefield sign-posts	240
View of Thiépval	240
A broken-down ambulance on the battlefield	241
A view in Delville Wood	242
View of Flers	243
View of Flers: The main street	243
One of the roads of Flers	244
Taking up boarding for bottom of trenches	244
Red Cross men carrying wounded over the top of the trench in Thiépval village	245
Comfort! An officer's dug-out, with his washing-stand and his bedding out to air or dry	246
Australians cheer the King	247
A model place for watering horses	248
A few plum-puddings that Fritz will soon receive: trench-mortar ammunition	249
Travelling water-butts	250
Transport men cleaning their harness at a pond after the wet weather	251
Infantry waiting to advance on the 25th of September	252
Waiting to advance on the 25th of September	253
A scene of desolation; once a village	254
A bombing party off to the attack	255
View of Morval, which we captured on the 25th of September	256
General view of Morval, which we captured on the 25th of September	257
The entrance of a captured German dug-out	258
Ruins of Combles	259
View of Combles	260
Some of the large ammunition left when the Huns had to clear out of Morval	261
One of the Boche gun-emplacements at Combles. Note the great baulks of timber	262
Combles: Main street	263
View of square at Combles	264
Clearing up a battlefield after an advance	265
Laying a railroad as we advance	266
Indian cavalry despatch-rider coming back from Flers	267
Big guns ready to move up	268
A mishap to a despatch-rider's bike	269
One of our many light railways	270
Slinging a big gun round to haul up into position	271
Taking up a big gun with a twelve-horse team and the help of the gun crew	272
How our artillery dealt with a German battery at Martinpuich	273
"Cab, sir!" Found in a captured village	274
Moving-day in a captured village	275
A scene on the battlefield, near Ginchy	276
A light railway engine made out of the parts of a discarded motor-car	277
Taking up medical stores	278
Motor machine-guns taking cover in a sunken road	279
A parade of the wounded walking cases	280
A light railway taking up its own rails to lay as we advance	281
The church bells of Montauban	282
The military cemetery, showing the grave of Colonel Fuchs, of the Russian Imperial General Staff, who was killed recently, while attached to the British armies in France	283
Where the British line joins up with the French the two batteries have a tug-of-war	284
A South African at home	285
The mail arrives	286
A scene in one of the German trenches in front of Guillemont, showing the havoc wrought by the British bombardment	287
Wounded men waiting to be taken away to the clearing station	288
Cleaning a captured German machine-gun	289
Stretcher-bearers on their way near Ginchy to bring back the wounded	290
A scene near Guillemont: An armoured motor-car	291
A scene on the battlefield near Courcelette	292
Waiting their turn to advance	293
Waves of infantry going with a Tank	294
German prisoners marching back past one of our Tanks	295
A large German shell which did not explode. By the side of it is one of the smaller brand, commonly called a whizz-bang	296
How bad water is guarded	296
How Tommy's food is cooked. The field kitchen works always in spite of wet weather	297
Group of our gallant airmen in front of one of our machines	298
A scene on the road	299
Engineers on the road	300
Mr. Massey coming out of a German dug-out	301
Some of the German prisoners taken on September 15th	302
New Zealanders on the rank to get things from the field canteen	303
The cavalry are very anxious to get to work	304
Heavy trench-mortar pit	305
A rest on a shattered motor-car	306
Albert Church	307
Worcesters returning from the trenches through the rain	308

Illustrations

	PAGE
Rolling a big pile up for bridging purposes	309
A wounded Tommy showing his helmet with a piece blown out	310
A cavalry patrol	311
A few of our empties	312
Returning from the trenches. "And everywhere that Tommy went, the goat was sure to go"	313
The French official kinematographer taking a close picture of one of our wounded	314
Taking up ammunition along the very muddy roads	315
Moving up the guns	316
Carrying a wounded man down to an ambulance	317
Inspection of the Guards by H.R.H. the Duke of Connaught: H.R.H. the Duke of Connaught calls for three cheers for His Majesty the King	318
Middlesex Regiment returning from the trenches in the pouring rain	319
Tommies arriving home at Mud Terrace	320
In a captured German dug-out. The Germans have made some very fine dug-outs	321
"I would like to borrow your coat, old chap"	322
Coldstreamers march past the Duke of Connaught after the inspection	323
At the inspection of the Guards by H.R.H. the Duke of Connaught	323
The Duke of Connaught inspects Irish troops	324
H.R.H. the Duke of Connaught issued an order for the police to allow the villagers up close to see the inspection	325
Inspection of the Guards by H.R.H. the Duke of Connaught. Guards marching past H.R.H. the Duke of Connaught after the inspection	326–7
The massed drums and pipes of the Guards at the inspection	326–7
At the inspection: Passing down the line	328
British soldiers' graves in France	329
Wiring parties going up to the front line after heavy rain	330
An early morning scene on the battlefield before the assault on the 15th of September	331
"Woodman, spare the tree." Highlanders in a wood	332
In a new trench	333
Cigarette firms send the different batteries cigarettes, and the sergeant is seen receiving a packet	334
Highlanders working on the roads	335
Free soup for our Tommies	336
Working on the roads	337
Some men of a navvy battalion at work on the Ancre	338
Wood is used for making up the roads on the Somme. Scene in a wood	339
The cook saves a large one for himself	340
The snob and the cook are opponents at this game, while Tommy looks on. The man on the left made this board and chessmen himself	341
Returning from leave and nearing the old spot again	342
Tommy at home in his winter quarters	343
Big shells for one of our guns	344
Clearing up German trenches at St. Pierre Divion	345
Bringing up big shells for our guns	346
A wintry scene on the Western Front	347
A scene on the Somme in the recent snowstorm	348
Boche machine-guns captured at Beaucourt-sur-Ancre	349
A smashed-up mill near St. Pierre Divion	350
Prince Arthur of Connaught decorating a French sergeant. With him is General Fayolle, commanding 6th Army	351
Prince Arthur of Connaught decorating a French General	352
Officers laying out the decorations	353
Returning for more ammunition	354
A water refilling point	355
On the road to the trenches	356
Returning from the trenches	357
Muddy mules	358
Moving up the guns	359
An army chaplain helping along a Boche prisoner taken on the 23rd	360
Muddy wheels of an ammunition-cart	361
Clearing away mud on the Somme	362
Feeding the guns and upsetting the Huns	363
Thrashing for their own straw for the men	364
After being rescued from the mud	365
Collecting Boche rifles left at St. Pierre Divion	366
A kite-balloon about to ascend	367
Cleaning up his rifle. The only way to wash the woodwork	368
Tommies going up to the trenches	368
Resting in their cage. Boche prisoners taken on the 13th in St. Pierre Divion	369
Once a trench, but now a small river	370
A corner of the great heap of bombs and stores left by the Germans when they were driven out of St. Pierre Divion	371
Field kitchens on the Western Front	372
A message for the Hun	373
The mill at Beaucourt-sur-Ancre	374
The observer of a kite-balloon testing the telephone before ascending	375
A scene on the Ancre	376
Sending a message to the Hun	377
Watering Canadian artillery horses at the front	378
A scene on the roadside	379
One of our armoured petrol engines	380
A busy scene at a watering-point for horses	381
Some of the material collected by parties detailed to clear up the battlefield	382
Smoke-bombs just exploded	383
The weather is very bitter in France. Note the frost on the trees	384
General Gourard visits a school of instruction for officers	385
A scene on the Ancre	386
A scene on the Ancre	387
Another scene on the Ancre	388
Bringing in a wounded Canadian through the mud	389
A German gun after our artillery got through with it. On ground captured by the Canadians	390
Serviceable winter clothing for our troops	391
Two smiling Canadians at their rest billets with German helmets	392

IN ABOUT 8 FORTNIGHTLY PARTS.　　1st EDITION, 100,000 COPIES.　HUTCHINSON'S NEW PART WORK　PART I.　8d. NET

SIR DOUGLAS HAIG'S
GREAT PUSH

THE BATTLE OF THE SOMME

A popular, pictorial and authoritative work on one of the Greatest Battles in History, illustrated by about **700** wonderful **OFFICIAL PHOTOGRAPHS AND CINEMATOGRAPH FILMS** and other authentic pictures

BY ARRANGEMENT WITH THE WAR OFFICE

Searching German Prisoners

GREAT VALUE FOR EIGHTPENCE

THIS PART CONTAINS **81 WONDERFUL REPRODUCTIONS** OF THE FAMOUS **WAR OFFICE CINEMATOGRAPH FILMS** AND **OFFICIAL PHOTOGRAPHS** OF THE BATTLE OF THE SOMME, BEAUTIFULLY PRINTED ON THE BEST ENGLISH ART PAPER.

LONDON : HUTCHINSON & Co.

A REMARKABLE NEW REMEDY

FOR

OBESITY, RHEUMATISM, LUMBAGO, GOUT, SCIATICA, NEURITIS & NERVOUS DISORDERS.

Splendid Success of Mr. Vernon-Ward's Electrical Treatment.

A Perfectly Harmless and Natural System Widely Prescribed by Leading Doctors.

IN health the circulation of the blood performs three important duties. It keeps every part of the body supplied with an adequate proportion of life-giving elements extracted from food; it regulates the quantity of fat stored up; and it collects Uric Acid and various waste products that are continually accumulating in the system and disposes of them before they can do any harm.

Muscular exercise is necessary in order to keep the circulation in full activity. If regular muscular movement is insufficient even in regard to only certain muscles, unhealthy conditions are set up, and various disorders result according to a person's constitution. In some people this lack of constant exercise by allowing an abnormal amount of fat to be stored up produces Obesity. When Uric Acid is allowed to accumulate, Rheumatism, Lumbago, Gout, or Sciatica occur. Others again have Neuritis, Neurasthenia, and Digestive troubles owing to lack of a proper supply of rich nourishing blood. Further, Obesity or Uric Acid disorders may not be general; often only parts of the body are affected.

Although lack of muscular activity produces these disorders, ordinary exercise will not restore a heathy condition again. Changes have taken place in the case of the heart, lungs, or other organs of the body that either make it unsafe to indulge in sufficient exercise or rob one of the energy to partake of it. This is why physical drill as a cure is so unsatisfactory.

Why Mr. Vernon-Ward's Treatment Succeeds where All Other Methods Fail.

In Mr. Vernon-Ward's new Electrical Treatment a means has been discovered of effecting rapid relief and cure by awakening circulatory and muscular activity throughout the body, or at particular areas without either the least fatigue or slightest danger. The Treatment is so harmless and gentle in action that leading doctors are regularly prescribing it even to youthful and elderly patients.

This splendid Treatment administered with so much success by Mr. Vernon-Ward is taken in perfect comfort under ideal conditions without elaborate preparation or lengthy visits. All the patient is required to do is to rest for a little while in a specially constructed chair while a gentle current, perfectly free from pain or sensations, passes through the affected parts. The results are quite permanent, and not only is the particular disorder quickly relieved and cured, but the health is wonderfully invigorated at the same time. It is impossible to accomplish such extensive improvement by any other means, for massage, baths, exercises, or drugs are merely superficial and temporary and have no lasting effect.

Free Particulars will be Supplied at Personal Interview or by Post. Why not Call or Write To-day?

If you are heavier than you should be, or desire the measurements of your bust, waist, hips, or limbs reduced, or if you are a sufferer from Rheumatism, Lumbago, Gout, Sciatica, Neuritis, or Nervous disorders, full details regarding Mr. Vernon-Ward's new Electrical Treatment will be given free of charge or obligation. A personal call is preferable, but if this is impossible at present, particulars will be sent gratis and post free on application to 2, Vere Street, Cavendish Square, W. (facing Marshall & Snelgrove's and New Bond Street), or to the Brighton Establishment, 91, King's Road, Brighton (a few doors from the Grand Hotel).

The King and The Somme Film.

His Majesty the King, after being shown the pictures of the famous War Office Film of the Battle of the Somme, remarked:—"The public should see these pictures that they may have some idea of what the Army is doing, and what war means."

THE famous War Office Cinematograph Film of the Battle of the Somme needs no introduction to intending subscribers to this book. Many millions of people, who have soldier-relatives or friends taking part in the Battle, the greatest in which the brave soldiers of Britain, her Dominions, Colonies and Dependencies have ever fought, have already seen the film, whilst the majority of those who have not yet done so will, in all probability, see it within the next few weeks.

Under the title of "SIR DOUGLAS HAIG'S GREAT PUSH," Messrs. Hutchinson & Co. have prepared an important work with the object of placing within the reach of everyone **a permanent record** of the Great Battle. It will contain popular letterpress accompanied by fine reproductions from this Wonderful Film (now reproduced in book form for the **first time** by arrangement with the War Office), and from the Official Photographs.

All those who have seen the Film will appreciate the opportunity of possessing in volume-form the fine intimate pictures of the Battle itself and the colossal preparations that led up to it, which were on a far larger scale than anything that had hitherto been thought possible.

A great number of these photographs were taken **in the** front line trenches by the Operator, under the direction of the War Office, while the actual Battle was raging, and of course at considerable risk to himself.

As you turn over the illustrated pages of this book at home in your armchair you seem to be transferred to the very front of the Front, and to watch the actual events as they are happening—just as you would have done had you been looking on at the time. You see **War as it really is;** the camera takes in everything and spares nothing.

In selecting the illustrations the Publishers have had the film carefully examined inch by inch, and only the very finest pictures of each subject will be included.

The work will therefore form a unique record of a great page in History, and from an educational point of view its historical value cannot be too greatly emphasized.

We owe it to the men who are giving their lives in the cause of liberty to preserve the record of their glorious sacrifices—we owe it to the generations yet to come, to pass on to them the inspiring example of those who are dying for them, and we owe it to ourselves to know and understand the spirit that is beating back the storm designed to overwhelm us.

Part I. of "Sir Douglas Haig's Great Push" is now before subscribers, and from it they will be able to realize what a beautiful volume the work will make when complete. Its cost is trifling—8d. a fortnight—just over a halfpenny a day—while the complete volume will only amount to a few shillings.

Part II. will be ready on Tuesday, October 10th.

It contains 76 beautifully-printed illustrations, which carry the reader up to the morning of the attack—July 1st. Such interesting subjects as the following are included:

- A GERMAN SHELL BURSTING BEHIND OUR TRENCHES.
- THE WILTSHIRE REGIMENT ON THEIR WAY TO THE FRONT.
- A WIRING PARTY GOING UP TO THE TRENCHES.
- CHURCH SERVICE ON THE EVENING BEFORE THE ATTACK.
- THE EAST YORKS STARTING FOR THE TRENCHES.
- A SUPPLY OF "PLUM PUDDINGS." THESE BOMBS ARE MOST EFFECTIVE IN SMASHING THE ENEMY'S BARBED WIRE ENTANGLEMENTS.
- FIRING "PLUM PUDDINGS" FROM TRENCH MORTARS.
- CARRYING BOMBS UP TO THE MORTARS.
- BOMBARDING THE GERMANS WITH 9·2-INCH HOWITZERS.
- HIGH EXPLOSIVE SHELLS FIRED BY THE 12-INCH HOWITZERS CREATING HAVOC IN THE ENEMY'S LINES.
- A COMPLIMENTARY MESSAGE TO "FRITZ."
- FIRING 12-INCH HOWITZERS.
- SHELLS TEARING UP THE ENEMY'S DUG-OUTS.
- ROYAL WARWICKSHIRES HAVING A MEAL IN CAMP ON THE EVENING BEFORE THE GREAT ADVANCE.
- ROYAL WARWICKSHIRES FEASTING.
- CONTINUOUS SHELL-FIRE FOR FIVE DAYS OVER BEAUMONT HAMEL.
- A FURTHER MOVING UP OF TROOPS. A NEW BATTALION OF THE ROYAL WARWICKSHIRES.
- ROYAL WARWICKSHIRES RESTING ON THEIR WAY TO THE TRENCHES.
- ROYAL WARWICKSHIRES IN RESERVE.
- THE FIELD ARTILLERY IN ACTION.
- DEAD HORSES ON THE BATTLEFIELD.
- THOUSANDS OF "FLYING PIGS" BEING FIRED BY 9·45-INCH TRENCH MORTARS TO SMASH UP THE ENEMY'S TRENCHES AND DUG-OUTS.
- "IRON RATION."
- OPERATING THE 15-INCH HOWITZER. (GRANDMOTHER.)
- "GRANDMOTHER" MANNED BY THE ROYAL MARINE ARTILLERY.
- "GRANDMOTHER" BEING LOADED.
- "GRANDMOTHER" FIRING.
- A TERRIFIC BOMBARDMENT OF THE GERMAN TRENCHES. SHELLS BURSTING.
- A LANCASHIRE BATTALION AWAITING INSTRUCTIONS.
- A LANCASHIRE BATTALION PASSING THROUGH A COMMUNICATION TRENCH TO THE FIRST LINE.
- BOMBERS TAKING UP SUPPLIES, Etc.

Mr. LLOYD GEORGE, Secretary of State for War, sent the following message to introduce the great Somme Film, when shown for the first time at the Scala Theatre:—

> The Battle of the Somme, furious and desperate as it has been, is a first and most important phase of what is an historical struggle; unique in its scope and world-wide significance.
>
> I am convinced that when you have seen this wonderful picture, every heart will beat higher in sympathy with its cause and purpose, which is no other than that every one of us at home and those abroad shall see what our men at the front are doing and suffering for us, and how their achievements have been made possible by the sacrifices made at home.
>
> **Be up and doing also! See that this picture, which is in itself an epic of self-sacrifice and gallantry, reaches everyone. Herald the deeds of our brave men to the ends of the earth. This is your duty.**

It should be remembered that this work will not be limited to the first film of the Battle, which millions have seen, but it will include others just as magnificent which have yet to be shown, and these it is the intention of the publishers to give in their chronological order in the later Parts.

As there has been an enormous demand for Part I. and it is difficult to reprint, owing to the great shortage of labour, those who would like to add this important work to their library should fill in the order form below for Parts I.—VIII., and hand it to their bookseller or newsagent with as little delay as possible.

Orders will only be executed in strict rotation.

ORDER FORM

To M ....
BOOKSELLER or NEWSAGENT,

....

Please send me Part II., Price 8d., and the following parts as published, of "Sir Douglas Haig's Great Push," *for which I enclose* ....

Name ....

Address ....

General Sir Douglas Haig introducing General Joffre to Lieutenant-General Sir Pertab Singh.

HISTORICAL INTRODUCTION

AUGUST, 1914—JUNE, 1916.

WHEN on August 1st, 1914, Germany finally dissipated the last lingering hopes of peace by declaring war upon Russia, she probably flattered herself that the intervention of Great Britain, with her hands full of the Ulster crisis, was an unlikely event, and she most certainly believed that, even if we did enter the contest, we should be powerless to avert or even delay, to any appreciable extent, the triumph which she so confidently anticipated. The war, as the Kaiser and his advisers saw it, would be but a matter of a few months, possibly of a few weeks. While Russia was held in check on the Eastern frontier, the French and the slender forces of their British allies would be crushed, and Germany would emerge from the struggle indisputably the greatest of the world's Powers, with enormous indemnities, which would pay her war bill and abundantly compensate her for the injury that might be inflicted on her commerce by the British

A sentry going up to his post.

Navy. How little did they foresee that the marvellous courage and tenacity of the little army which they, in their arrogance, affected to regard as an almost negligible factor, would enable it to hold the legions of the War Lord at bay, the while the nation behind it prepared for victory on a scale that was to astonish the world!

On August 16th, twelve days after Great Britain had declared war, our first Expeditionary Force, consisting of two army corps and one cavalry division, landed in France, and on the 21st our troops crossed the Belgian frontier and began coming into position on the extreme left of the Allied line, on a front of about twenty-five miles, extending from Condé on the west, just inside the French frontier, past Mons to Binche. Field-Marshal Sir John French was Commander-in-Chief; the 1st Army Corps was under the command of Sir Douglas Haig, one of the youngest of our lieutenant-generals; the 2nd under that of General Sir Horace Smith-Dorrien, who had done brilliant work in South Africa; and Major-General Allenby commanded the cavalry division. Liége, after a gallant defence, had fallen on the 15th; on the 20th the Germans had entered Brussels, and on the extreme left of the advancing tide of invasion their great howitzers were already thundering against the forts of Namur. The 5th French Army held the line of the Sambre, with its headquarters at Charleroi; and the plan of the French Staff was to meet

A view in Mametz after the bombardment.

Historical Introduction

A view of the guns and mortars captured at the beginning of the Great Offensive.

the enemy's onset along the Charleroi–Mons line, and after breaking the first attack, assume the offensive, and advance, with Namur as their pivot. The success of this operation would raise the siege of that fortress, and open the way for the reoccupation of Brussels and a junction of the British left with the Belgian Army.

On the 22nd, the defence of Namur having unexpectedly collapsed, the French were fiercely attacked in front by Von Buelow's army, while two army corps, under Von Hausen, pressed upon their right flank and rear and threatened their line of retreat. Under the stress of this converging attack the 5th Army gave way, and began its retreat southwards. Unfortunately, in the confusion of the retreat, the Staff work broke down, and no information of the collapse of the Sambre defence reached Sir John French until the afternoon of the following day, by which time he found himself engaged, not only with the army of Von Kluck, whose attack he had been expecting, but also with the right wing of Von Buelow's victorious force. Against the vastly superior numbers opposed to them the British made a superb stand, and the losses sustained by the enemy in their attacks in mass formation were very great.

When darkness interrupted the battle our line was still practically intact; but during the night the memorable retreat from Mons began, though the bulk of the army did not abandon the position it had

Searching German prisoners.

so gallantly defended until the early hours of the 24th. The retreat—one of the greatest in history—was conducted in masterly fashion, and the courage and endurance displayed by our men during their long forced marches along the sun-baked high roads, with the enemy pressing hard on their rear, were beyond all praise. Its chief incidents were the desperate night-battle in and around Landrecies and about Maroilles on August 25th, and Smith-Dorrien's heroic rearguard action at Le Cateau, on the following day, which saved our 2nd Corps from being enveloped and destroyed.

BRINGING IN THE WOUNDED.
This man is actually under fire. He brought in no less than twenty wounded men in this manner.

The southward movement continued until the Allies had crossed the Marne, in the first days of September, when Von Kluck, under the pleasing illusion that the British, whom he had been driving for a week, had by this time been reduced to an undisciplined mob, had the temerity to march his right wing across our front, in the hope of driving a wedge between the 5th Army and the British. The Allied commanders at once decided that the moment had come to abandon the defensive and attempt a counter-stroke, and on September 6th a new French army, moving up from the direction of Paris, was thrown against the German right, while the British attacked in front. The counter-stroke was completely successful, and the Battles of the Marne, in which the tide of German invasion was stemmed and rolled back, will undoubtedly rank amongst the most decisive in the world's history.

Meanwhile, in the Eastern theatre of war the Russians, in the hope of relieving the pressure on their Allies, had invaded East Prussia and gained victories at Gumbinnen and Frankenau. But they sustained a terrible defeat at the hands of Von Hindenburg at Tannenberg (August 26th–31st), when the Army of the Narev was almost destroyed. Having been tempted, however, to advance into Poland, Hindenburg was completely defeated in a series of engagements known as the Battle of Augustovo, and in his turn, narrowly escaped destruction. In Galicia the Russians were carrying all before them, the main armies of Austria had been defeated in four great battles, and Lemberg was in their hands. At sea the British had gained the victory of the Heligoland Bight, in which the German cruisers *Mainz* and *Köln* were sunk (August 28th). Beyond Europe the war had spread to every quarter of the globe where Germany possessed a square mile of territory. In the Far East Japan, which had declared war against her on August 23rd, was,

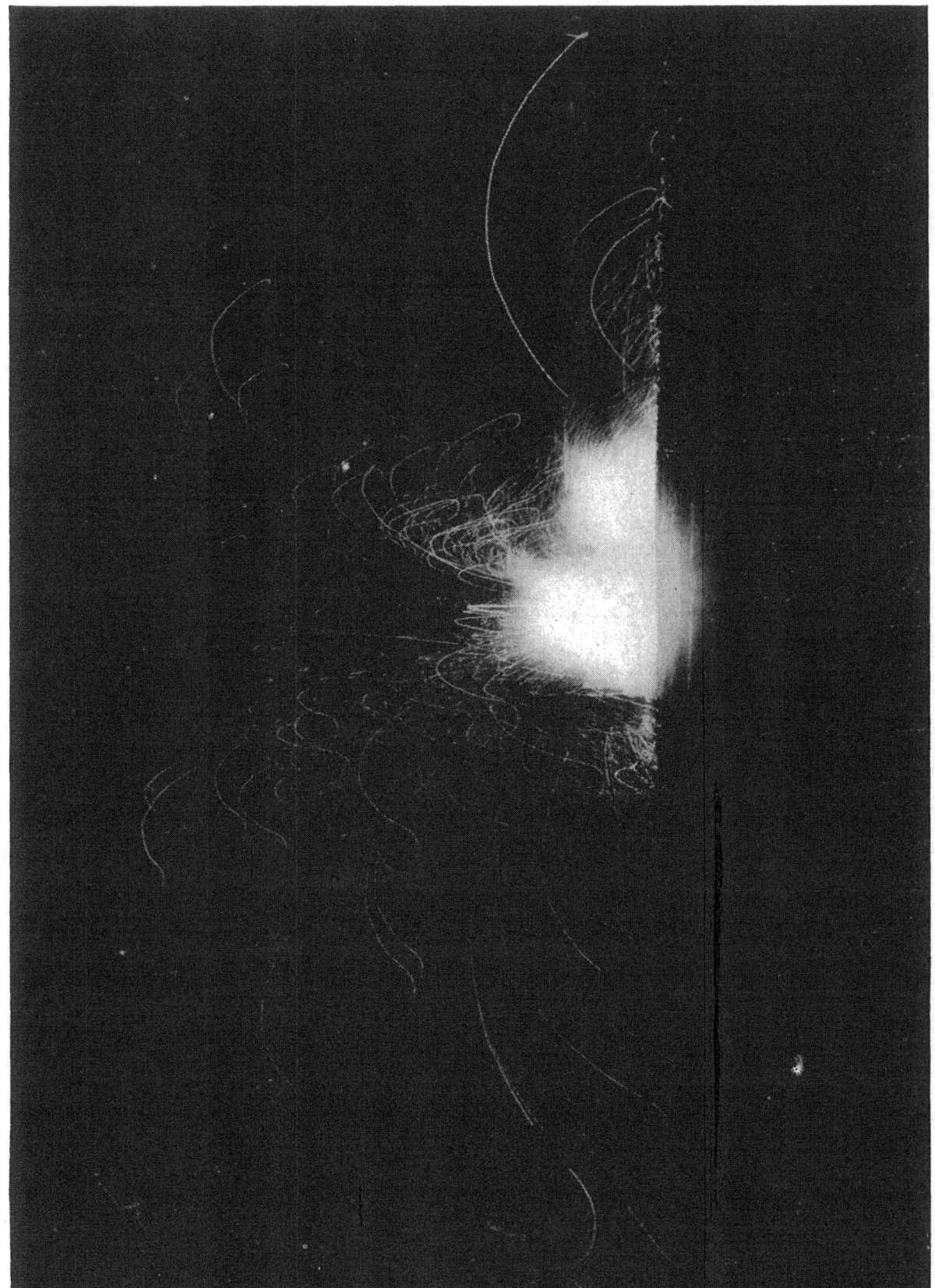

A star shell bursting at night near our lines.

Canadian Infantry entrenched in a wood.

with British assistance, besieging the fortress of Tsing-tau, the capital of the important German colony of Kiao-chau, and Samoa, New Pomerania and the other German possessions in the Pacific were being successively seized by the Australians and New Zealanders. In Africa Togoland had already passed into the hands of the Allies, fighting was proceeding in the Cameroons, and hostilities were about to extend to " German East " and " German South-West."

After its defeat in the Marne battles, the baffled army of Von Kluck retreated in good order across the Aisne, on the heights above which strong defensive positions had already been prepared. The Allies pressed hard upon the retreating enemy, and on September 13th the British forced the passage of the river in the face of almost unexampled difficulties; and on the following day, after many hours of the most stubborn fighting, established themselves in an entrenched position on the northern bank. On

An anti-aircraft gun firing at night.

the 16th, they were reinforced by the 6th Division under Major-General Keir, and during the next two days held their ground in the face of determined counter-attacks. For three weeks the battle degenerated into a sullen trench warfare, when the approaching fall of Antwerp, the possession of which would leave the Germans free to advance against Calais, Boulogne and Havre, necessitated a north-eastward movement to cover the Channel coast. By the third week in October we had fought our way to a line extending from a few miles north-east of Ypres to the Béthune–La Bassée canal, where we stood on the defensive, and for three weeks beat back the most desperate attacks of the very flower of the German Army. More than once our thin line seemed on the point of crumbling away beneath the weight of the overwhelming masses that were continually being hurled against it, but happily the valour and endurance of our troops saved the situation. In this terrific conflict, known as the First Battle of Ypres, the German casualties are believed to have exceeded a quarter of a million; the Allied losses amounted to 100,000, of which 40,000 were British.

In the first week in October, the Germans, under Hindenburg, taking advantage of the fact that defects in the provision of equipment were seriously delaying the main Russian mobilization, invaded Poland in immense force and advanced upon Warsaw; but after an obstinately-contested battle in the vicinity of the city, which lasted from the 16th to the evening of the 18th, the invaders were defeated and compelled to fall back to the frontier, Hindenburg ruthlessly sacrificing thousands of his men in the retreat in order to save the guns and transport.

At the end of October, Turkey, whose attitude since the beginning of hostilities had been highly suspicious, openly joined the Central Powers, and her intervention necessitated the despatch of a considerable force from India to the Persian Gulf and other troops to Egypt, where the Khedive Abbas II., having thrown in his lot with Turkey, was deposed. At sea we had to deplore the loss of Admiral Cradock and of H.M.S. *Good Hope* and *Monmouth* in an engagement off Coronel with a much superior German force

Red Cross men in the trenches attending to a wounded man.

under Admiral von Spee (November 1st); but a spacious revenge was taken when, five weeks later (December 8th), Von Spee's squadron was sunk by Admiral Sturdee off the Falkland Islands. Good news also came from South Africa, where the rebellion engineered by Maritz and Beyers, as well as a subsidiary movement, of which De Wet was the moving spirit, had been effectually crushed by the prompt action of General Louis Botha. On November 7th the fall of Tsing-tau marked the end of German influence and power in the Far East.

Little fighting of any importance took place on the Western Front during the winter months; but with the approach of spring, by which time our army had been greatly augmented, hostilities on a large scale recommenced, and in the fierce Battle of Neuve Chapelle (March 10th–12th, 1915) we advanced our front some considerable distance, though our main objective, the capture of the Aubers ridge, was not attained. On April 17th we carried the important German position of Hill 60 and held it for some days against a furious bombardment and determined counter-attacks, but it was eventually recaptured. During

Australian pioneers at work behind the trenches previous to the Great Advance.

German prisoners being brought in from Contalmaison.

the last days of April and the first part of May the Ypres salient was again the scene of a stubborn and sanguinary conflict, in which the enemy made use of a new weapon—the diabolical poison-gas. The chief episodes of the Second Battle of Ypres were the heroic stand of the Canadians, which undoubtedly saved the situation at the most critical stage of the battle, the fight for the Frezenberg ridge, the terrific shelling of our cavalry front on May 13th, and the brilliant charge of our dismounted 8th Brigade—the 10th Hussars, the Blues and the Essex Yeomanry—on the same day.

On May 9th we took the offensive in the Festubert region, between Festubert and Bois Grenier, the movement being intended mainly as an auxiliary to the French thrust in the Artois; but though some ground was won, most of our gains could not be held and we made little progress. Another advance, which began on the morning of the 16th, immediately east of Festubert, was more successful and resulted in the piercing of the enemy's lines on a total front of four miles.

At the beginning of February, Egypt became a theatre of hostilities, and a Turkish force of some 12,000

His Majesty the King on the battlefield looking at the grave of an unknown British soldier.

men endeavoured to pass the Suez Canal, but was easily repulsed. Towards the middle of the same month, a considerable naval force, British and French, was concentrated at the entrance to the Dardanelles, and on the 19th began operations against the outer forts. By the 26th these had been destroyed, but the real defences of the Straits—the forts at the Narrows—proved a more difficult problem, and, after three battleships had been lost through floating mines and others had sustained serious damage from gun-fire, a combined movement by sea and land was decided upon. On April 25th, a British force under Sir Ian Hamilton succeeded after desperate fighting and heavy casualties in effecting a landing on the shores of the Gallipoli Peninsula; while a French force landed at Kum Kale, on the Asiatic side of the Straits. But the obstacles which confronted us in so difficult a country were immeasurable, and though the great offensive movement early in the following August at one time promised a successful issue, our hopes were not realized, and during the early part of the winter the peninsula was gradually evacuated. Seldom, however, has failure been redeemed by more superb heroism.

On May 7th, 1915, the barbarous sinking of the *Lusitania* by a German submarine, a crime hailed with enthusiastic applause in Germany, sent a thrill of horror through the civilized world. A few days later, General Botha successfully crowned his wonderful march through German South-West Africa by the occupation of Windhoek, and yet another huge tract of territory was wrested from the grip of the Hun. On the 23rd, Italy, the third member of the Triple Alliance, which, on the outbreak of hostilities, had declined to aid the Central Powers, on the ground that the war was one of aggression on their part, declared war upon Austria, amid great popular rejoicings, and on June 2nd the Italians crossed the Isonzo.

Italy could scarcely be accused of coming to the succour of the victor, for at the moment she joined the Allies their prospects seemed darkening. The French were certainly making some progress in the Artois and elsewhere, but, as a set-off against this, the British had suffered grievously at Ypres, the Dardanelles expedition was not succeeding, and Mackensen was driving the Russians to the San; indeed, on the day after the Italian Army crossed the Isonzo Przemysl, which had been captured by our ally

A sentry in the trenches looking through an improvised periscope.

towards the end of March, was retaken by the enemy. Hopeful signs, however, were not wanting, for Britain, at last awakened to the magnitude of the danger which threatened her, had resolved to set her house in order, and on May 26th the Liberal Government gave way to a Coalition Ministry—a " Ministry of all the Talents." On June 16th a Ministry of Munitions was established, with Mr. Lloyd George at its head, and munition factories began to spring up all over the country.

During the summer attention was chiefly focussed on the progress of Mackensen's gigantic " drive." A tremendous phalanx of men in close formation, whose advance had been prepared by a thunderstorm of shell, could only be countered by a machine of the same quality; and that the Russians did not at this time possess. No valour could withstand so terrible an ordeal, and back and back the Czar's armies fell, fighting heroically whenever a chance of making a stand presented itself, only to be obliged to retreat anew. Przemysl and Lemberg were retaken; Bialystok, Grodno, Ivangorod, Kovel, Kovno, Warsaw itself, fell into the hands of the enemy. But, thanks to the genius of the Grand Duke Nicholas, the Russian

Historical Introduction 15

The Great Assault of July 1st.

armies were saved, and it was abundantly clear that it was their inferiority in artillery and shells alone that had brought them so near disaster. For whenever they got to grips with their adversaries they broke them. The situation spurred the Russian people to a mighty effort, and, like ourselves, they set all their industrial machinery to the task of supplying the munitions which would assure them the victory.

The end of September witnessed a welcome renewal of activity along the Allied front in the West. On September 25th the French in Champagne advanced against the German lines between Auberive and Tahure, and, as the result of that and the two subsequent days' fighting, much ground was gained and heavy loss inflicted on the enemy. On the same day on which the Battle of Champagne began the French 10th Army attacked the Vimy heights and the British 1st Army advanced against the La Bassée–Loos lines; while north of the La Bassée Canal four attacks were undertaken by us from Givenchy, Neuve Chapelle, Bois Grenier, and in the south of the Ypres salient respectively. The net result of the fighting, which continued until the end of the month, was the carrying of the enemy's first-line trenches on a front of 6,500 yards, while their reserve line was broken up, and in one case their last position pierced. Over 3,000 prisoners were captured and a great quantity of war material fell into our hands.

At the beginning of October, Bulgaria entered the war on the side of the Central Powers. Serbia,

Indian Cavalry on the battlefield.

menaced with invasion by her ancient enemy, as well as by the Central Powers, called upon Greece to fulfil her treaty obligations. But the latter declined, on the pretext that these referred only to an attack on Serbia by Bulgaria, and not to an invasion by other Powers; and by the middle of November Serbia had been completely overrun, and her aged King and the remnant of his army were in exile. An Allied force had landed at Salonika on October 5th, but it was too inferior in numbers to the invaders to render the Serbians any effective assistance.

The early part of the winter of 1915–16 in the West was a period of almost complete stagnation. On the Eastern front, the Russians assumed the offensive in the Bukovina and advanced on Czernowitz, but failed to take it. But in Asia Minor they utterly routed the Turkish forces opposed to them, and on February 16th the great fortress of Erzerum fell into their hands. In Western Africa we completed the conquest of the Cameroons, but bad news came from Mesopotamia, where General Townshend's force, shut up in Kut-el-Amara, was, after an heroic defence, obliged to surrender.

German dead in a German first-line trench.

With the approach of spring there was a great increase of activity. At the end of February the Germans commenced their great attack on Verdun, where every yard of ground they gained was dyed red with German blood. On the other hand, Russia, now abundantly supplied with heavy artillery and munitions, assumed the offensive along the whole Austrian front and began dealing out a series of staggering blows to the armies of the Dual Monarchy, who were soon almost everywhere in full retreat. On the British front there was some fierce fighting in the Ypres salient, in which the Canadians again greatly distinguished themselves, and also about Neuve Chapelle, which resulted in a substantial gain of ground, and was regarded as a happy augury for the coming offensive. On June 1st the great naval battle off the coast of Jutland afforded one more proof of the immeasurable superiority of the British seaman over the German. A few days later (June 6th), to the inexpressible grief of the whole Empire, the cruiser *Hampshire*, which was on her way to Russia with Lord Kitchener on board, went down off the Orkneys. But our grief at the tragic end of the great soldier was tempered by the reflection that his work had been practically accomplished, and that nothing remained for us but to set in motion the mighty machine which his genius had created and perfected.

The German trenches being blown up by a great mine before the assault.

Position of British Front Line July 13th 1916.

An interesting map to illustrate the first few days of the Great Push. Notice the network of trenches which our armies in the field had to take before making any appreciable headway.

For many weeks previous to the Great Advance preparations on a vast scale were taking place behind the firing line along the entire British front in Picardy.

SIR DOUGLAS HAIG'S GREAT PUSH

THE BATTLE OF THE SOMME

CHAPTER I

PREPARATORY ACTION

TOWARDS the end of June, 1916, it became apparent that the moment was at hand when the "Big Push" on the Western Front, so long expected and so ardently desired, might at length be attempted with every prospect of success. For months the Allied Staffs had been making ready for this stage. Never has the world witnessed preparation on so colossal a scale—a preparation which had converted Great Britain into a vast arsenal and a first-class military power—and it is hardly conceivable that the world will ever witness the like again. But it was known that the enemy, too, had not wasted these months, and that we should do well to presume that every device or plan that military genius can conceive or apply for the strengthening and elaboration of their system of defences must have been carried out with the greatest thoroughness and scientific precision; that every eventuality that could be foreseen had been provided against.

In the great Champagne and Artois offensives of last year our advance was in nearly every case successful as regards the first line of the enemy's trenches; but it was thereafter frequently held up by local

This illustration shows activities on the part of the Army Service Corps and Artillery behind the British line between Fricourt-Mametz. The position of these places will be found on the map facing this page.

A platoon of the Buffs (East Kents) answering roll-call at Bray prior to going forward to the front-line trenches.

centres of resistance which had survived our preliminary bombardment, and rarely effected any serious breach in the second lines; while the casualties sustained were very heavy. Happily, we had not failed to profit by the experience so dearly purchased, and, recognizing that artillery had become the decisive arm, so long as the present fixed lines exist, and that it was only when our artillery and its provisions were at length superior that we could hope for success, we resolved to wait until the huge national effort thrown into the output of munitions under the auspices of Mr. Lloyd George had progressed sufficiently to become a chief factor in Armageddon. Never again, if it could by any possibility be prevented, must our heroic infantry find themselves, when they approached within sight of their goal, up against unbroken lines of wire, and unsuspected shelters from which cunningly concealed machine-guns spat unceasing streams of lead. Never again must they be forced to relinquish the ground which their valour had won, because the trenches into which they had fought their way were rendered untenable by the fire of batteries which an adequate artillery preparation should have enabled us to destroy. And so we waited; and during these months of relative quiescence Sir Douglas Haig's command, the main army of the Empire, grew and grew until it had become, with its reserves, one of the four most powerful armies in existence and second to none in equipment and ability. But there was no intention of compromising success by a premature offensive, and it was not until it had been supplied with an artillery as formidable in proportion to its size as had yet been known in this Titanic struggle, with all its stupendous mechanism, and—what was of even greater

A platoon of the Bedfords moving up on the evening before the attack.

While these great preparations were going on, industrious French peasants continued their daily work in the fields just outside the firing line.

—A few seconds later we see mules carrying baggage—

Here the stretcher-bearers are seen marching by,—

—and so on until the whole battalion and its accompaniment passes.

—and then more troops with a motor-cyclist rushing past at over thirty miles an hour,—

A BATTALION OF THE ROYAL WELSH FUSILIERS MOVING UP ON THE EVENING BEFORE THE ATTACK.

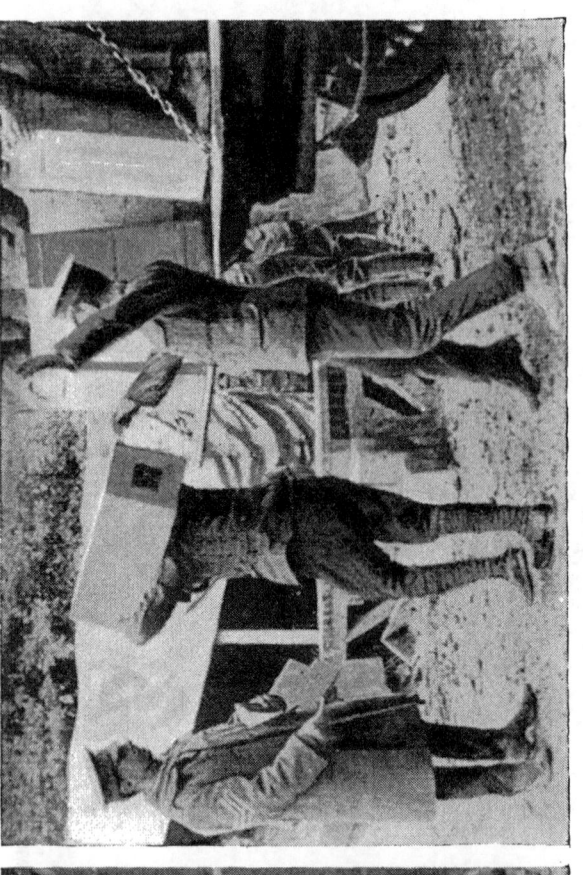

Here you see one of our men lifting a box containing shells off the transport wagon,—

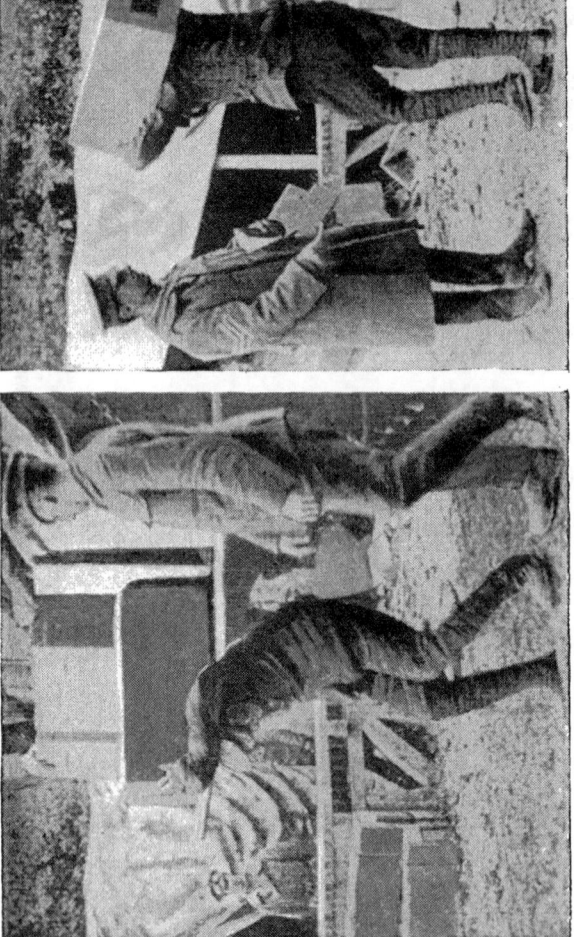

—and takes another box,—

—No sooner is one box lifted from the wagon than another man comes forward—

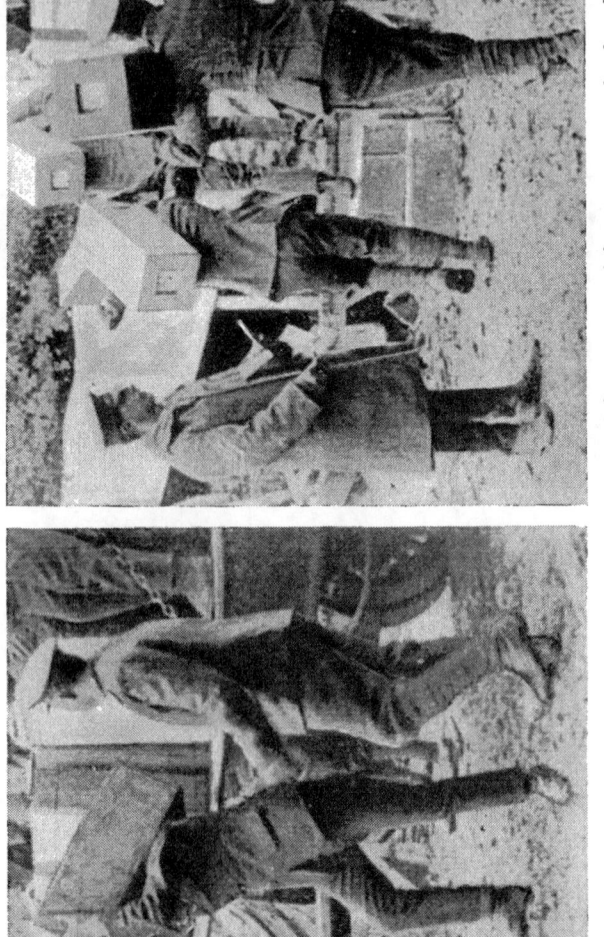

—and this goes on until the wagon is emptied and a pile made of the boxes of ammunition ready to fill the limbers.

UNLOADING BOXES OF SHELLS FROM TRANSPORT WAGONS.

The Great Push

There were vast stores of ammunition and dozens of empty limbers drawn up ready to be filled with shells. They were taken to the guns and fired on the German trenches. The piles of ammunition can be seen on the left, and the limbers on the right.

importance—with almost inexhaustible stocks of shells, that it was judged that the moment to strike had come.

"To-day our artillery has been more active than usual along the whole front." In these laconic terms, Sir Douglas Haig, in his dispatch of Saturday, June 24th, 1916, announced the beginning of the tremendous artillery preparation which was to pave the way for the great offensive movement in the West. On the morning of that day, guided by our aeroplanes, which had been gradually establishing an unquestioned superiority over the German aircraft, and the kite-balloons which floated in security over our lines, while the enemy's balloons had, for the most part, been driven down, the British batteries, giving tongue along a line of eighty miles, from the Yser to the Somme, began to operate in colossal unison against the German front. Our gunners overwhelmed the enemy's front with an unceasing deluge of explosives. On long stretches of the hostile lines their entanglements were swept away like matchwood, their parapets blown to atoms, their communication-trenches and support positions reached; while in some places the great shells sought out the enemy in their billets and rest-camps, destroyed their batteries, blew up their ammunition-stores, and swept the ground behind their lines so effectually that it was impossible for food or water to be sent up to the trenches, and their occupants had to subsist on iron rations.

On the 25th, a fierce bombardment was maintained along the whole front, the German positions about Neuville-St. Vaast, south of Vailly, and to the north of the Ypres–Menin road being most heavily shelled. The cannonade continued throughout the night and all the next day, and in the evening Sir Douglas Haig reported that "four large explosions had been caused by our heavy artillery in the enemy's rearward lines, between Pozières and Montauban," and that "considerable damage had been caused to hostile defensive works, notably near Longueval, Gommecourt, Givenchy-en-Gohelle, north of the Loos salient, opposite Wytschaete, and to the east of Wieltje." On the 26th, the German lines from Thiépval southwards to La Boiselle and Fricourt were subjected to a terrific bombardment. A correspondent calculated that in less than half an hour five hundred shells had fallen over Thiépval, while simultaneously La Boiselle was being slashed with fire, and above Fricourt there was a continual flash of bursting shells through the smoke which shrouded it.

This devastating torrent of projectiles not only caused enormous damage to the enemy's defences and

The casualties amongst horses have been very heavy in the War, and members of the Artillery pay great attention to the needs of each animal. The illustrations show horses being brought to water at troughs specially set up

Every regiment has its mascot, and here we see the mascot of the Royal Field Artillery, caught in France.

wrought havoc amongst those who manned them, but simply ate up the countryside for miles and transformed the whole appearance of the landscape. Woods, copses and orchards that had been green before were shattered and stripped of their foliage as completely as though summer had suddenly changed to winter; solid buildings came tumbling down as though they had been made of cards; châteaux, farms, whole villages, sank into shapeless heaps.

The Great War has witnessed many terrible bombardments: our own artillery preparation at Neuve Chapelle, that of the French between La Targette and Carency on May 9th, 1915, and the German bombardment of our cavalry front at Ypres a few days later—to speak only of the Western theatre. But, taking its range and weight together, this was unparalleled. Moreover, it went on, more or less, day and night for a week. It was heard in Calais, in Amiens, in Paris itself; and in the calm of those summer nights dwellers on our own southern cliffs and hillsides listened to the faraway thunder which told them that the full weight of Britain's inexhaustible resources was at length beginning to be turned against the Hun, and that his doom was assuredly sealed.

A striking testimony to the terrible effect of the British fire is borne by the correspondent of the *Liberté*, in a dispatch to his journal, dated June 29th: "During the last twenty-four hours," he says, "the bombardment by the British, in spite of bad weather, has increased in violence all along the front; its intensity on certain points being frightful. The roar of the cannonade is uninterrupted, causing the earth to tremble far away from the scene of action. Shell follows shell at only a few seconds interval. Not only have the first-line trenches been completely wrecked over a considerable extent and some entirely obliterated, but the British artillery has

A transport wagon coming up to where the limbers are, and bringing from the base hundreds of shells. Notice the empty cartridges lying about; all are taken back, refilled, and freshly charged ready to be used again in the guns.

Here you see the shell just after it has burst in a German trench.—

—No sooner has this done its damage than another shell is hurled in close proximity,—

—and a few seconds afterwards the débris, etc., thrown up into the air by the explosion, drops again,—

—and then all we see is the smoke being gradually wafted away by the wind.—

—This continued every few minutes of the day along the entire front for five days before the attack.—

—As a result, by the time July 1st came, the German trenches were destroyed and very heavy casualties inflicted.

HEAVY BOMBARDMENT OF THE GERMAN TRENCHES.

Here you see the man in the foreground ready to receive the shell;—

—it is thrown to him;—

—he then passes it on to the man at the limber,—

—who catches it and puts it in the limber.

REFILLING LIMBERS WITH 18-POUNDER SHELLS AFTER "DUMPING" THE EMPTY CASES.

reached the second and third lines of the enemy's defences. Two munition depôts, both five miles to the rear, have been blown up; prisoners taken wear a dazed and bewildered expression."

This terrific cannonade was not the only means by which we sought to harass, injure and demoralize the enemy during this week of preparation. Gas-clouds were repeatedly launched against their trenches, and it was subsequently ascertained that many hundreds of Germans who had escaped the bombardment had succumbed to the diabolical method of attack which they themselves had invented. To this must be added the new form of infantry attack. Here again we were taking a leaf out of the German book, for the Huns had been the first to work out the theory of the new tactics and to apply the practice At Verdun, after bombardment by their massed batteries had continued for a given time, they sent out thin lines of skirmishers again and again, until it appeared that the French front positions were sufficiently pulverized and cleared of men and machine-guns to offer an easy prey to an advance in force. Only then were their dense columns of assault sent forward to occupy the ground which the big guns had conquered in advance. The French displayed boundless ingenuity in deceiving the enemy, and often put up a desperate resistance where little or none had been expected. But, on the whole, the new process proved sound and minimized the German losses. Now, however, the Hun found it turned against himself and employed with infinitely more daring and success than ever he had used it. Night after night our patrols and raiding-parties went out, penetrating the German lines at many points, while curtain fire was carried over the enemy's support and communication trenches. In these deadly scuffles with grenade, bayonet, bludgeon and rifle-butt our men easily had the better. They inflicted heavy casualties on the enemy,

UNPACKING SHELLS.
The lid has been torn off, the packing extracted,—the shell taken out and handed down, —and passed up to the limber.

while sustaining comparatively slight losses themselves, and on nearly every occasion brought back prisoners, so that gradually we learned the name and position of nearly every battalion confronting us. Above all, our raiding-parties brought back reports upon the state of the enemy's trenches and of the damage effected along the whole German front.

During the night of June 25th–26th, in the neighbourhood of Armentières, two raids were carried out by the Anzacs, one against Prussian, the other against Saxon, troops, at points of the enemy's line some three miles apart. Each raid was similar in its operation. About half an hour after midnight, our trench-mortars got to work, slicing through the enemy's barbed wire and smothering their trench with a hail of bombs; while, at the same time, our heavy guns began shelling the communication-trenches

Throughout the preparatory action from June 25th–30th British guns were giving the enemy no rest. There was an ample supply of ammunition, thanks to the munition workers, and an immense number of shells were fired. The illustration shows a 4·7 gun being loaded.

to prevent the German supports from coming up. Then the Anzacs—all picked men—who had trained for the enterprise as though for an athletic contest, scrambled over their parapet, armed with bombs and bludgeons, and, notwithstanding some machine-gun fire, raced across No Man's Land at such a pace as almost to escape casualties. Once they entered the hostile trench, the affair was as good as over, for the Huns, demoralized by the fire of the mortars and by the suddenness of the attack, had no stomach for a hand-to-hand encounter. A few tried to defend their position with bombs, which, in their panic and confusion, inflicted far more loss upon their own comrades than upon the enemy. But the majority offered little resistance, some surrendering at once, with piteous appeals for mercy; and the raiders were able to enter the dug-outs and take at their leisure whatever they required. But, though it was an easy matter enough to take prisoners, all the strength and persuasive powers of the Anzacs were needed to get them across to our lines, when the order was given to retire, so terrified were they of their own

Here the same gun as shown on the previous page has been loaded and its sights adjusted ready to fire.

artillery and machine-gun fire, and several of them had literally to be hauled along. One huge Queenslander, while with one hand he pulled his prisoner, limp as a sack of potatoes, over our parapet, held out the other to the officer in charge of the way out, who had made a sporting bet with the men, and

The same gun is here shown immediately after being fired. Notice the recoil due to the force of the explosion.

All day long the limbers were being filled with shells as fast as the guns could fire them. Here we see the men passing up the ammunition to the limbers hand to hand.

shouted: "I've won that five francs, sir." Both raids were completely successful; more than a dozen prisoners were brought back, a bomb-store and other material of value destroyed, and many Germans killed by the firing or by the attacking parties. A curious episode was the discovery of a body of the enemy's wirers at work, who, thanks to an ingenious manœuvre, were entirely wiped out by our mortars.

On the same night, a raid on a more important scale was carried out by a party of the Royal Munster Fusiliers at another section of the line, after the way had been prepared by a terrific shelling of the hostile trenches. On this occasion, the Germans, who appear to have been made of sterner stuff than those with whom the Anzacs had had to deal, put up a stout fight. But nothing could stop the rush of the Irishmen, who bombed and bludgeoned the enemy until all resistance was at an end. The victors, however, sustained a good many casualties, two of their officers being killed and two others severely wounded. One of the wounded officers, Lieutenant A. H. Batten-Pooll, who was in command of the raiding-party, was subsequently awarded the Victoria Cross, for the splendid courage and devotion to duty he had displayed: "At the moment of entering the enemy's lines," says the *Gazette*, "he was severely wounded by a bomb, which broke and mutilated all the fingers of his right hand. In spite of this, he continued to direct operations with unflinching courage, his voice being clearly heard, cheering on and directing his men. He was urged but refused to retire. Half an hour later, during the withdrawal, while personally

The shell is then placed in a round partition in the limber, a cord being tied to the end to enable it to be withdrawn without delay.

assisting in the rescue of other wounded men, he received two further wounds. Still refusing assistance, he walked unaided to within one hundred yards of our own lines, when he fainted, and was carried in by the covering party." It is interesting to note that, according to an officer of the Munsters, the most deadly instrument of destruction in this encounter was a short, heavy bludgeon, in the shape of a shillelagh, the use of which we are led to believe is the prescriptive and hereditary right of all Irishmen.

During the great activity on the part of our gunners, regiment after regiment was being moved up to the front-line trenches. This particular illustration shows the Hampshires moving up to the attack. Notice the two men in the foreground carrying Lewis quick-firing guns.

During the succeeding days the raids continued with increasing daring and success.

"During last night," wrote Sir Douglas Haig, in his report of June 28th, "raids and patrols entered enemy's trenches at several points, bombing the enemy and inflicting casualties. Near Angres, one of the raiding parties found enemy's trenches badly damaged by shell-fire, and the enemy had apparently suffered from the gas which we had successfully discharged from our trenches. A particularly successful raid was carried out by the Highland Light Infantry near the Vermelles–La Bassée road, when forty-six prisoners and two machine-guns were captured and two enemy mine-shafts destroyed, with a loss of only two men wounded." And on the 29th: "During the past twenty-four hours a large number of our reconnoitring and raiding parties entered the enemy's trenches at various

These are followed by members of the Army Medical Corps carrying a stretcher. They are seen wearing their white armlet with a Red Cross on it.

One of our guns drawn up to a favourable position at the back of the firing line.

points along the entire front of the British Army. All these enterprises were successful in achieving their objects, inflicting heavy casualties on the Germans and capturing prisoners and warlike stores. In several instances our troops remained for a considerable period in the German lines, repelling hostile counter-attacks across the open. One of these enterprises took place after a discharge of gas, and our troops on entering the German trenches found a considerable number of dead. Our casualties were insignificant."

Meanwhile, whenever the weather permitted, our aircraft displayed great activity and rendered

One of the many large "dumps" of empty cases which could be seen over the entire front after the great artillery preparation previous to the attack.

It was just about to be fired when this photograph was taken.

Preparing to clean out the barrel.

The gun is here shown being carefully sighted.

The recoil.

A 6in. HOWITZER IN ACTION SHELLING THE GERMAN FIRST-LINE TRENCHES AT MAMETZ.

The Lancashire Fusiliers being addressed by their Divisional Commander on the eve of the battle.

splendid service, both in reconnoitring and in engaging the enemy's machines and destroying their kite-balloons. On June 24th no less than six German balloons, out of a total of fifteen attacked, were destroyed by them, the whole six being seen to fall in flames. On the 27th numerous encounters took place on the enemy's side of the line. Five of our machines engaged four Fokkers, two of which were brought down;

Several 6in. howitzers preparing to fire on the German first-line trenches at Mametz.

while two more of the enemy's machines were driven down in the course of the day. Our own casualties were one machine missing.

The weather during the three following days was unfavourable for aerial work, but on the 30th, as the result of one of the few combats in the air which took place, an enemy aeroplane was driven down with a damaged engine, while an important railway depôt was attacked with powerful bombs, and a large number of other bombs were dropped on depôts, railway-junctions, batteries, trenches and other points of military importance in the enemy's lines. Everywhere along the front our airmen had established the most marked superiority, and on the 29th, at a point a few miles north of the Somme, a correspondent counted twelve of our kite-balloons poised above our lines, so that the observers in their hanging baskets could see far across the enemy's trenches to their battery positions, while there was not a single hostile balloon opposite them. The fact that to the immense weight of metal which our gunners were continually pouring upon the German positions, the enemy's artillery made but a comparatively feeble reply, was no doubt largely due to the disadvantage under which it laboured in being thus deprived of its eyes. However, it is probable that on all sections of the front our guns had at this time the mastery in numbers.

But the problem before us was one of the greatest difficulty.

One of the guns illustrated above is here shown actually at the time of the discharge.

Our attack was not, like that of the Germans at Verdun, localized against a salient. We had to probe and tear along the whole front, keep the harassed enemy taut, anxious and perplexed over a line eighty miles in length, and prevent them, if we could, from divining the hour and direction of our main purpose. Otherwise, when the advance began, we might find that they had concentrated formidable reserves and a great mass of artillery and machine-guns on the threatened sector, which would render it impossible for us to break through, except at a cost too terrible to contemplate. However, at the end of a week of preparation, the reports brought back by our raiding parties of the havoc wrought by our bombardment upon the enemy's trenches, and the demoralized condition of the majority of the prisoners brought in, some of whom asserted that they had had no food for three days, owing to the barrage of fire which had prevented supplies from reaching them up to the communication-trenches, appeared to justify the belief that the moment to strike had come ; and it was decided that the advance should begin at 7.30 on the morning of July 1st.

East Yorks on the march to the front line.

The country chosen for our main attack stretches from the Somme for some twenty miles northwards. It is—or rather was, before War had laid its devastating hand upon it—a pleasant country, a country of wooded hills and little valleys and fertile meadows and stretches of woodland, crossed at rare intervals by roads and railways and dotted here and there with villages and small market-towns ; a very different land from Flanders with its swamps and flats, or the Loos battlefields, with their dreary plain, pimpled with slag-heaps.

About three miles north of the town of Bray-sur-Somme lies a shallow and tortuous valley, with a single line of railway running along its bed. Beyond this hollow there rises a range of small hills, about ten miles in length, the highest point of which is only some five hundred feet above the sea. Through the hollow, in which lie Fricourt and Mametz, ran the first line of German trenches. On the rising ground beyond is Montauban, and beyond Montauban was the enemy's second line of defence, running south-eastward from Pozières past Bazentin-le-Grand and Longueval to Guillemont. Farther to the north, extending from the high ground above Thiépval in a south-easterly direction, was the third—or what

"Hot work at the guns." The gunners are busily engaged in putting over a curtain fire or barrage.

The vicious bark of the Canadian 60-pounders adds to the din of gun-fire. The gun just before discharging the shell—

—and just after, showing the recoil back. The manner in which the gun is protected by hundreds of sacks of earth should be noted.
ONE OF THE WONDERFUL CANADIAN 60-POUNDERS.

The Great Push 39

A view of the same Canadian gun as shown on the previous page taken from within the gun-pit. The German trenches at which the gun is aimed can be seen in the distance.

may be called, from the chief village on the line—the Martinpuich line of the enemy's defences. Once this line was in our hands we should look down the far slope of the range into the upper valley of the Ancre, and across this valley to Bapaume. Then for the enemy the security of Bapaume would be gone, and the German position west of a twelve mile line drawn from Bapaume to Arras would have begun to acquire the character of an almost peninsular salient.

On the evening of June 30th scenes of great activity might have been witnessed behind the British lines, and particularly at Bray, where a whole division was waiting to move forward to the firing-line. Munitions in vast quantities were arriving at the munition "dumps;" huge howitzer shells, 18-pounder shells for the field guns, "flying-pigs" and "plum-puddings" for the trench-mortars, belts of cartridges for the machine-guns, hand-grenades, and endless supplies of small-arms ammunition. Presently the troops began moving off: a battalion of the Royal Welsh Fusiliers; platoons of the Buffs, Bedfords and Suffolks; Lancashire Fusiliers and Royal Fusiliers, to whom the Divisional General delivered a brief address before they

Shrapnel bursting over the trenches keeps the Germans astir.

marched away; a battalion of the Hampshires; London Scottish, East Yorkshires, and Manchesters. All alike —English, Scots and Welsh —keen for the work which lay before them—for the spirit of the men was for an assault across the open and they were confident in the new power of our guns.

And our guns were not failing them; their voices were louder, more insistent, than ever that night, and the calm summer sky was rent with the incessant flashes of light, as shells of every calibre burst and scattered. Here a battery of 4.7-inch guns were giving the enemy no rest; there 6-inch howitzers were shelling the German first-line trenches at Mametz. At another part of the line 9.2-inch howitzers were bombarding the Germans and destroying their dug-outs. At others the "plum-puddings" from the trench-mortars were smashing the enemy's barbed wire; while the vicious bark of the Canadian 60-pounders added to the din, as they flung their shrapnel over the German trenches, and every now and

The London Scottish starting for the trenches, led by their pipers and drummers.

again "Grandmother," a great 15-inch howitzer, worked by men of the Royal Marine Artillery, coughed up one of her 1,400-lb. shells—a projectile powerful enough to smash a cathedral with one enormous burst.

The dawn of July 1st came. It was a perfect summer's morning, which after the miserable weather experienced during the past few weeks was hailed as a good augury, as well as an important aid to success. But it was cold, and over all the fields there was a floating mist, which, rising from the damp earth, lay heavily upon the ridges, so that the horizon was obscured.

All night troops had been moving up to the firing line—troops in steel helmets and full fighting kit. At one place, a battalion of the Worcesters might be seen fixing wire-cutters to their rifles for forcing the enemy's wire entanglements, if any part of them remained still intact. At another, a Lancashire battalion was awaiting instructions. Presently, the order to move forward came, and the men, fixing bayonets, filed through the communication-trench to the firing line. Behind them came a party of bombers bearing supplies of those deadly missiles which had not been seen on a battlefield for more than a century until the Japanese revived their use in a greatly improved form at the Siege of Port Arthur, but which have been employed with such murderous effect in the present war.

About six o'clock the full power of our artillery was let loose, and there was one continual roar of guns—of guns of every calibre from "Grandmother" to the 18-pounder field-gun, which beat the air with great waves and shocks of sound. Nothing like it had been seen or heard along our front before, and all the preliminary bombardment seemed insignificant in comparison.

"I do not know," wrote Mr. Philip Gibbs, special correspondent of the *Daily Chronicle*, "how many batteries we have along this battle-line or along the section of the line which I can see, but the guns seem crowded in vast numbers of every calibre, and the concentration of their fire was terrific in its intensity. For a time I could see nothing through the low-lying mist and heavy

This illustration shows the officers and men of the London Scottish wearing steel helmets, which saved many a life during the Great Advance.

SCALA THEATRE
CHARLOTTE STREET, W.
(GOODGE STREET TUBE STATION.)

AT THE FRONT
OFFICIAL WAR OFFICE FILMS.

KUT RELIEF FORCES.

SALONIKA.   FRENCH ARMY.
RUSSIAN ARMY.   EAST AFRICA, &c.

THE BATTLE of the SOMME

"There is no programme in London which gives so complete and vivid a description of the War on ALL FRONTS."
—*Evening News.*

THE KING'S ADVICE:

SEE THE SOMME WAR FILM AND WHAT WAR MEANS

"The public should see these pictures, that they may have some idea of what the Army is doing, and what war means."

This statement was made by the King after witnessing a programme of the Official War Office film "The Battle of the Somme," which was shown by command to the King and Queen at Windsor Castle.

—*Daily Express.*

DAILY, 3 and 8.

BOX OFFICE, 10 to 10.   'Phone: Gerr., 1,444 and 1,366.

SCALA THEATRE

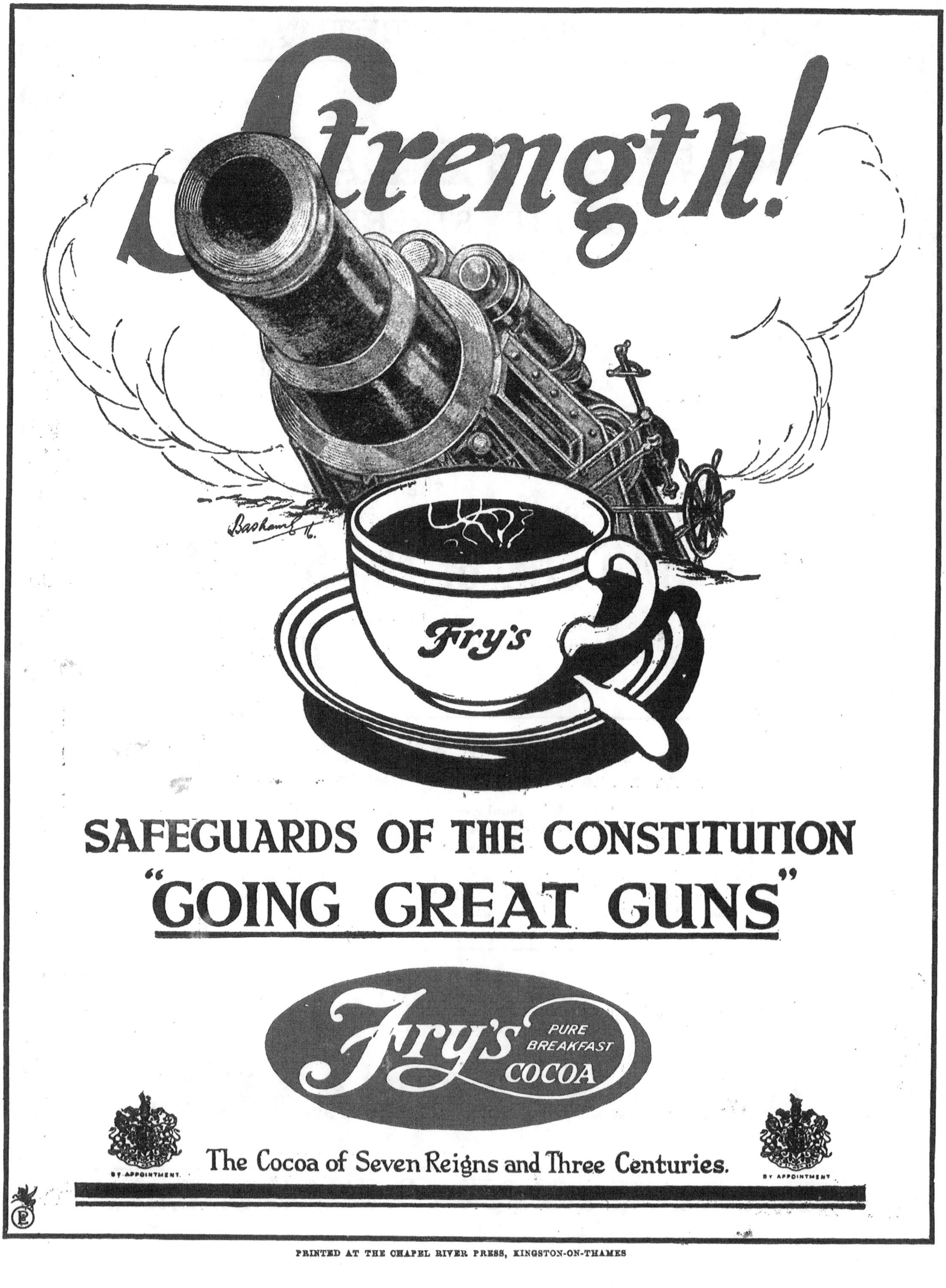

Strength!

SAFEGUARDS OF THE CONSTITUTION
"GOING GREAT GUNS"

The Cocoa of Seven Reigns and Three Centuries.

PRINTED AT THE CHAPEL RIVER PRESS, KINGSTON-ON-THAMES

ABOUT 8 FORTNIGHTLY PARTS. — HUTCHINSON'S NEW PART WORK — Part III. ready Oct. 24th. PART II. 8d. NET

SIR DOUGLAS HAIG'S
GREAT PUSH

THE BATTLE OF THE SOMME

A popular, pictorial and authoritative work on one of the Greatest Battles in History, illustrated by about **700** *wonderful* **OFFICIAL PHOTOGRAPHS AND CINEMATOGRAPH FILMS** *and other authentic pictures*

BY ARRANGEMENT WITH THE WAR OFFICE

A COMPLIMENTARY MESSAGE TO FRITZ

GREAT VALUE FOR EIGHTPENCE

THIS PART CONTAINS **78 WONDERFUL REPRODUCTIONS** OF THE FAMOUS **WAR OFFICE CINEMATOGRAPH FILMS** AND **OFFICIAL PHOTOGRAPHS** OF THE BATTLE OF THE SOMME, BEAUTIFULLY PRINTED ON THE BEST ENGLISH ART PAPER.

LONDON : HUTCHINSON & Co.

5,000,000 Letters

received every week from our armies in France, according to the Postmaster-General.

No wonder that there has been such a demand for Fountain Pens since the outbreak of war.

Which 20 Years ago set the Standard in
FOUNTAIN PENS

has so increased its sales that the nominal increase in cost of production has been more than counterbalanced. The present time has been thought opportune by some Fountain Pen makers to put up prices. The pens themselves are unchanged. The burden will fall largely on our soldiers and sailors and their friends. Send your soldier or sailor a "Swan" and save 20 per cent.

THERE IS NO ADVANCE IN PRICES OF "SWAN" FOUNTPENS.

Sold by Stationers and Jewellers everywhere.

Standard pattern, with slip-on cap, from 10/6 Up.
Safety pattern, with screw-on cap, from 12/6 Up.

Illustrated Catalogue post free on request.

MABIE, TODD & Co., Ltd.,
79-80, High Holborn, London, W.C.
LONDON FACTORY—319-329, WESTON STREET, S.E.

38, Cheapside, E.C.; 95a and 204, Regent St., W., London; 3, Exchange St., Manchester; Paris, Zurich, Sydney.

Associate House—
Mabie, Todd & Co., Inc., New York and Chicago.

Size 1, with fit-on clip, 11/6

Size 2c, "Safety," with screw-on cap, 12/6

Size 1, standard pattern, slip-on cap, 10/6

Size 1, with 2 rolled gold bands, 14/6

smoke-clouds which mingled with the mist, and stood like a blinded man, only listening. It was a wonderful thing which came to my ears. Shells were rushing through the air as though all the trains in the world had leapt their rails and were driving at express speed through endless tunnels in which they met each other with frightful collisions. Some of these shells, fired from batteries not far from where I stood, ripped the sky with a high-tearing note. Other shells whistled with that strange, gobbling, sibilant cry which makes one's bowels turn cold. Through the mist and the smoke there came sharp, loud, insistent knocks, as separate batteries fired salvoes, and great clangorous strokes, as of iron doors banged suddenly, and the tattoo of the light field-guns playing the drums of Death.

"The mist was shifting and dissolving. The tall tower of Albert Cathedral appeared suddenly through

A German shell bursting behind the British trenches.

the veil, and the sun shone full for a few seconds on the Golden Virgin and the Babe, which she held head downwards above all this tumult as a peace-offering to men. The broken roofs of the town gleamed white, and the two tall chimneys to the left stood black and sharp against the pale blue of the sky, into which dirty smoke drifted above the whiter clouds.

"I could see now as well as hear. I could see our shells falling upon the German lines by Thiépval and La Boiselle, and further by Mametz, and southwards over Fricourt. High explosives were tossing up great vomits of black smoke and earth all along the ridges. Shrapnel was pouring upon these places, and leaving curling white clouds, which clung to the ground. Below there was the flash of many batteries like Morse code signals by stabs of flame. The enemy were being blasted by a hurricane of fire."

And the fire did not come from the British guns alone, for our aeroplanes were sailing high over the German lines, and ever and anon swooping down to drop bombs upon their batteries and ammunition wagons. At 7.15 a new sound mingled with the general thunder of the artillery, as the trench mortars came into action along the whole length of our line, and thousands of " flying pigs " went whirling up in their peculiar vertical flight to descend upon the enemy's trenches and dug-outs. Then with a terrific roar a deep mine, packed with many tons of the highest explosives known to science, was exploded near La Boiselle, blowing a great gap in the enemy's defences, and a part of the Royal Engineers rushed off to wire the crater for occupation by our advance troops. Just before 7.30 our gunners lengthened their range and began to interpose a terrific barrage of fire between the enemy's first and second lines. No reinforcements could possibly make their way through that hail of shell. At the same time, clouds of smoke were liberated to form a screen for our infantry, who punctually at the half-hour swarmed out of their trenches and, with a mighty cheer, advanced to the attack. The " Great Push " had begun !

The Wiltshire Regiment on their way to the front.

CHAPTER II

In modern warfare, with large assemblages of troops and regular artillery preparations, surprise is exceedingly difficult, and the enemy were in no degree taken unawares. The best evidence goes to show that they had been expecting our attack to be delivered that morning, though they appear to have antedated it by a couple of hours. Since daybreak, indeed, certain sectors of our front had been heavily and continuously shelled, and the discharge of the smoke clouds was the signal for No Man's Land to be swept by a hurricane of lead from countless machine-guns. But, thanks to the smoke, it was blind shooting, and, though not a few of our men fell before even they had crossed our parapet, they were the victims of chance bullets.

On through the tempest of death swept our brave fellows ; men fell at every step, but their comrades kept steadily on ; the more casualties they saw in front of them, the louder they cheered, the faster they pressed forward ; and at 11.55 a.m. Sir Douglas Haig was able to report that " British troops have broken into German forward system of defences along front of sixteen miles."

For along great stretches of the enemy's lines our bombardment had wrought enormous damage, sweeping away the barbed wire, flattening the parapets, and blowing in the dug-outs, which in many places were found choked with dead bodies. Frequently, out of those dug-outs which had survived the storm of high explosives crept dazed and deafened men, who surrendered without a semblance of resistance ; indeed, at one part of the line the Germans did not even wait for our men to enter their trenches, but emerging from their shelters so soon as the British guns lifted, met the advancing troops in the open, holding up their hands in token of surrender.

A GREAT SUCCESS.

ALTHOUGH Part I. of "SIR DOUGLAS HAIG'S GREAT PUSH" has at the time of writing this prospectus only been published a few days, large repeat orders are already being received from all parts of the country, and the success of the work is assured.

The illustrations in Part II. carry subscribers up to July 1st, the Day of the Great Advance, and Part III. and the subsequent Part show the actual battle in progress.

Part III. will be ready on Tuesday, October 24th.

Among the various subjects covered by the Part there are illustrations of the following:

Just before the attack. Blowing up enemy trenches by a huge mine. Royal Engineers rushing off to wire the crater for occupation by the advance troops.

Setting up machine guns. Firing from top of trench parapet. Shrapnel bursting over first line German trenches.

THE ATTACK.

At a signal, along the entire 16-mile front, the British troops leaped over the trench parapets and advanced towards the German trenches, under heavy fire of the enemy.

A sunken road in "No Man's Land" occupied by Lancashire Fusiliers. (20 minutes after this picture was taken these men came under heavy machine gun fire).

Warwickshires advancing up a captured trench to relieve the Queen's in the front line.

British Tommies rescuing a comrade under shell fire. (This man died 30 minutes after reaching the trenches). Conveying the wounded by wheeled stretchers.

A Lancashire Battalion, which has been relieved after a successful attack, returns with prisoners. Friend and Foe help each other.

Royal Field Artillery moving up during Battle over ground where the Gordons' and Devons' dead are lying, after a glorious and successful charge on the ridge near Mametz.

These two batteries advanced under fire to a position beyond Mametz and were fortunate in having no casualties.

Remember, the Official Photographs and Cinematograph Films have been taken with certain definite objects.

They enable us to realise more fully the sacrifices made by our brave men at the Front, and how their achievements have been rendered possible by the untiring labour of our women and men in the Factories and kindred industries at home.

They also show Neutral Nations what we are doing, and in this way counteract the faked pictures from Germany.

And thirdly, do they not bring home to us this War as it actually is, and show us the great gallantry and cheerfulness of our men?

Cannot we and must not we emulate them in our stay-at-home life? They are doing their best and giving their best; we at home should give help just as much to bring the War to a conclusion by supplying them with all they need and doing all that we possibly can for them.

The Publishers hope and believe that the excellent pictures in this book will act as an incentive to the British public to take their lessons willingly, and carry out their respective duties with good hearts, until a lasting peace is won.

Some wonderful photographs and films have been taken in France daily by the official photographers since July 1st, and the best of these will appear in "SIR DOUGLAS HAIG'S GREAT PUSH."

The complete work will reveal War as it actually is, and will give you a permanent and authoritative account of the greatest battle in which the people of Great Britain, her Dominions, Colonies, and Dependencies have ever fought. It will be treasured in every home and be handed down from generation to generation.

FILL IN THE FORM BELOW TO-DAY.

ORDER FORM

To M ....
               BOOKSELLER or NEWSAGENT,

....

Please send me Part III., Price 8d., and the following parts as published, of "Sir Douglas Haig's Great Push," *for which I enclose* ....

Name ....

Address ....

HUTCHINSON'S LATEST 6/- NOVELS
AT ALL LIBRARIES AND BOOKSELLERS.

"The book is a tour de-force. One reads it delightedly, because the skill of the raconteur is great."—*Daily Chronicle.*

By LUCAS MALET.

"There is a delicate, almost hypnotic fragrance about Lucas Malet's new novel. The book is charmingly written, almost every sentence shining like a polished gem. Henrietta Pereira is a triumph of characterisation that would make any novel distinctive. No finer portrait could have been executed."—*Daily Telegraph.*

"Mr. Stacpoole is a master in the art of vivid presentation of both character and incident. In this book he has carried that art to a point truly Stevensonian."—*Land and Water.*

"Reveals him at the very top of his form."—*Sunday Times.*

THE REEF OF STARS
By H. DE VERE STACPOOLE.

"A breathless yarn of the tropics—a book full of colour and full of the excitement we thought to have felt the last thrill of when we left the pirate yarns of our boyhood behind. Most heartily to be recommended."—*The World.*

A NEW ALLEN RAINE

LOVE and the WHIRLWIND
By HELEN PROTHERO LEWIS

A fascinating and exciting novel. The wrenching asunder of closest family ties when love enters is shown with poignant effect. The contrasting characters are finely drawn, and through turmoil and tragedy true love shines unwaveringly. The exquisite scenery of the Welsh mountains is beautifully portrayed.

BOUNDARY HOUSE
By PEGGY WEBLING

"A delightful new story of London life with a quaint and original background.

MISS BRADDON'S LAST NOVEL

By M. E. BRADDON — **MARY** — By M. E. BRADDON

A posthumous full-length story of this delightful novelist, who held a first place for the reading public for half a century.

Bindweed
By GABRIELLE VALLINGS.

A vivid first novel by a great-niece of Charles Kingsley and cousin of "Lucas Malet."

"Revealing her talent for story-telling up to her last pages, she continues to do justice to her most conspicuous gift, that of vivid realization of possibility."—*Times.*

Given in Marriage
By B. M. CROKER

"Testifies to Mrs. Croker's unusual expertness as a story-builder."—*Morning Post.*

"Described with the skill that comes from knowledge, the characters she draws are very human and appealing.—*Pall Mall Gazette.*

THE ALTERNATE LIFE
By CURTIS YORKE

"Makes excellent reading.—*Aberdeen Free Press.*

"She has handled her theme so cleverly and so pleasantly. A thoroughly effective story."—*Globe.*

THE DISTAFF DREAMERS
By Mrs. Baillie Saunders

"An original and attractive story staged in a little corner of old London, where a piquant *rapprochement* takes place.—*The Times.*

A NEW NOVEL OF EXCEPTIONAL CHARM.
By the Author of "SUCCESS."

THE INHERITANCE
By UNA L. SILBERRAD.

"Miss Silberrad always tells a good story straightforwardly. 'The Inheritance' is a really enjoyable story."—*Daily Express.*

QUITE A NEW TYPE OF STORY.

THE MAN WITH A SQUARE FACE
By DOROTHY BLACK

A most delightful romance, breezy and refreshing, one to banish depression and weariness, it is indescribably attractive and wholesome.

LONDON: HUTCHINSON & Co., Publishers, PATERNOSTER ROW.

P.T.O.

IMPORTANT WAR BOOKS.

17th EDITION OF THE FAMOUS BOOK
THE FIRST SEVEN DIVISIONS
Being a detailed account of the fighting from Mons to Ypres
By LORD ERNEST HAMILTON (late Captain 11th Hussars)
(Revised and enlarged, with six additional Maps and an Index.)
In cloth gilt, 6s. net, with Maps.

"Easily the best war book. You can read it again and again."—*Morning Post.*
"A book for which the English-speaking peoples have been waiting since the beginning of the war."—*Daily Express.*

AN ENTIRELY NEW WORK OF ESPECIAL INTEREST.
ON THE ROAD FROM MONS With an Army Service Corps Train
By its COMMANDER
In crown 8vo, cloth gilt, with Map, 3s. 6d. net.

A straightforward personal record of the difficulties and dangers overcome by an A.S.C. Train in carrying supplies, etc., for the famous 19th Brigade. The author—one of the first five British officers to land in France in advance of the B.E.F.—commanded his train to the Aisne. It consisted of 200 to 300 vehicles and about 500 horses, split up into sections, and ran great risks of capture or destruction.

AN INTENSELY HUMAN BOOK.
From Dug-Out and Billet: An Officer's Letters to his Mother
In crown 8vo, cloth, 2s. 6d. net.

"'From Dug-Out and Billet' has a pathos all its own. The letters are very intimate, and were no doubt published out of sympathy with others to whom the War has meant unspeakable sacrifice."—*Graphic.*

London: HURST & BLACKETT, LTD.

A Selection from HUTCHINSON & CO.'S War Books.

A BOOK EVERYONE IS READING.
With the Zionists in Gallipoli
By LT.-COLONEL J. H. PATTERSON, D.S.O.
Author of "The Man-Eaters of Tsavo" and "In the Grip of the Nyika."
In crown 8vo, cloth, with Maps, 6s. net

'Neath Verdun
By MAURICE GENEVOIX
With an Introduction by ERNEST LEVISSE
Translated by H. GRAHAME RICHARDS.
In cloth, 6s. net.

"This will surely be one of the comparatively few war books which contemporaries will read and re-read and hand on to posterity."—*The Times.*

AN IMPORTANT NEW WORK.
Through the Serbian Campaign
By GORDON GORDON-SMITH.
With a Preface by M. S. BOSHKOVITCH, formerly Serbian Minister in London.
32 Illustrations and Maps. *In cloth gilt, 12s. 6d. net.*

The story of Serbia's loyalty to her Allies, and her heroism, told by one who accompanied her Army throughout.

"It is a book of monumental industry, as full of knowledge as an egg of meat, and with much illuminating thought."—*Glasgow Herald.*

The Causes and Consequences of the War
By YVES GUYOT
Late French Minister of State, &c.
In one large volume, cloth gilt, 10/6 net.
Translated by F. APPLEBY HOLT, B.A., LL.B.

The Soul of Germany
By THOMAS F. A. SMITH, Ph.D.
(Late English Lecturer in the University of Erlangen).

"This illuminating book, derived from the pain begotten wealth of twelve years' experience should be on the shelves of everyone who desires to identify the German of Louvain and Dinant with the German of Germany."—*Morning Post.*

9 Large 6/- editions sold out. New Cheap Edition, now ready, 2/6 net.

DEEDS THAT THRILL THE EMPIRE
True Stories of the Most Glorious Acts of Heroism of the Empire's Soldiers and Sailors during the Great War.
WITH A FOREWORD BY THE EARL OF DERBY K.G.
With over 700 Original Drawings by Leading Artists; and many Fine Coloured Plates.
WRITTEN BY WELL-KNOWN AUTHORS
Volume I Now Ready.
In demy 4to 440 pages, 462 black and white illustrations and 12 coloured plates bound in handsome cloth gilt and gilt edges, 10/6 net. And in various leather bindings.

A BEAUTIFUL LASTING RECORD OF BELGIUM'S RUINED WORKS OF ART.
BELGIUM THE GLORIOUS: Her Country and Her People
Written by well-known Authorities
Edited by WALTER HUTCHINSON, M.A., F.R.G.S., F.R.A.I., F.R.S.A., Barrister-at-Law.

In 2 handsome volumes, with 18 beautiful coloured plates, over 1,100 artistic black-and-white drawings, and 13 maps.
Net price, 10s. per volume.

A wiring party going up to the trenches.

This illustration and the one on the opposite page—

But terrific and prolonged though our artillery preparation had been, there were points where the enemy's defences were still comparatively intact. In places, such as the corner of the wood at Fricourt, and in the trench known as "Danzig Avenue" on the ridge by Mametz, their machine-guns had been so effectually hidden as to escape our bombardment, for no artillery can destroy every cache; and here the Germans offered a desperate resistance, emerging from the enormously deep dug-outs, such as are easily excavated in this hilly and chalky country, in which they had remained secure, and working their machine-guns with the utmost skill and determination. The Danzig trench was eventually cleared by the Gordon Highlanders and Manchesters, though not until they had sustained heavy casualties. For the machine-gunners fought their deadly weapons to the last moment, many refusing to surrender, and being bombed or bayoneted where they stood. A pathetic incident in the attack on the Danzig trench was the death of the Manchesters' pet dog, who had accompanied his master in the charge. Both master and dog were killed at the same moment, and were found afterwards lying a few paces apart.

By the evening the village of Mametz was entirely in our hands, and several field-batteries had been brought up and were shelling the high ground beyond it. The village presented a terrible sight. Such had been the devastating effect of our artillery that there was scarcely a house which had even a part of the wall rising to second story height, while the church looked like the pedestal of a statue. In places the German trenches had been virtually filled in by our shell-fire; many of the dug-outs were completely blocked, and in those where the doorways

The East Yorks marching to the trenches.

—show fine panoramic views of the Manchesters' church parade on the evening before the attack.

were clear our stretcher-bearers descended by flights of twenty or twenty-five steps, to find at the bottom heaps of dead, among whom were a few men who still breathed.

Fricourt offered a more difficult problem. The Germans had laboriously organized the defences of the village, and the position was all the more advantageous to them, as the houses are built in échelon formation, as it were, and sweep up in a gentle slope to the eminence that culminates in the wood of Fricourt. The enemy had fortified the outer girdle of houses which followed the railway line, and had armed the interior line with small forts full of machine-guns. Hence, the principal streets could be taken in enfilade, in the event of the first line being broken. The wood itself had been likewise the object of special attention on the part of the German engineers, and opposed formidable obstacles to our advance.

The German first-line trenches in front of Fricourt had been reduced to a mere wreckage of earth, and those behind were in little better case; but there were deep dug-outs which had remained untouched, and during our bombardment men were sheltering there with machine-guns and long periscopes, through which they could see the British lines. The moment the first wave of men broke over our parapet these machine-gunners rushed up the steps, and from behind what cover the débris of their shattered trenches afforded them, raked our advancing lines with streams of bullets. Attached to each gun-team was a crack rifle shot, who had orders to pick off the officers, and so deadly was the marksmanship of the snipers that by the time one North-Country battalion had crossed the one hundred and fifty yards to the enemy's first line they

Rank and file of the East Yorks. Notice their jolly faces.

had scarcely any officers left. Once our men were upon them, however, bayonet or bomb quickly put an end to their powers of mischief, and the victors pushed on to the second and third lines, which were carried after some fierce fighting. Beyond the third line, to the left of Fricourt, lay a work called Crucifix Trench, the possession of which would greatly facilitate our capture of the village; and against this some Yorkshire troops advanced, though the intervening ground was being very heavily shelled and machine-guns from Fricourt were enfilading them viciously. As they approached the trench, they were saluted with a storm of bombs by the Germans who occupied it. They returned the compliment, and then, rushing through the gaps in the parapet, followed up the effect of their bombs with such good work with the bayonet that in a very short time all resistance ceased and the Crucifix was in our hands. Further progress was impossible that day, since just beyond the captured trench

A huge "dump" of "plum-puddings." These bombs are most effective in smashing the enemy's barbed-wire entanglements.

was a wood called Shelter Wood, at the south-east corner of which the enemy had erected a redoubt bristling with machine-guns. Substantial progress, however, had been made on the other side of Fricourt, so that the village was partially surrounded, while Montauban to the north-east, which our bombardment had reduced to a rubbish heap and to one vast series of shell-craters so deep and so broad that it looked like a field of extinct volcanoes, had been captured.

The attack on Montauban was carried out mainly by Lancashire troops, supported by the Bedfords and Home County battalions. On the right centre two battalions found themselves in a tract of ground known as the Warren, and most fittingly named, since it was a perfect honeycomb of mine-craters, shell-burrows, bashed-in trenches and broken wire-entanglements; and, while floundering through these obstructions, came under a galling machine-gun fire. But, pushing on with the utmost resolution, mostly in what is known as artillery formation, so as to present as small a target as possible to the enemy's gunners, they wriggled their way along, killing or capturing all the Germans whom they

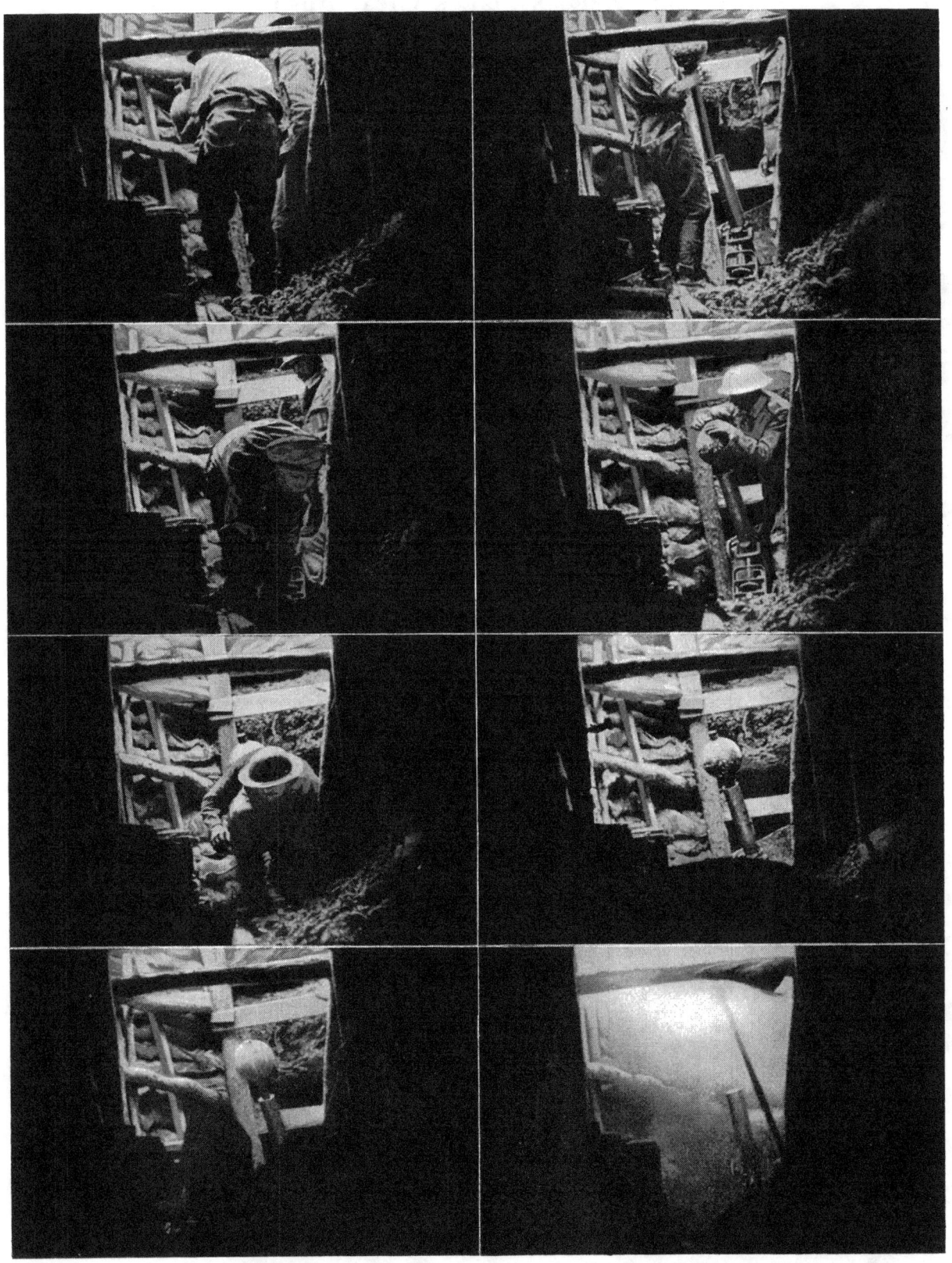

FIRING "PLUM-PUDDINGS" INTO THE GERMAN TRENCHES.

These eight wonderful pictures show the consecutive steps in the firing of a trench-mortar. Commencing at the top from left to right we see the "plum-pudding" fetched and placed in the mortar; one of the men then retires into the dug-out, while the other sets the fuze; he in his turn retires, and we see the bomb just before, at the very moment of, and then immediately after the discharge.

A sergeant organizing the supply of bombs and an officer checking them.

encountered, until they had cleared the Warren and linked up with their comrades on the outskirts of Montauban. From every mutilated house in the ruined village came the rattle of machine-guns and the crackling of rifle fire, but nothing could stay the advance of the Khaki tide, which swept over the pulverized German trenches and into the streets of Montauban as the surf sweeps over ribbed sand. Here for a while there was a furious hand-to-hand struggle. But the Germans had to give way, and slowly but surely they were pressed back through the further end of the village, until they broke and scurried for the shelter of their second line. Montauban was ours. A large number of prisoners were captured here, the greater part of whom had taken refuge from our bombardment in cellars and dug-outs. On the entry of our troops these came out of their hiding-places and surrendered, some of them falling on their knees and begging piteously for mercy, so demoralized were they by the frightful fire to which they had been subjected. To their credit, it should be mentioned, however, that some of the enemy were made of sterner stuff, and in more than one instance parties of them preferred death to surrender. Thus, a handful of snipers had remained concealed in a deep dug-out containing several orifices and bolt-holes which had been overlooked by our troops when they carried the trenches in front of the village, and, as soon as the charge had passed, they began sniping in all directions. Several of our men had fallen before the firing was located, when a rush was made to the spot, and the Germans were called upon to surrender. No

The men carrying up the bombs from the "dumps" under the direction of a non-commissioned officer.

response being made to this invitation, bombs were thrown down the stairways; but these must have been ineffective, for, when our men had retired, the firing from the rear promptly broke out again. Finally a hole was made in the top of the dug-out, in which a powerful charge of aminel was inserted and detonated, with apparently satisfactory results.

Some hundreds of yards east of Montauban, in the direction of Péronne, a very

Men at work loading a 9'2-inch howitzer.

brilliant little piece of work was accomplished by a force which had been left in reserve. Here stood a disused brick-yard, which had been converted into a formidable German *fortin*, bristling with machine-guns and trench-mortars, and which, despite the pounding it had received from our artillery, showed, by the incessant fire which proceeded from it, that it was still a place to be reckoned with. Upon this our men advanced, and passing through the squall of bullets which burst upon them as coolly as though they were rehearsing an attack upon a home parade-ground, carried it with one rush, the defence promptly collapsing as soon as they reached the entrance to the place.

The loss of Montauban was a serious blow to the enemy, who at once turned their guns upon the position, while in the course of the afternoon their infantry counter-attacked in determined fashion. But our men clung to the ground they had won with splendid determination throughout the bombardment, and when the assault was delivered, met it with so withering a machine-gun and rifle fire, that it was completely broken up. Meanwhile, terrific fighting was in

Bombarding the Germans with 9'2-inch howitzers.

progress on the extreme left of our offensive, over a stretch of about four miles from the Ancre Valley northwards to Gommecourt. About the Gommecourt salient the German defences were as perfect as defences could well be, their dug-outs being so deep and so solidly built that they were practically indestructible. The enemy had concentrated a great mass of artillery and an enormous number of machine-guns here, in the belief that the British main attack was to extend from Lille to Roye. The big guns barraged our front and support trenches with a most infernal fire; while the machine-guns were in position within a few seconds of our own bombardment lifting, and so numerous were these deadly weapons that their clamour as they spat their streams of lead amongst our advancing troops is said actually to have drowned the noise of the artillery. In places where the rain of bombs from our trench-mortars was smothering their trenches, the enemy, with great courage, came out into No Man's Land and worked their guns in the open.

Through this inferno of bullets and explosives our troops advanced as steadily as on parade, not a man faltering save those who fell, and with bomb and bayonet forced their way into and across the German first-line trenches, onwards to their second line, and even in places to their third. But, under the murderous fire to which they were exposed their losses were so great that no lasting success was possible; they could not hold the ground they had won, and though a party of some one hundred men belonging to a Lancashire battalion actually succeeded in fighting their way into a village bristling with machine-guns beyond the enemy's third line, at a point south-east of Hébuterne, they appear to have been entirely wiped out, since not one of them was seen again.

Further to the right, where the troops engaged were chiefly Midland and West of England battalions, and where there was a sanguinary hand-to-hand struggle for the possession of the German first-line trenches some Territorials,

High-explosive shells fired by the 12-inch howitzers. This type created great havoc in the enemy's lines.

pushing on in advance of their comrades, penetrated as far as a small wood called Pendant Copse, south-east of Serre, from which place they sent urgent messages calling for help. But no reinforcements

Preparing to load a heavy howitzer Hoisting the shell.

A complimentary message to Fritz.

The Battle of the Somme

Ramming a shell into a 12-inch howitzer.

could possibly have lived through the terrific shell-fire which was sweeping the intervening ground, and the gallant Territorials appear to have shared the fate of the Lancashire lads.

Further south still, near the German stronghold of Beaumont-Hamel, from which machine-guns in concrete emplacements swept No Man's Land like a scythe, Ulster battalions, advancing with their battle-cry of "No Surrender!" carried three lines of German trenches, repulsed repeated counter-attacks, and captured a number of prisoners; but their losses were terrible, and eventually what was left of them were obliged to retire.

South of the Ancre more success rewarded the heroism of our men. By one o'clock in the afternoon some ground had been gained about Authuille and Ovillers, north of La Boiselle; a part of La Boiselle itself was in our hands, and the Lincolns, and other troops past La Boiselle to Contalmaison. They had to make their way through very heavy shell-fire, and were furiously enfiladed by machine-guns from La Boiselle and the high ground above it, the bullets pattering down like rain. They took the first line of German trenches, which had been blown to atoms with the bodies of the men who held them, and quickly bombed out the defenders of the second. But, as they passed La Boiselle and approached the enemy's third line, they had to encounter a perfectly appalling fire. "It seemed to me," observed one of the Lincolns, "that there was a machine-gun to every five men of the enemy." And it

Preparing the gun previous to firing.

our troops were fighting in the village of Contalmaison, two miles east of our original front, part of which had also been captured, though our gains here could not be held.

A really memorable feat of arms was the advance of the Royal Scots,

The gun in position after being fired.

was not only machine-guns which mowed them down; the sky above them was white with the puffs of the bursting shrapnel, and high-explosive shells and trench-mortar bombs churned up the ground on every side. Nevertheless, the German trenches were reached and carried, the Royal Scots charging in such determined fashion with the bayonet that all the fight was knocked out of the enemy, and the other battalions, as they came up at the double, had little to do but take prisoners.

About Authuille, where the troops engaged were the Dorsets, Manchesters, Highland Light Infantry and Borderers, there was some very hard fighting, for, though the German first-line trenches had been so pulverized by our bombardment that they were easily taken, the second offered a stubborn resistance; and it was only after a veritable battle of bombs that it was eventually broken down.

Further north, a furious struggle was in progress for the possession of Thiépval. Between Ovillers

These high-explosive shells are fired by the 12-inch howitzers, which have created such havoc in the enemy's lines.

and Thiépval the fortified ridges, rising hereabouts to nearly five hundred feet, dominated all our lines of attack, and assaults in the old way, such as those of the Russians at Plevna, were child's play compared to this task. The Thiépval defences had been subjected to a terrific bombardment for days past, but they were of immense strength, some of the dug-outs in the first line of trenches going thirty feet below ground, and in some cases having trap-doors leading to still lower chambers. Built with the most remarkable solidity and equipped as if for permanent habitations, these caves were for the most part shell-proof and were stored with bombs, grenades and machine-guns. The retention of Thiépval was of the most vital importance to the enemy, since, if it fell, they had no place of equal strength to oppose our advance over the sector to the north, where stand Beaumont-Hamel and Gommecourt, and here they had posted some of their best troops, the machine-gunners having been sworn to fight to the death, while behind their lines was a great concentration of artillery. Notwithstanding the hellish fire which swept through them, our troops advanced with the most superb bravery, carried the first

ROYAL WARWICKSHIRES IN CAMP.

Two good panoramic views of the Royal Warwickshires in camp behind the firing-line on the evening before the Great Advance. Everything is being prepared for the great battle to be commenced on the next day.

The Royal Warwickshires waiting to receive their portion of stew.

Men of the Royal Warwickshires having a meal in camp on the evening before the Great Advance.

line of trenches and pressed on beyond them, though at several points, where they had not stopped to clear out the dug-outs in which the enemy were in hiding, or to search for all the machine-gun emplacements, the Germans, emerging from their hiding-places, rushed to their guns and poured a stream of bullets into the backs of the men who had gone forward.

A view taken from the British trenches showing a shell bursting over Beaumont-Hamel. Here shells were fired continuously day and night for five days previous to the Great Push.

Little progress, however, could be made on the northern side of Thiépval, where the enemy's fortifications on a steep ridge just above the river defied all the valour and resolution of our troops.

All this time, from every part of the long battle-front, a continual stream of wounded men was flowing back to the casualty clearing-stations behind the British lines. The serious cases were brought back on stretchers; the others walked along unaided or with the assistance of comrades, often wounded themselves, or rode on lorries, which had taken up ammunition and were now bringing back casualties, sometimes fifty or more on one lorry.

"They were wonderful men," writes Mr. Philip Gibbs, the special correspondent of the *Daily Chronicle*, "so wonderful in their gaiety and courage that one's heart melted at the sight of them. They were all grinning, as though they had come from a jolly in which they had been bumped a little. There was a look of pride in their eyes as they came driving down like wounded knights from a tourney. They had gone through the job with honour and had come out with their lives, and the world was good and beautiful again in this warm sun, in these snug French villages, where peasant men and women waved hands to them, and in these fields of scarlet and gold and green.

"The men who are going up to the battle grinned back at those who were coming back. One could not see the faces of the lying-down cases, only the soles of their boots as they passed; but the laughing men on the lorries—some of them stripped to the waist and bandaged roughly—seemed to rob war of some of its horrors; and the spirit of our British soldiers shines very bright along the roads of France, so that the very sun seems to get some of its gold from these men's hearts."

Other men were coming back too, sometimes in batches of a dozen or more, sometimes in long

A further moving up of troops. Reserves were being marched up to the reserve trenches over the greater part of the British lines previous to July 1st, in order that there might be no shortage of men in any section where our losses were particularly heavy.

columns—men in green-grey uniforms, round, peakless caps, and high boots. They were German prisoners, Prussians and Bavarians chiefly, with a sprinkling of men from Baden and other States. On the whole they were tall, strongly-built men, and not a few of them were obviously superior to the artisan or peasant types, which formed the majority, but they were all alike haggard, worn and dirty. Some were wounded and were being helped along by their comrades or their captors, the worst cases being carried on stretchers. Here, a German who had been badly hit in the left foot was hopping along with his arm round the neck of a British soldier; there, two unwounded Germans were supporting the tottering steps of one of their wounded foes. A curious sight was presented by a long column of prisoners several hundred strong coming from the direction of Mametz. At the head of this column strutted three privates of the Gordon Highlanders, all blood and dirt and rags, with their rifles at the slope, like pipers at the head of a Scottish battalion; while the rear was brought up by a wounded officer of the same regiment with his arm in a sling, who subsequently remarked, laughingly, that "he couldn't equal the swagger of those three Jocks in the lead." At a spot near Authuille, a wounded corporal of the Dorsets might have been seen driving before him five stalwart Huns, whom he had taken prisoners single-handed. He brought them into our lines, and then, without waiting to have his hurts attended to, hurried back to assist an officer of his battalion

A battalion of the Worcesters fixing wire-cutters to their rifles for forcing the German barbed-wire entanglements.

A new battalion of the Royal Warwickshires resting on their way to the trenches.

Royal Warwickshires resting in reserve.

Another illustration showing the Royal Warwickshires resting.

whom he had seen lying wounded in a shell-hole.

Not a few of the prisoners were so utterly nerve-shattered by the dreadful effects of our bombardment that they appeared to imagine that it was intended to shoot them, and when they reached the British lines held up their hands whenever they passed a group of our men. The treatment they received at the hands of their captors, who gave them food and water, which many declared they had not tasted

A field battery brought up across the captured German trenches, in action within two hours of the Germans retiring.

for two or three days, owing to the impossibility of getting supplies up the communication trenches in the face of our intense fire, and distributed cigarettes amongst them, went far to reassure even these poor wretches; and after their papers had been taken and their identification books examined and handed back, and they were able to smoke and satisfy the cravings of hunger, most of the prisoners appeared quite resigned to their fate. True, here and there sullen and angry faces might be seen— faces of men who scowled at their captors and muttered imprecations upon the hated English under their breath. But these were the exception, and the majority seemed pleased enough to be out of the war, with the prospect before them of regular meals and sleep undisturbed by the thunder of the guns and surprise visits from raiding parties.

Throughout the day our aeroplanes were very active and afforded valuable assistance to our operations. Numerous enemy headquarters and railway centres were attacked with bombs, and much

Two dumb victims—horses killed in bringing the battery up.

The catch of a 9·45-inch trench mortar being released to enable it to be revolved on its base.

In the three following illustrations the gun is being pushed round for the gunners to load with a "flying pig," as the ammunition is called.

Here the gun is shown being lowered and loaded.

It is then raised again—

—and revolved back to its former position and prepared for firing.

The men then retire, and the bomb is fired into the German trenches.

damage inflicted. In one of these raids our escorting aeroplanes were attacked by twenty Fokkers, which were beaten off, two of them being driven down and destroyed. An attack was made by some of our machines on a railway train between Douai and Cambrai, one of our airmen descending to below nine hundred feet and dropping a bomb on one of the trucks, which exploded. Other pilots saw the whole train in flames and heard explosions which seemed to indicate that the train was loaded with ammunition. Several long-distance reconnaissances were carried out, despite numerous attempts by the enemy's machines to frustrate them; and our kite balloons were in the air the whole day, while the German balloons were conspicuous by their absence.

The principal achievement of the second day of the great battle was the capture of Fricourt. The

A huge shell, weighing 1,400lb., ready to be fired by the 15-inch howitzer, or "Grandmother," as it is called. Notice the message chalked on it by one of the gunners.

ground which we had won the previous day had been heavily shelled by the enemy during the night, but our men had held on to it with splendid determination; and early in the morning, having been strongly reinforced, they resumed the offensive, one body of troops working round to the north, and another fighting their way round the south side, until the salient had been contracted too narrowly for further successful resistance. Then the village was attacked simultaneously in front and flank, the troops concerned in the latter movement being a new division which had yet to win its spurs. It won them handsomely, and by two o'clock in the afternoon Fricourt was ours.

The village, like Mametz and Montauban, was merely a heap of ruins, while the trenches in many places had been simply pounded to bits. Behind the remnant of one parapet lay a German grenadier, still clasping in his clenched right hand the grenade which he was about to throw when death overtook him. Further away was a group of three infantrymen, who had been struck down together by a shell

The Battle of the Somme

and half buried beneath a fallen wall. In every corner, in every shell hole or wrecked dug-out, were dead and yet more dead. In one part of the trenches they lay thick, tall, fine men for the most part, one, who was covered with wounds, being quite a giant. Another was lying on his back, with his face turned up to the blue sky, and his hands raised above his body, as though in prayer. Before our final attack was delivered most of the enemy had filtered out in retreat, leaving some

These shells tore up the ground and made great craters, which would be large enough in many cases to hold a motor 'bus.

of their wounded behind them. But about one hundred and fifty men, who had taken refuge in dug-outs, emerged from their hiding-places and came forward, holding up their hands. They belonged to regiments of the 14th Reserve Corps and were mostly from Baden, and asserted that they had had nothing to eat or drink since the early hours of the previous day, the intensity of our bombardment, which they described as terrible, having prevented supplies from reaching them. A prisoner of another kind was taken at Fricourt, in the shape of a fox-terrier puppy, left behind by his German master. The poor little fellow was promptly adopted by one of our battalions.

Fricourt taken, our men advanced to gain possession of the high ridge above the village. The enemy's guns swept the ridge with a storm of shrapnel and high explosive, while from the upper part of the Fricourt Wood came the incessant clatter of machine-guns. However, our attack did not falter, and by the end of the day considerable progress had been made.

Meantime, heavy fighting was taking

Over twenty shells, each weighing 1,400lb., before they were fired by "Grandmother" on the German lines.

place at other spots between the Ancre and the Somme, particularly about La Boiselle, part of which had fallen into our hands the previous day. Here the enemy offered a most stubborn resistance, their machine-guns being very numerous and admirably served, while their artillery in the rear kept up a continuous deluge of shrapnel. But, notwithstanding the terrible fire through which they had to make their way, our brave fellows were not to be denied, and slowly but surely they pushed forward, until by the evening they had succeeded in penetrating into the village. The final effort, which was to give us possession of the place, was, however, reserved for the morrow.

During the day excellent work was again performed by our aircraft. In the forenoon several attempts at offensive action on our side of the line were made by the German airmen, several machines swooping down together. All these attempts were successfully repulsed, and subsequently our airmen assumed

Operating the 15-inch howitzer, or "Grandmother," manned by the Royal Marine Artillery.

the offensive, in their turn, and held the enemy's aeroplanes far behind the German lines, with the result that the machines which were observing for our artillery were able to do their work without interruption. A very large number of aerial combats took place over the enemy's lines, in the course of which six hostile machines were brought down, while five others were driven down in a seriously damaged condition. On our side, seven machines were reported missing.

CHAPTER III

VERY early on the morning of July 3rd a great bombardment began from both sides, the enemy shelling the places we had taken from them, and our guns putting a heavy barrage on their positions. The British batteries were concentrating upon the German lines behind Fricourt and Mametz Wood and La Boiselle, shells from our heavies screaming continuously through the air, while the field-guns seemed

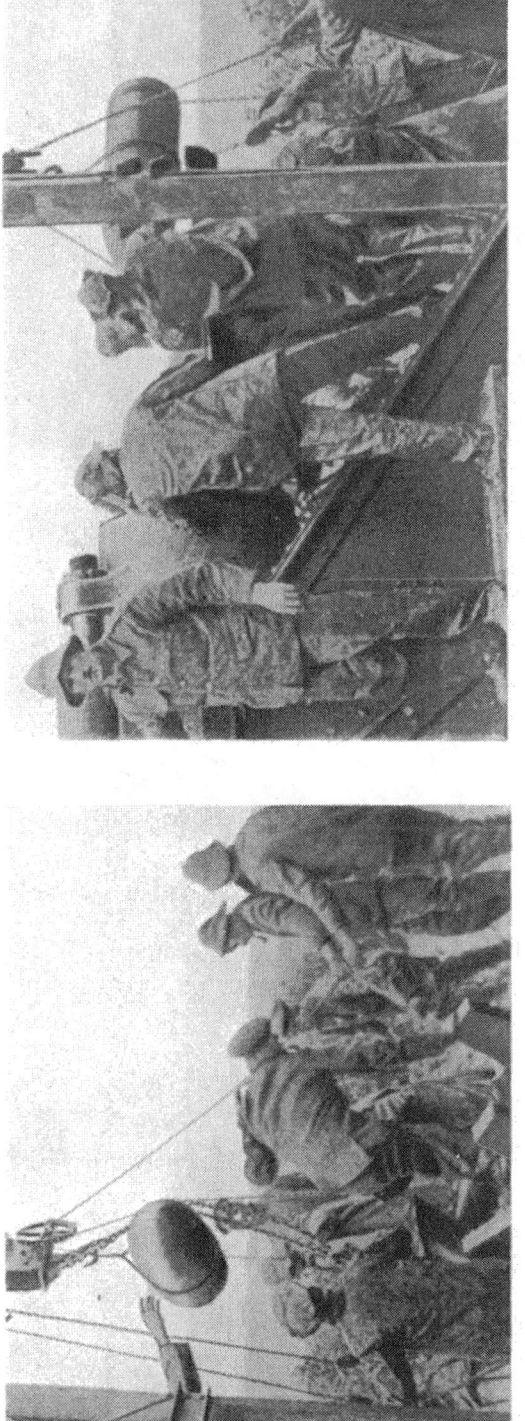

Here the shell is being hauled up from the ammunition wagon.—
—It is then pulled in and—
—placed on a receiver,—
—from which position it is rammed into the gun.

LOADING A 15-INCH HOWITZER, OR "GRANDMOTHER."

A 15-INCH HOWITZER, OR "GRANDMOTHER," FIRING ITS 1,400lb. SHELL.

The morning of the attack, July 1st, 1916.

to be firing with almost the rapidity of Maxims. The enemy were replying chiefly on the ground about La Boiselle, and there was one spot near the northern end of the La Boiselle Wood where British and German shells seemed to meet and mingle their explosions. " In what was once a village," writes the special correspondent of the *Daily Chronicle*, " there were dense clouds of smoke, which rose up in columns and then spread out like a pall. In the very centre of this place, which looks like one of Dante's visions of hell-fire, one of our soldiers was signalling with a flaming torch. The red flame moved backwards and forwards through the wrack of smoke, and was then tossed high, as a new burst of shrapnel broke over the place where the signaller stood." Here, as at other points of the line, however, the British fire was by far the most intense, and it was observed that many of the German shells appeared to come from an extreme range by high-angle fire. From which circumstance it was inferred that the enemy, having been unable so far to bring up supports to strengthen their defence, had withdrawn their artillery far to the rear, in order to minimize the risk of capture.

All the forenoon our troops were gradually working their way forward in the vicinity of La Boiselle until the village was partially surrounded. Then a mass of artillery was concentrated upon it and poured in such a tornado of shell that nothing could be seen of the place for the smoke which enveloped it. This bombardment proved to be the *coup de grâce*, for when the guns lifted our infantry closed in on the position, and the remnant of the garrison surrendered, though one machine-gunner went on working his deadly weapon until he was overpowered and made prisoner. It was well that his life was spared, for he was a right gallant fellow, who had stuck to his gun, notwithstanding that he had received no less than nine wounds. Beside another machine-gun the whole of the team were lying dead ; a single shell had accounted for them all. Some two hundred and fifty Germans were captured here, all that were left of a whole battalion which had originally garrisoned the village, and with them an heroic doctor, who was binding the wounded in a dug-out, whither he had had them carried from the dressing-station, which

Terrific bombardment of the German trenches.

had been demolished by our fire. This same doctor afterwards did much good work amongst our own wounded, under heavy fire from his compatriots' guns which had been promptly turned upon the captured position. Just before the remnant of the La Boiselle garrison capitulated, an entire battalion of the 186th Prussian Regiment surrendered to the British between Fricourt and Contalmaison. This battalion, composed for the most part of stalwart fellows recruited along the Upper Rhine, had been rushed up to replace very heavy casualties, and, on detraining, was at once sent into the trenches. Our artillery was, however, ready for the new-comers and directed a rain of shrapnel upon the place where they were debouching from a communication trench, and with deadly effect, since the trenches at this point were too shallow and wide to afford them much protection from our fire. This continued for a quarter of an hour, at the end of which the survivors, to the number of twenty officers and some six hundred men, perceiving our infantry advancing to the attack, prudently decided that they had had enough of it, and, emerging from the trench, came towards them with signs of surrender. The whole rout of them was

A Lancashire battalion awaiting instructions.

Anzacs resting for a few minutes on their way to the trenches.

—to the first line. Notice the spade which is carried by the man seen on the extreme left.—

In a reserve trench. Ready to line the front trenches. Having fixed bayonets, the men pass through the communication trench—

—The bombers taking up supplies very soon pass as we watch at this corner.— —and so they file past.

TROOPS MOVING UP A COMMUNICATION TRENCH INTO THE FRONT LINE.

The Loyal North Lancashire Regiment parading for the trenches.

SCALA THEATRE
CHARLOTTE STREET, W.
(GOODGE STREET TUBE STATION.)

AT THE FRONT
OFFICIAL WAR OFFICE FILMS.
KUT RELIEF FORCES.

SALONIKA.   FRENCH ARMY.
RUSSIAN ARMY.   EAST AFRICA. &c.

THE BATTLE of the SOMME

"There is no programme in London which gives so complete and vivid a description of the War on ALL FRONTS."
—*Evening News.*

THE KING'S ADVICE:

SEE THE SOMME WAR FILM AND WHAT WAR MEANS

"The public should see these pictures, that they may have some idea of what the Army is doing, and what war means."

This statement was made by the King after witnessing a programme of the Official War Office film "The Battle of the Somme," which was shown by command to the King and Queen at Windsor Castle.
—*Daily Express.*

DAILY, 3 and 8.

BOX OFFICE, 10 to 10.   'Phone: Gerr., 1,444 and 1,366.

SCALA THEATRE

Did you buy this book because you are fond of pictures?

If so, the **DAILY SKETCH** will appeal to you. It is the premier picture paper. Happenings all over the world are illustrated in its pages — and you can watch the progress of the war *daily*—almost as if you were a spectator!

The best week-end picture paper is the
ILLUSTRATED SUNDAY HERALD.

PRINTED AT THE CHAPEL RIVER PRESS, KINGSTON-ON-THAMES

IN ABOUT 8 FORTNIGHTLY PARTS.　　HUTCHINSON'S NEW PART WORK　　Part IV. ready Nov. 7th. PART III. 8d. NET

SIR DOUGLAS HAIG'S
GREAT PUSH

THE BATTLE OF THE SOMME

A popular, pictorial and authoritative work on one of the Greatest Battles in History, illustrated by about **700** *wonderful* **OFFICIAL PHOTOGRAPHS AND CINEMATOGRAPH FILMS** *and other authentic pictures*

BY ARRANGEMENT WITH THE WAR OFFICE

The Assault on July 1st.

GREAT VALUE FOR EIGHTPENCE

THIS PART CONTAINS **84 WONDERFUL REPRODUCTIONS** OF THE FAMOUS **WAR OFFICE CINEMATOGRAPH FILMS** AND **OFFICIAL PHOTOGRAPHS** OF THE BATTLE OF THE SOMME, BEAUTIFULLY PRINTED ON THE BEST ENGLISH ART PAPER.

LONDON : HUTCHINSON & Co.

SCALA THEATRE
CHARLOTTE STREET, W.
(GOODGE STREET TUBE STATION.)

AT THE FRONT
OFFICIAL WAR OFFICE FILMS.
KUT RELIEF FORCES.

SALONIKA.   FRENCH ARMY.
RUSSIAN ARMY.   EAST AFRICA, &c.

THE BATTLE of the SOMME

"There is no programme in London which gives so complete and vivid a description of the War on ALL FRONTS."
—*Evening News.*

THE KING'S ADVICE:

SEE THE SOMME WAR FILM AND WHAT WAR MEANS.

"The public should see these pictures, that they may have some idea of what the Army is doing, and what war means."

This statement was made by the King after witnessing a programme of the Official War Office film "The Battle of the Somme," which was shown by command to the King and Queen at Windsor Castle.
—*Daily Express.*

DAILY, 3 and 8.

BOX OFFICE, 10 to 10.   'Phone: Gerr., 1,444 and 1,366.

SCALA THEATRE

promptly packed off to our rear, with such dispatch that scarcely a life was lost from the fire of their friends, which was sweeping the intervening ground.

Meanwhile, fierce fighting was in progress at other points between the Ancre and the Somme, and particularly about Ovillers, where in the early morning we were successful in capturing a portion of the hostile defences. Elsewhere we succeeded in holding all the ground we had gained, notwithstanding heavy shelling and repeated counter-attacks.

Throughout the day our aircraft again displayed great activity and an astonishing boldness. Our bombing aeroplanes, penetrating far behind the enemy's lines, attacked the important railway centres at Cumines, seven miles south-east of Ypres, on the Franco-Belgian frontier, Combles, ten miles east of Albert, and St. Quentin, on the Lille–Paris trunk line, twenty miles behind the German battle-front, at

A big railway gun firing.

each of which places considerable damage was inflicted. On these expeditions hostile aeroplanes were encountered in great numbers and much fighting took place, which in practically every instance terminated to our advantage, four of the German machines being brought down, while at least three others were driven to the ground in a damaged condition.

During the night the enemy, who had by this time been reinforced by numerous battalions drawn from all parts of their line, made most determined efforts to regain possession of La Boiselle, where our position was as yet far from consolidated. But our troops, fighting with the greatest gallantry, repulsed every attack, and, although the Germans contrived to recapture a small portion of the trenches south of the village, elsewhere they could make no impression on the defence.

On other sectors of our front trench warfare activity continued, and the Germans attempted to retaliate for the losses they had suffered at the hands of our raiding parties by a raid in considerable force on our trenches to the south of Armentières. But this attack, which had been preceded by a heavy bombardment, found our men well prepared, and broke down completely before our machine-gun and rifle fire. Severe losses were inflicted on the enemy, who retreated in con-

Setting a machine-gun on the top of the parapet.

fusion, leaving some of their wounded behind them.

On the other hand, several successful raids were carried out by the British, one by the Rifle Brigade and another by the Sherwood Foresters being particularly successful.

Heavy thunderstorms, with torrential rains, which rendered artillery observation difficult, interfered somewhat with offensive operations during the greater part of the 4th, and the work of our troops chiefly consisted in minor local advances, with a view to consolidating the ground already gained. In the afternoon the enemy made a determined bombing attack on that part of their original first line of trenches which we had captured to the south of Thiépval, but it was easily repulsed, with considerable loss to the assailants. Between Thiépval and the Ancre the Germans heavily shelled our newly-won trenches, but without causing us to abandon any portion of them, and on the northern parts of our front there was considerable artillery activity about Loos and the Hohenzollern Redoubt. During the night there was heavy fighting between the Ancre and the Somme, and we made further progress at certain important points. The German artillery fire was intense in certain sectors, and in the neighbourhood of Thiépval, after a fierce bombardment, the enemy launched two most determined attacks against our new trenches. Both, however, were beaten off with loss.

After the first four days of battle there was something approaching a lull of twenty-four hours; that is to say, though fighting still continued all along the front, and particularly between the Ancre and the Somme, where some fierce hand-to-hand work and bombing took place, it was mostly in the nature of local struggles for the possession of certain strong points, and no movement of importance was undertaken by the British. In the result our troops advanced slightly in certain sectors and held the ground they had won elsewhere, breaking up several determined attacks,

A machine-gun being adjusted.

in which the enemy's casualties were very heavy. Many more prisoners fell into our hands, and on the evening of the 5th Sir Douglas Haig reported that the total number taken during the last five days now amounted to over six thousand. During the night of the

Just before the attack. Blowing up the enemy trenches by a huge mine. The photographs show successive stages in the explosion.

Troops coming through a wood.

5th–6th, to the south of the La Bassée Canal, after the discharge of gas and smoke clouds, some highly successful raids were made into the enemy's front line. In one of these a party of the Royal Welsh Fusiliers, a regiment whose bomb-throwers had on several occasions performed brilliant work — notably, at Festubert in May, 1915, when a mere handful of them cleared five hundred yards of hostile trenches and took over one hundred prisoners — particularly distinguished themselves. Bursting into the German trenches with one irresistible rush, the Welshmen destroyed three mine shafts, captured a trench mortar and a machine-gun, killed or put out of action some one hundred and fifty of the enemy and brought back forty-three prisoners. In another raid the Highland Light Infantry successfully entered the enemy's trenches west of Hulluch (two miles north-east of Loos), where they destroyed a machine-gun emplacement, killed a number of Germans, and brought back several prisoners.

An officer in our front-line trenches watching the explosion of the mine shown on page 75.

On the 6th we made a further slight advance near Thiépval, where a number of prisoners were captured, and some progress at other points, as the result of successful bomb attacks. The British artillery was very active all along the line, and one of our heavy batteries secured direct hits on a German battalion in column of route, inflicting many casualties. Low clouds interfered with the work of our aircraft ; but in the Bapaume area one of our aeroplanes, dropping to an altitude of three hundred feet, successfully bombed a train from which reinforcements were alighting.

The night was an exceedingly lively one all along the line and particularly between the Ancre and the Somme, an area which seemed to be ablaze with fire in all its forms : jets of flame from the gun-muzzles, orange flashes from the bursting shrapnel, volcanic eruptions caused by the high-explosive shells, and cascades of white, red and green stars. The enemy heavily bombarded our new positions at Bernafay Wood, Montauban and near La Boiselle, using in some places lachrymatory (tear) shells ; while the British batteries pounded Mametz Wood, the German trench to the west of it, Contalmaison village and the wood and shallow valley on its western side, and at the same time, liberally sprinkled the German communications to the rear with a mixture of explosives. To the east of La Boiselle there was severe fighting,

Engineers rushing off to wire the crater for occupation by the advance troops.

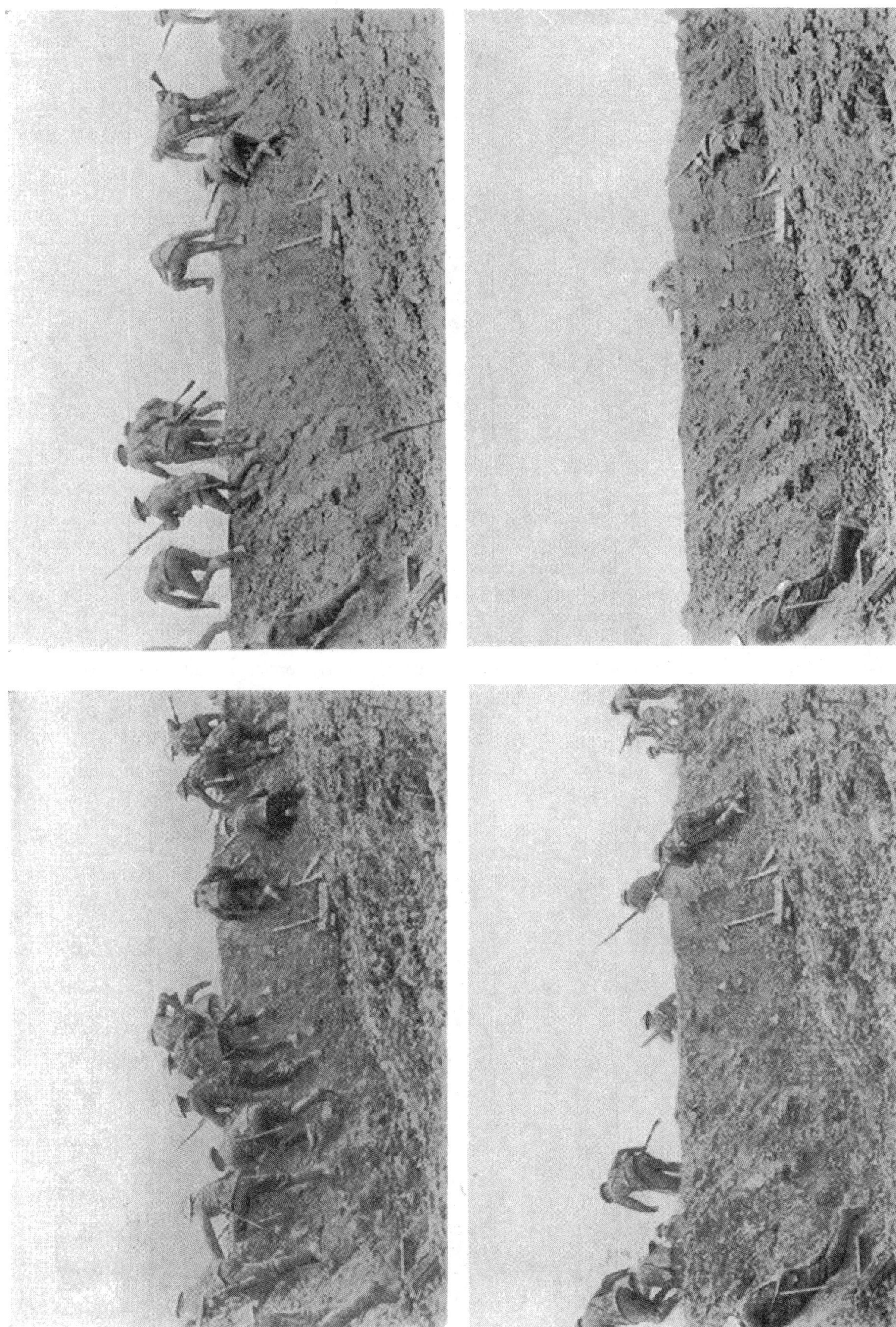

At a signal along the entire 16-mile front the British troops leaped over the trench parapet and advanced towards the German trenches under heavy rifle and machine-gun fire. It will be noticed that in the above pictures two men who had raised themselves to spring forward were killed as soon as their heads appeared above the parapet, and slipped back and lay still.

A panorama of a part of our line showing on the —

in which the enemy suffered heavy casualties, and we succeeded in capturing another trench on a front of one thousand yards and firmly establishing ourselves there. South-west of Thiépval the Germans made a determined attack on our new lines, but it was effectually broken up. In the Loos salient and opposite Hulluch the enemy's artillery was very active, while our guns retaliated by shelling the German communication trenches and billets. We successfully sprung two mines opposite Auchy and Hulluch.

Towards morning the British gun-fire increased in violence, and from Thiépval southwards the German positions were subjected to a furious bombardment, which clearly foreshadowed a resumption of our offensive on a large scale. The enemy's reply was relatively feeble. "I could see his shells," writes Mr. Beach Thomas, the special correspondent of the *Daily Mail*, "dancing a rather jerky *chassé* to and fro along certain sections of our approaches and trenches. His method was consistent: first, a high-explosive shell on the supposed trench; then, two or three seconds later, a high shrapnel over the ant-heap he thought he had exposed. But the volume was never really great. We may

A panoramic view of the assault on La Boiselle on July 1st, showing—

—extreme left of the picture a machine-gun in action.

accept it, I think, as undoubted that the enemy has never since the Marne lost so many guns by direct hits. Observation has been splendid, and artillery accurate, as well as incomparably weighty. Many of the remaining batteries have skedaddled behind the third highly-fortified line of defence."

With the dawn the British resumed a vigorous offensive in certain sectors along the southern part of the line, while the Germans simultaneously launched heavy attacks on our new trenches in the vicinity of the Ancre and north of Fricourt, with the result that violent fighting was soon in progress along the whole front between the Ancre and Montauban. The triangle, Ovillers, La Boiselle, Contalmaison, was the centre of a furious conflict; while actions hardly less serious were proceeding northwards around Thiépval and southwards about Fricourt. North-west of Thiépval the enemy, advancing in great force and with the utmost determination, succeeded in temporarily regaining two or three hundred yards of their lost ground; but to the south of the village, after a fierce preliminary bombardment, the British obtained a brilliant success by carrying by assault the immensely strong work known as the Leipzig Redoubt. This redoubt is situated in a salient of the German line, and during the past twenty months the enemy had exercised all their ingenuity over its fortification.

—our troops rushing to occupy the trenches after our artillery bombardment.

Here our troops are shown advancing over the barbed-wire entanglement.

Further to the south our troops forced their way across five hundred yards of German front-line trench into the village of Ovillers, where savage fighting continued throughout the day. Repeated bombardments had reduced the once pleasant village to a shapeless mass of unutterable ruin. Nothing was left of it but heaps of débris. There was not a wall, or even a part of a wall, standing two feet high. The guns had swept it flat. But beneath the surface the whole place was caverned and tunnelled like the catacombs, and, though our heavy shells had opened up some of these subterranean hiding-places and filled them with dead and wounded, many were still intact; and in every one of them lurked men with machine-guns, who issued forth as soon as our artillery lifted and raked our advancing ranks with streams of bullets. There were bombers concealed there, too, who came out whenever a favourable opportunity presented itself, hurled their grenades and then bolted for cover again. Nevertheless, despite the fiercest resistance, the British contrived to make progress. Above ground, amidst the shattered trenches, in shell-craters,

A sunken road in "No Man's Land" occupied by the Lancashire Fusiliers. (Twenty minutes after this was taken these men came under heavy machine-gun fire.)

and in ditches, our men fought with bomb, bayonet and rifle-butt. Below, they worked forward by sap and mine, blowing up vaults and floors. There were grapples to the death between parties of men meeting underground in the darkness of deep cellars and dug-outs quarried out of the chalk subsoil; and in some places the German machine-gunners in their cunningly-concealed emplacements were suddenly assailed by men who rose out of holes in the earth or broke through the adjoining walls and brained those who resisted with their picks. Many a gallant deed was performed by our troops that day, by the end of

Warwickshires advancing up a captured trench to relieve the Queen's in the front line.

A long white line. A common sight in France.

British troops attacking German trenches at Mametz.

which most of the southern end of the village was in our hands. One of the most notable was that of a young officer who, followed by a couple of men, ran towards a machine-gun, which was doing deadly work, and knocked out both gun and team with a well-aimed bomb. East of La Boiselle we followed up our success of the previous night by advancing our line over a maze of German trenches on a front of more than a mile to a depth of five hundred yards; while to the north of Fricourt, linking up with the above attack, we drove the enemy from two fortified woods and three lines of trenches.

Our great movement, skilfully planned and heroically executed, threatened at once a disastrous breach in the German line and an enveloping movement of an alarming character, and about 10 a.m. the 3rd Division of the Prussian Guard, which had been hurriedly brought up some days before from Valenciennes, was thrown into the struggle east of Contalmaison, in a desperate effort to force us back. Around Contalmaison our artillery, heavy and light, had just started to put a terrific barrage, and straight into this

A scene in the trenches at night on the 1st July, after the first day of the battle.

inferno of fire, by an awful stroke of chance, marched the Prussian Guard, advancing in close formation, as though on parade. The sight was appalling. The first ranks were literally mown down, dead and wounded being piled upon one another in ghastly heaps; one whole battalion was almost annihilated. But the Prussian Guard, though not equal to those splendid regiments which had faced us at the Marne, at Ypres and at Loos, was still the *corps d'élite* of the German Army, and through the hurricane of shells it struggled on. Then, as the advancing troops drew near our lines, our artillery lifted, and, after a fierce burst of machine-gun and rifle fire, the British infantry—chiefly Lancashire and other North-Country troops —charged with the bayonet. A fierce hand-to-hand struggle ensued, and for a time the issue hung in the balance. But our supports came up and flung themselves into the mêlée, and before this fresh cataract of steel the Prussian Guard wavered, recoiled and fell back upon the village of Bazentin, pursued by the fire of our batteries, which had again come into action and played upon the retreating enemy with murderous effect.

British Tommies rescuing a comrade under shell-fire. (This man died thirty minutes after reaching the trenches.)

The losses of the Prussian Guard were terrible. The 2nd Battalion of the 2nd Regiment was almost destroyed; it was reported to have no more than thirty survivors. The 3rd Battalion of the 2nd and the 10th of the 9th Regiment are estimated to have lost half their effectives, and the other units of the 3rd Division suffered hardly less. The enemy left on this part of the field three thousand dead and several thousand wounded.

The tragic episode of the defeat of the Prussian Guard is graphically described by a British soldier belonging to one of the battalions who took part in the repulse of the enemy:

"What I shall always remember most about the fierce counter-attack made upon us by the Prussian Guard east of Contalmaison, after we had made a splendid advance, is the immense number with which they advanced to the assault and the terrific yells they uttered as they came on. . . . It was a strange sight to see such big fellows howling at the top of their voices. They were all giants; not one of them could have been under six feet two inches, much bigger in the main than our Life Guards. In size they could have eaten us little chaps, but we weren't afraid of them. We could see as they got closer that they were mostly new troops, for their helmets, uniforms and equipments were brand new, and there was a lack of that easiness which you associate with seasoned soldiers. They didn't carry any heavy haversacks like we do when we advance; that was so they should be able to run all the better.

"I never witnessed such an awful spectacle in my life as that which happened about a hundred yards from our positions. Our artillery had been heavily shelling the ground over which an enemy must pass, and as these fellows, pressing forward, neared our line, a perfect hurricane of shells smashed into them, knocking the big chaps over like ninepins. The ground was simply heaped up with dead before they reached us. Then a ding-dong fight took place, which looked at one time like turning out critical for us, when reinforcements came along. Our fresh troops heavily counter-attacked and drove the great fellows back, taking a plentiful yield of dead. Before that we had cut mightily into them with rifle and machine-gun fire. In hand-to-hand fighting the crack Germans were not much class. Their hearts were in the wrong place, and we got at least seven hundred prisoners. They were not the same Prussian Guard that we had up against us at the beginning of the War."

The appearance of the Guard in the battle was rightly regarded as a phenomenon of great importance, and one which could not fail to afford much encouragement to our troops, furnishing as it did a striking proof that, in the opinion of the German General Staff, the German Second Army alone was not equal to the task imposed upon it by the attack of the

Stretcher-bearers bringing in the wounded on wheeled-stretchers.

A CAPTURED GERMAN TRENCH.

A view of an old German trench. Ovillers can be seen in the background. The white chalk trench can be followed for miles.

A captured German trench after our bombardment.

The Battle of the Somme

Allies along the Somme Valley. The summoning of the Guard, however, was only one example of the way in which hurried concentrations were now being imposed upon the enemy, for in the first five days of the battle the French had noted the presence among the forces opposed to them of not less than sixteen battalions separate from their normal organization, which had been brought up in all haste and thrown pell-mell into the struggle. Exactly the same thing appears to have been happening at almost the same moment 2,500 miles away in the Eastern theatre of hostilities. " In a word," observes Mr. Hilaire Belloc, " the Great War has produced in the enemy a phase of exhaustion, in which his rapid and sufficient concentration upon the increasing number of points where he must suffer attack from now superior opponents has already become a matter of bewilderment and strain for him, and is about

These four pictures show one of our Tommies bringing a seriously wounded man along a trench to a dressing-station.

to become a matter of acute peril and anxiety. There lies before him—perhaps at some distance of time still, but now inevitable—a last phase, in which it will become a matter of attempting the impossible."

The destruction of the Prussian Guard appeared to decide the fate of Contalmaison, upon which our troops were now steadily closing in. This village, part of which, it will be remembered, had been captured by us on the first day of the battle, though the ground gained was subsequently lost, lies at the southern end of the Pozières ridge, and constitutes a position of great natural strength, every defensive feature of which had been most ably exploited by the enemy. The approaches to it were defended by a network of trenches, with strong redoubts here and there, and several fortified woods and copses. Some of the outer works, pounded into ruin by our guns, had already fallen, but the more important were still in the enemy's hands, and their possession was fiercely disputed. However, our gallant fellows were not to be denied, and troops advancing from the direction of Shelter Wood carried in brilliant fashion a powerful redoubt to the south-west of the village, while, after an unsuccessful assault, another body of our men succeeded in capturing a similar work on the eastern side. A third redoubt, triangular in shape, situated

Bringing in the wounded during the battle.

on the confines of a small, narrow wood, south-west of Contalmaison, offered a most stubborn resistance, and changed hands more than once before the rising British tide all along the line rendered it no longer tenable by the enemy. The last serious obstacle to our success was overcome when an observer had the good fortune to locate the position of some machine-guns placed at the junction of two trenches to the east of the wood just mentioned, which had been causing considerable mischief. The spot was quickly submerged by our artillery and trench-mortars, and our men, advancing rapidly both on the left and right, carried the cemetery, Acid Drop Copse and the remaining defences; and by noon Contalmaison was in our hands.

It was a splendid feat of arms, but unfortunately circumstances subsequently compelled us to abandon a considerable part of the ground so gallantly won. In their triumphant rush through Contalmaison, our men omitted to make a sufficiently thorough search for hidden machine-guns; and one or two of those deadly weapons, whose whereabouts had escaped their notice, had been so placed as to command the shallow valley on the western side of the village, with the result that our advance from that direction was held up and the troops who had carried Contalmaison left unsupported. The German artillery, too, at once began shelling the captured position heavily; while towards evening a strong counter-attack began to develop from the north. At the same time, the enemy were reported to be streaming out of Mametz Wood, apparently with the intention of attacking the village on its eastern side. Rain had been falling heavily throughout the day, and the troops holding Contalmaison, who had fought so bravely and so long, were drenched to the skin, and utterly worn out by their exertions in the heavy ground, and in no condition to continue the conflict. In these circumstances, it was decided to evacuate the village itself, and to confine ourselves to holding the outskirts in the neighbourhood of the cemetery and Acid Drop Copse, which would leave us in a sound position for further attack.

Despite this temporary check, which was to be brilliantly retrieved four days later, our troops had every reason to congratulate themselves on the success of the day's operations, in which we had not only made substantial advances at several important points and carried defences upon which Teutonic ingenuity had exhausted all its resources, but inflicted heavy casualties on the enemy and captured a large

Miners in a mine-chamber laying a charge.

Bringing in a wounded German prisoner and placing him in one of our dug-outs.

The first batch of German prisoners to come in after the successful assault on the 1st of July.

number of prisoners. Most of these belonged to the ill-fated 3rd Division of the Prussian Guard, which had been so utterly broken that it had ceased to exist as a fighting unit. Those survivors who had not fallen into our hands were subsequently withdrawn from the line. The *morale* of the men as well as their fighting force had been smashed. Some of them stated that they had been brought from Valenciennes to Cambrai, from which point most of their officers were sent on by motor-car, while the troops marched long distances through unknown country to the front. The officers who had remained with them had no maps and no local knowledge, and an ominous feeling prevailed that they were marching to disaster. They professed themselves astonished at the strength of our artillery and its deadly accuracy, and still more at the dash of our infantry when they learned that they had been up against men of the " New Army." " We thought that they were the Guards," remarked one of them.

Bringing in the wounded on stretchers through the trenches during the height of the battle.

Despite the unfavourable weather, our aeroplanes once more rendered valuable service. In addition to active co-operation with the artillery and important reconnaissance work, they bombed the hostile aerodrome at Douai, completely wrecking a hangar and doing other material damage. In several instances our airmen displayed great daring in attacking troops which were being brought up to the trenches; and a German officer prisoner stated that his battalion came under strong machine-gun fire from an aeroplane at an altitude of 300 feet. This same battalion was soon afterwards heavily shelled by our long-range guns, so that by the time it reached the trenches it could have had but very little stomach left for fighting.

On the northern part of our front the enemy showed some activity near Neuville St. Vaast and Roclincourt. To the north-east of the latter place they exploded a mine, without, however, doing any damage to our defences, and the explosion of another mine amongst the existing craters near the Hohenzollern Redoubt was equally ineffective. On the other hand, the British sprang a mine north-east of Hulluch and destroyed a hostile gallery.

Helping along a wounded German prisoner.

The night was comparatively quiet, and was chiefly spent by us in improving the forward positions gained during the previous day's fighting; but in the neighbourhood of Gommecourt our field-guns and trench-mortars carried out a lively bombardment of the German trenches.

On the 8th fighting was principally on our extreme right flank, where an important success rewarded the efforts of our troops. East of Bernafay Wood, at the angle made by our advance with that of the French, lies a dense wood, triangular in shape, and measuring some 1,400 yards from north to south, with a southern base of 400 yards. This wood, called by our Staff maps the Bois des Trônes, though the correct name, according to the French ordnance map, is the Bois des Troncs, is a position of considerable strategic importance, since it is situated within two miles of the German station at Combles, one of the enemy's most important nerve centres in this region, with roads branching from it whereby Péronne might be threatened from the north; and the Germans, recognizing this, had protected it by strong trenches,

Stretcher-bearers bringing in a wounded man.

a perfect network of wire-entanglements, and a little arsenal of machine-guns. The problem before us, however, was not so much to gain possession of Trônes Wood as to hold it when it was in our hands, since it was so completely commanded by the artillery of both sides as to constitute a very death-trap for the troops, whether British or German, which happened to be in occupation.

Nevertheless, the position was of so much importance that it was decided to wrest it from the enemy at all costs, and, after a fierce preliminary bombardment, in which the British and French artillery combined with great effect, we

Placing the wounded man under the charge of a R.A.M.C. man.

Bringing in German prisoners.

German prisoners—wounded and unwounded—being brought in near Carnoy.

stormed a line of trenches and captured the southern end of the wood. The enemy's losses from the combined Anglo-French bombardment were very severe, the captured trenches being filled with dead, while 130 prisoners and several machine-guns were taken.

But this successful assault was merely the first phase in one of the grimmest conflicts in the Picardy battles. Not even the struggle for Mametz Wood, of which we shall presently speak, exceeded in savage obstinacy and swaying vicissitudes the grapples in the Bois des Trônes.

Hardly had we established ourselves at the southern end of Trônes Wood than the German guns began to shell the captured position heavily, and this bombardment was followed by the launching of a heavy counter-attack across the open. It broke down completely, however, before the fire of our

A captured mine-crater.

18-pounders and the French 75's, and the enemy retired in disorder, leaving the ground over which they had advanced covered with their dead and wounded.

In the neighbourhood of Ovillers, where our troops had laboured throughout the night erecting barricades to cut off the enemy from the southern end of the village, we worked our way steadily forward, both above and below ground. A party of our men, creeping forward under cover of the ruins, succeeded in establishing a bombing-post to the left of the village, from which they bombed the enemy most effectively; while another body of troops, by a sudden forward movement, for which the Germans were unprepared, managed to take up a line across the south-western end of Ovillers, which enabled their comrades to link up from various points and placed us in a very advantageous position for a further advance. Despite the cloudy weather, our aeroplanes and kite-balloons performed much useful work, taking photographs of the enemy's positions and directing the fire of our batteries. Our bombing aeroplanes, penetrating far behind the German lines, dropped bombs on their billets and caused a heavy explosion in one of their ammunition depôts, the smoke from which gushed out in dense masses and rose to a vast height, when it spread out like the foliage of some gigantic tree. One of our machines, while returning, was attacked by three hostile aeroplanes, with which, though disabled, it maintained a running fight for twenty minutes, and afterwards landed safely in our own aerodrome. Except in this instance the German machines were careful to keep far behind their own trenches; indeed, very few of them were seen during the day.

In his reports on the 8th, Sir Douglas Haig announced that "during the past few days we had captured twenty guns, 51 machine-guns, and a large number of automatic rifles, trench-mortars, *minenwerfer*, canister-throwers and search-lights, together with a mass of other war material which had not been scheduled."

During the night there was a good deal of fighting between the Ancre and the Somme, though of a

Signallers operating during the British advance.

much less violent character than that which had marked the past two days. The Germans made no fresh attempt to recapture their lost positions, while, on the other hand, we continued our offensive about Ovillers and made some further progress.

In another sector we captured a group of fortified buildings, and near Givenchy sprang three mines, which played havoc with the hostile defences. Further north, along a part of the sector held by the New Zealanders, there was a very fierce little affair indeed. After a heavy bombardment of the Anzac trenches, the enemy advanced in great force and succeeded in entering them at one point. This success, however, was of very brief duration, for the New Zealanders at once organized a counter-attack, and, after half an hour's stubborn hand-to-hand fighting, the Germans were driven out with heavy loss, our trenches being found full of their dead and wounded.

July 9th was characterized by considerable activity on the part of the German guns, and artillery duels took place in several sectors of the battle-front. The British offensive was chiefly confined to the neighbourhood of Ovillers, where we again made steady progress, despite very stubborn opposition. In the course of the afternoon, the enemy, in an attempt to retrieve to some extent their losses of the past

Bombardment of Fricourt on the 2nd of July.

One of the captured mine-craters.

Samples of captured machine-guns, etc.: German trench-mortar, German machine-gun, Russian machine-gun, and automatic rifle.

Captures made during the first days of the advance: Two periscopes with cases, one telephone, one gas-helmet and one first aid for gas-poisoning (Selbstretter) are shown.

week, launched two violent counter-attacks in mass against our new positions in and near Trônes Wood. But, as in the case of their fruitless efforts of the previous day, both attacks were completely broken up by the effective fire of our artillery.

During the day the Royal Flying Corps carried out several successful bombing attacks against various detraining centres, ammunition depôts and aerodromes. Numerous aerial combats took place, as the result of which one German machine was destroyed and several others driven to the ground in a damaged condition. These successes, however, were not gained without cost, as one of our aeroplanes was brought down by a direct hit from an anti-aircraft gun, while three other machines were reported missing.

There was no rest for the troops on the right of the British line that night. At 8 p.m., after bombarding our positions in Trônes Wood with all manner of missiles, the enemy launched two further violent

A view of a trench, Ovillers.

attacks against it, one coming from the east, the other from the south-east. The first was completely repulsed; but the second, after a furious struggle, succeeded in penetrating the southern end of the wood, though the Germans were almost immediately driven out again. Later in the night, yet another desperate attempt—the fifth within less than thirty-six hours—was made to expel us from the wood; but it was completely crushed by our fire. The enemy's casualties in these five fruitless attempts were very severe. North-west of Contalmaison we captured a small copse and three guns; while on the Flanders front, near Hooge, we made three successful raids into the enemy's front line.

CHAPTER IV

THE 10th witnessed further fierce fighting in Trônes Wood, and a conflict of an equally desperate character in another wood—the Bois de Mametz.

The Bois de Mametz is a large, irregular stretch of dense woodland, more than two hundred acres in extent, rising from the valley between Montauban and Contalmaison. So tight and twisted was the growth of trees and saplings, unthinned for two seasons, that to force a way through the stems and branches would have been a far from easy task, even had there been no opposition to encounter, whereas the Germans had spared no pains to increase the difficulties presented by Nature. They had stretched through the wood successive lines of barbed-wire nets; had cut paths and avenues for hidden machine-guns to rake, and had installed several heavy batteries there. It was an ugly place to attack, and the wood itself had hitherto resisted all our efforts, though some progress had been made against its outlying defences. But, notwithstanding the immense difficulty of the undertaking, it was resolved to persevere with it; and early in the afternoon of the 10th a battalion of a famous Welsh regiment and other troops advanced to the assault by short, sharp rushes, keeping time with the British artillery, which furiously shelled the ground ahead of them as they went forward; and, after an obstinate struggle, carried the first line of hostile trenches and gained a firm footing in the wood. Some of our men, with dare-devil courage, pushed on too fast and too far, right into the zone swept by the fire of our own guns;

An aeroplane going out to reconnoitre.

and but for a timely warning which an artillery officer in an advanced observation post managed to convey to our gunners, the consequences might have been serious. It was impossible, however, to make further progress that day, for torrents of bullets were swishing through the trees from the enemy's machine-guns, while their artillery was shelling us heavily; and until our own guns had taken some of the heart out of the defence it would have been folly to attempt a fresh advance. And so our men lay down under whatever cover they could find or dig, and there they hung on all through the night, while shells burst continually over them and machine-guns clamoured unceasingly through the glades.

Meanwhile, on the right, another violent forest battle was in progress. In the course of the afternoon, undeterred by the failure of their five previous attempts to regain possession of Trônes Wood, the enemy, after a heavy bombardment, advanced to the attack yet again, in greater force than ever and with unabated courage. Shrapnel, rifle and machine-gun took a terrible toll of the assailants, as they came on in serried ranks across the open. But, reckless of loss, they still pushed forward, and, by sheer weight of numbers, succeeded in driving us from the wood. The special correspondent of the *Liberté* relates

A kite-balloon ascending during the advance.

Two photographs showing an interior of a signal exchange during the battle.

PART IV. WILL BE READY ON TUESDAY, NOVEMBER 7TH.

There are many large, magnificent pictures in this Part, including:—

ROYAL FIELD ARTILLERY MOVING UP DURING BATTLE OVER GROUND WHERE THE GORDONS' AND DEVONS' DEAD ARE LYING, AFTER A GLORIOUS AND SUCCESSFUL CHARGE ON THE RIDGE NEAR MAMETZ.

THESE TWO BATTERIES ADVANCED UNDER FIRE TO A POSITION BEYOND MAMETZ, AND WERE FORTUNATE IN HAVING NO CASUALTIES.

ONE OF FIVE UNSUCCESSFUL GERMAN COUNTER-ATTACKS AT LA BOISELLE.

SCENE IN "DANTZIG ALLEY"—A GERMAN TRENCH MORTAR CAPTURED AND HELD BY A BATTALION OF THE MANCHESTERS.

ACTIVITY AT MINDEN POST WHILE THE BATTLE RAGED FURIOUSLY. ARRIVAL OF WOUNDED TOMMIES—THE FIRST LINE TRENCHES ARE JUST OVER THE CREST, ABOUT 200 YARDS AWAY.

STRETCHER CASES FOR AMBULANCE—WOUNDED AWAITING ATTENTION AT MINDEN POST—SHOWING HOW QUICKLY THE WOUNDED ARE ATTENDED TO.

WITH THE AUSTRALIANS IN FRANCE — SCENES BEHIND THE ANZAC TRENCHES.	SOME MACHINE GUNS CAPTURED BY OUR TROOPS ON 1st JULY.	AUSTRALIAN MACHINE GUNNERS RETURNING FROM THE TRENCHES.
ROYAL ENGINEERS MOVING THEIR HOME.	CANADIAN INFANTRY IN THE TRENCHES WEARING THE NEW STEEL HELMETS.	A MONSTER GUN IN ACTION.
BRINGING IN THE WOUNDED.	FIELD GUN CAPTURED NEAR MONTAUBAN.	A GERMAN LOOK-OUT POST IN MAMETZ WOOD.
FOUR PHOTOGRAPHS SHOWING R.F.A. MOVING UP.	GERMAN FIELD GUN CAPTURED.	ANTI-AIRCRAFT GUNS ABOUT TO FIRE ON HOSTILE AIRCRAFT.
A VIEW OF FRICOURT.	CAPTURED GERMAN TRENCH MORTAR.	A VIEW IN MAMETZ WOOD.
ROYAL FUSILIERS RESTING AFTER THE STORMING OF LA BOISELLE.	CAPTURED GERMAN TRENCH MORTAR.	BRINGING UP WATERPIPES TO SUPPLY THE MEN IN THE FRONT LINE WITH WATER.
A VIEW IN OVILLERS.	CAPTURED GERMAN FIELD GUN.	A LITTLE MUSIC BY THE BLACK WATCH AFTER COMING BACK FROM THE CAPTURE OF LONGUEVAL.
MEN OF A WEST INDIAN REGIMENT WATCHING A BOSCH AEROPLANE BEING CHASED BY ONE OF OUR PLANES.	CAPTURED GERMAN 10-c.m. FIELD GUN.	
	A MACHINE GUN AND AN AUTOMATIC RIFLE CAPTURED.	A BIG HOWITZER IN ACTION.
ARTILLERYMEN EXAMINING A GERMAN GUN, CAPTURED BY THE ROYAL IRISH, PRIOR TO FIRING INTO THE GERMAN LINES WITH IT.	CAPTURED GERMAN TRENCH GUN.	THE MASCOT OF THE ANZACS.
	A NIGHT SCENE WITHIN THE AUSTRALIAN LINES.	LABOUR BATTALION MAKING A ROAD OVER GROUND RECENTLY CAPTURED.

ORDER FORM.

To M ....
BOOKSELLER OR NEWSAGENT.

Please send me Part IV., and the following Parts as published, of "SIR DOUGLAS HAIG'S GREAT PUSH," for which I enclose..................................

Name..

Address ....

The Sunday Times

LONDON'S BEST INFORMED WEEKLY NEWSPAPER

COL. FEYLER'S WAR ARTICLES

A Special Feature of "THE SUNDAY TIMES" is the weekly war article contributed by Col. Feyler, the eminent Swiss strategist, whose accuracy of information and insight has won for him recognition, even in official circles, as the premier writer on the war in this or in any other country.

IN ABOUT 8 FORTNIGHTLY PARTS.   HUTCHINSON'S NEW PART WORK   Part V. ready Nov. 21st. PART IV. 8d. NET

SIR DOUGLAS HAIG'S
GREAT PUSH

THE BATTLE OF THE SOMME

A popular, pictorial and authoritative work on one of the Greatest Battles in History, illustrated by about **700** *wonderful* **OFFICIAL PHOTOGRAPHS AND CINEMATOGRAPH FILMS** *and other authentic pictures*

BY ARRANGEMENT WITH THE WAR OFFICE

ANTI AIRCRAFT GUNS ABOUT TO FIRE.

GREAT VALUE FOR EIGHTPENCE

THIS PART CONTAINS **51 WONDERFUL REPRODUCTIONS** OF THE FAMOUS **WAR OFFICE CINEMATOGRAPH FILMS** AND **OFFICIAL PHOTOGRAPHS** OF THE BATTLE OF THE SOMME. BEAUTIFULLY PRINTED ON THE BEST ENGLISH ART PAPER.

LONDON : HUTCHINSON & Co.

5,000,000 Letters

received every week from our armies in France, according to the Postmaster-General.

No wonder that there has been such a demand for Fountain Pens since the outbreak of war.

THE "SWAN"

Which 20 Years ago set the Standard in

FOUNTAIN PENS

has so increased its sales that the nominal increase in cost of production has been more than counterbalanced. The present time has been thought opportune by some Fountain Pen makers to put up prices. The pens themselves are unchanged. The burden will fall largely on our soldiers and sailors and their friends. Send your soldier or sailor a "Swan" and save 20 per cent.

There is no advance in prices of "Swan" Fountpens.

SOLD BY STATIONERS & JEWELLERS EVERYWHERE

Standard pattern, with slip-on cap, from 10/6 Up.
Safety pattern, with screw-on cap, from 12/6 Up

Illustrated Catalogue post free on request.

MABIE, TODD & CO., Ltd.,
79-80, High Holborn, London, W.C.
LONDON FACTORY—319-329, WESTON STREET, S.E.

38, Cheapside, E.C.; 95a and 204, Regent St., W., London; 3, Exchange St., Manchester; Paris, Zurich, Sydney.

Associate House—
Mabie, Todd & Co., Inc., New York and Chicago.

Size 1, with fit-on clip. 11/6

Size 2c. "Safety," with screw-on cap, 12/6

Size 1, standard pattern, slip-on cap, 10/6

Size 1, with 2 rolled gold bands, 14/6

that, as the last British troops retired from the wood, an officer shouted mockingly to the Germans: "Good-bye for the present, gentlemen; you'll soon hear from us again." They did indeed! For scarcely had they installed themselves in what our men now called "Hell Hole Wood" than our guns proceeded to give the Boche a double dose of his own medicine, and poured a deluge of shells upon it, which broke and splintered and slashed the tree-trunks as though innumerable sharp axes were being hurled against them. Thus, by a singular coincidence, the Germans in Trônes Wood and the British in Mametz Wood were each undergoing a similar ordeal at the same time; but our men stood it infinitely better than the enemy, and the renewal of the attack at dawn found their spirit unbroken.

Bringing in a wounded soldier.

On through that terrible Mametz Wood, the gloom of which was brightened by the flash of the bursting shells, went our brave fellows. The stumps and fallen débris of smashed and splintered timber made a barrier almost as formidable as barbed wire, and the enemy's machine-guns swished destruction through the wreckage. But still they pressed on, Welshman and Englishman vying with one another in their sublime indifference to the death which rained upon every yard. Once they had to draw back, while for half an hour the British artillery fiercely pounded the ground in front of them. Then forward they went again, and with bomb and bayonet forced their way onwards, killing the machine-gunners, who fought their murderous weapons to the last, and carrying line after line of the hostile trenches, while the "cleaners" who followed the fighting force dived down into the dug-outs and raked out the ambuscaders who lurked there; and before mid-day the greater part of the wood was in our possession. A heavy howitzer, three field-guns and 296 unwounded prisoners, including three officers, fell into our hands.

Royal Engineers moving their home.

This splendid success had been preceded by another. It will be remembered that during our successful advance on the 7th some of our troops had carried the village of Contalmaison, but that they had been subsequently obliged to retire and fall back to a strong position south of the village. Here they established a machine-gun post, which was to do valuable service in the next attack. Since then our artillery had given the Germans in Contalmaison no rest and had subjected the defences to a merciless pounding; while our successful advance into Mametz Wood precluded the danger of any interference from that direction. Everything, therefore, promised well for the success of a fresh attack.

The Royal Field Artillery moving up during the battle over ground where the Gordons' and Devons' dead are lying.

The way for our advance upon Contalmaison was prepared by a furious bombardment, our batteries first concentrating upon the positions in front of the village, and then upon the village itself, which they shelled with terrific intensity. Meanwhile, Bailiff Wood, to the west of Contalmaison, had been carried by a dashing assault, and the prospects on the western side were so good that it was decided to make the effort here, instead of from the south, in spite of the distance to be covered. The Germans had expected us to attack from the south, and most of their machine-guns were trained that way, when towards five o'clock on the morning of the 11th our troops advanced upon them from the west.

We had to traverse some 1,100 yards of open ground, and our infantry advanced in four waves, in extended order, leaving their packs behind them, in order to push forward the more rapidly. They went across in magnificent style, and, though their casualties were numerous, by seven o'clock the whole of Contalmaison was in our possession.

The fire of our artillery powerfully contributed to this success. Never, indeed, had our guns performed their part better. They worked throughout in the most perfect harmony with the plan of the infantry attack, and the clockwork precision with which the barrage or curtain of fire was lifted in stages just in front of the advance was truly admirable.

There was some fierce hand-to-hand fighting here and there in Contalmaison, in which about two hundred Germans who refused to surrender were killed. But the majority of those who had survived the bombardment and were unwounded began streaming out of the village in disorderly retreat before our troops entered it. As the sequel showed, they would have been far wiser to remain where they were and surrender, for, bolting across the open in a north-westerly direction, they were caught by the barrage which our artillery was putting between Contalmaison, Pozières and Bazentin, and by machine-gun fire from the advanced post held by the troops who had made the attack on the 7th, with the result that the rout became a shambles.

Another photograph showing the Royal Field Artillery moving up.

A view of Fricourt, captured on the 2nd July by the British.

Anti-aircraft guns about to fire on hostile aircraft.

The Battle of the Somme

The effect of our gunfire had been terrible in Contalmaison. The shells from our heavies had smashed the houses to pieces, even penetrating to the cellars, and, according to the statements of prisoners, of whom nearly two hundred were captured, including a battalion commander and four other officers, at least half of the troops holding the place had been either killed or wounded. There is no reason to suppose that they were guilty of exaggeration, as, when our men entered the village, they had in many spots to walk over the bodies of the dead. The prisoners, of whom over seventy were taken in a lump in one cellar and over fifty in another, were for the most part in a pitiable condition, and in some cases so exhausted from want of food and nerve-shaken from the strain of our bombardment that they could scarcely stand. One of these unfortunates had a tragic tale to tell. He, with other men of the 122nd

Canadian Infantry in the trenches, wearing the new steel helmets.

(Bavarian) Regiment, had been sent into Contalmaison some days before. Soon the rations which they had brought with them were finished, while, owing to the intensity of our gunfire, it was impossible for fresh supplies to reach them, the communication-trenches having become veritable death-traps. They suffered much from hunger, and still more from thirst, and their casualties increased steadily. So many of the dug-outs had been destroyed by our artillery that there was not nearly sufficient room in the others for all to find shelter; and the only dug-out for his company was one which would not hold more than twenty men, even when packed close together. They had therefore to take refuge there in turn, while outside the British shells were bursting everywhere. At intervals two or three would be ordered out to make room for others, who sometimes entered bleeding from wounds which they had received while waiting to be admitted. Those whose places they took went out pale and trembling, knowing that very probably death or mutilation awaited them. When the British carried the village, of the men then in the dug-out there was scarcely one unwounded; and they were thankful indeed to be able to surrender and have their hurts attended to, for, though they had a doctor with them, they had no bandages left.

We were not suffered to remain long in undisturbed possession of Contalmaison, as the German guns were very quickly turned upon the village, and the bombardment was followed by a determined counter-attack. It was, however, beaten off with heavy loss to the enemy, and the place remained definitely in our hands.

The Germans' success in their capture of Trônes Wood, after six costly assaults, was of short duration. About nine o'clock on the morning of the 11th, after an artillery preparation so terrific that it was visible from miles away, our troops advanced to the attack. "The shock was terrible," writes the correspondent of the *Liberté*. "For a moment the Germans fell back before the irresistible advance of the British, but,

Men of a West Indian Regiment watching a German aeroplane being chased by our planes.

reinforcements having been quickly brought up, they counter-attacked furiously. The mêlée was awful along the whole line, and there were frequent and bloody hand-to-hand fights. An eye-witness of the battle tells me that it was disputed with almost incredible fury. The Germans had engaged not less than three divisions, which our Allies victoriously resisted. It was only at three o'clock in the afternoon, after more than six hours' incessant struggle, that the British, thanks to a daring manœuvre, gained the advantage. They pretended to retreat at the centre of the front of attack, during which troops operating on the extreme right swept forward, enveloping the Germans, who let themselves be taken in the trap. The Germans, to avoid being completely surrounded, were obliged to retreat. Even so they left five hundred prisoners in the hands of their adversaries, without counting the machine-guns and cannon they had lost. The day of July 11th will remain as a glorious date in the history of British valour."

In his report that night Sir Douglas Haig thus summarizes the result of the operations since the beginning of the battle on July 1st:

Artillerymen examining a German gun captured by the Royal Irish, prior to firing into the German lines with it.

Activity at—

Scenes in "Dantzig Alley," captured and held by a—

—Minden Post.

—battalion of the Manchesters.

"After ten days and nights of continuous fighting, our troops have completed the methodical capture of the whole of the enemy's first system of defence on a front of 14,000 yards (nearly 8 miles). This system of defence consisted of numerous and continuous lines of fire-trenches,

A captured trench mortar.

support-trenches and reserve-trenches, extending to various depths of from 2,000 yards (1⅛ miles) to 4,000 yards (nearly 2½ miles), and included five strongly fortified villages, numerous heavily wired and entrenched woods, and a large number of immensely strong redoubts. The capture of each of these trenches represented an operation of some importance; and the whole of them is now in our hands."

Considerable reinforcements would appear to have reached the enemy in the course of the 11th, and during the night several determined counter-attacks were launched against our new positions. In Trônes Wood, where the Germans had hung on like grim death to the northernmost fringe, they succeeded in regaining a little ground, and in Mametz Wood they also met with some success. But elsewhere their attacks were beaten back with loss. Between the main battle-field and the sea our troops were actively engaged in bombarding the enemy's positions and raiding their front trenches. South-east of Loos a party of the Royal Irish Fusiliers penetrated the German trenches at a point where they were strongly held and remained there for twenty minutes, during which fierce hand-to-hand fighting took place, and many of the enemy were killed. Our own casualties were slight. Opposite the Hohenzollern Redoubt (two and a half miles north of Loos), two companies of the Seaforth Highlanders succeeded, after obstinate fighting, in forcing their way into another part of the enemy's trenches. Many Germans were killed or wounded; one of their machine-guns was destroyed; several dug-outs crowded with the enemy were successfully bombed, and some prisoners were taken.

The 12th was marked by sharp fighting about Contalmaison and in the Mametz and Trônes Woods, with results highly favourable to the British. Against Contalmaison the Germans launched two heavy attacks, both of which, however, com-

One of the five unsuccessful German counter-attacks at La Boiselle.

pletely broke down under our fire. In Mametz Wood we not only regained all the ground lost during the night, but drove the enemy, notwithstanding that they had been strongly reinforced, right out of the wood, and by the evening every yard of the place was finally in our grip. In Trônes Wood,

Australian machine-gunners returning from the trenches.

Labour Battalion making a road over ground recently captured.

Stretcher cases for the ambulance.

where the number of German dead who covered the ground showed that their success of the previous night had been very dearly purchased, we also made some progress.

During the night of the 12th–13th and the following day there was no change in the situation, though fighting continued at various points and there were heavy artillery duels in certain sectors. West of Wytschaete (between four and five miles south of Ypres) and on the southern side of the La Bassée Canal the enemy attempted to raid our trenches, but were driven back in each case by our fire. Although the weather during the 13th was unfavourable for aerial work, our aeroplanes were very active over the German lines, and several encounters took place between them and hostile machines, the latter being in every instance driven off. One of our aeroplanes was, however, reported missing.

The battle had now been in progress for a fortnight, almost every day of which had witnessed the most fierce and obstinate fighting. On the left of our attack, from Hébuterne down to Thiépval, the splendid courage and self-sacrifice of our men had not yet been rewarded by success, and that side of the German fortress-lines, though broken in places, still remained practically intact. But through the southern bastion we had been steadily storming our way, and had pushed forward up the high ground from the Fricourt ridge to the Montauban ridge.

With Contalmaison finally and securely in our hands, with the whole of Mametz Wood captured, and the enemy ejected from all but the northern fringe of Trônes Wood, the time had now arrived for the second phase of the Great Push—the attack upon the German second system of defences. This movement was fixed for daybreak on Friday, July 14th—the National Day of France—and, as in the case of our first advance on July 1st, was prepared by a tremendous bombardment of the hostile trenches, which began on the evening of the 11th and increased in violence as the moment for the attack approached.

The wounded waiting their turn for treatment.

Terrific as had been our gunfire on the former occasion, this second bombardment would appear to have been even more wonderful and terrible; indeed, the infernal grandeur of the spectacle presented during the night preceding the assault was one which no one who witnessed it is ever likely to forget. Let us listen to the vivid description of Mr. Philip Gibbs, the special correspondent of the *Daily Chronicle*:

"The hell of war encircled us, and its waves of sound and light beat upon us. Our batteries were firing with an intense fury. The flashes of them were away back behind us—where the heavies have their hiding-places—and over all the ground in front of our new line of attack. They came out of the black earth with short, sharp stabs of red flame, whose light filled the hollows with pools of fire. And the sky and the ridges of ground and the earthworks and ruins and woods across our lines were blazing with the flashes of bursting shells. . . . Along the German second line, by Bazentin-le-Grand, Bazentin-le-Petit and Longueval, at the back of the woods, our shells were bursting without a second's pause and in great clusters. They tore up the ground and let out gusts of flame. Flame fountains rose and spread from the German trenches above Pearl Wood. The dark night was rent with all these flames, and hundreds of batteries were feeding the fires.

"Every calibre of gun was at work. The heavy shells, 15-inch, 12.9, 8-inch, 6-inch, 4.7, came

A wounded soldier being handed a cigarette after his wounds have been dressed.

overhead like flocks of birds—infernal birds with wings that beat the air into waves and came whining with a shrill, high note, and stooped to earth with a monstrous roar. The light batteries, far forward, were beating the devil's tattoo—one, two, three, four; one, two, three, four—with sharp knocks that clouted one's ears. I sat on a wooden box on the top of an old dug-out in the midst of all this fury. There was a great gun to my left, and every time it fired it shook the box, and all the earth underneath, with a violent vibration."

As the first glimmers of the dawn showed in the eastern sky our fire reached its most devastating intensity of concentration on the sectors chosen for assault, and the tumult of noise became positively overwhelming. Then, towards 3.30 a.m. there was a moment of hush. It was the guns lifting in anticipation of the attack. At 3.25 the assault was launched, while our artillery broke into a new uproar and began furiously barraging the enemy's communication and support trenches. From the German lines came the clamour of machine-guns spouting their streams of bullets amongst our advancing troops, upon whom their artillery also got to work with shrapnel and high explosive. But the enemy's fire was neither so intense nor so accurate as on July 1st, and failed completely to stay the onward rush of our men, who pushed forward in the fullest assurance of victory; and at 10.4 a.m. Sir Douglas Haig reported that "our troops had broken into the hostile positions on a front of four miles and had captured several strongly defended localities."

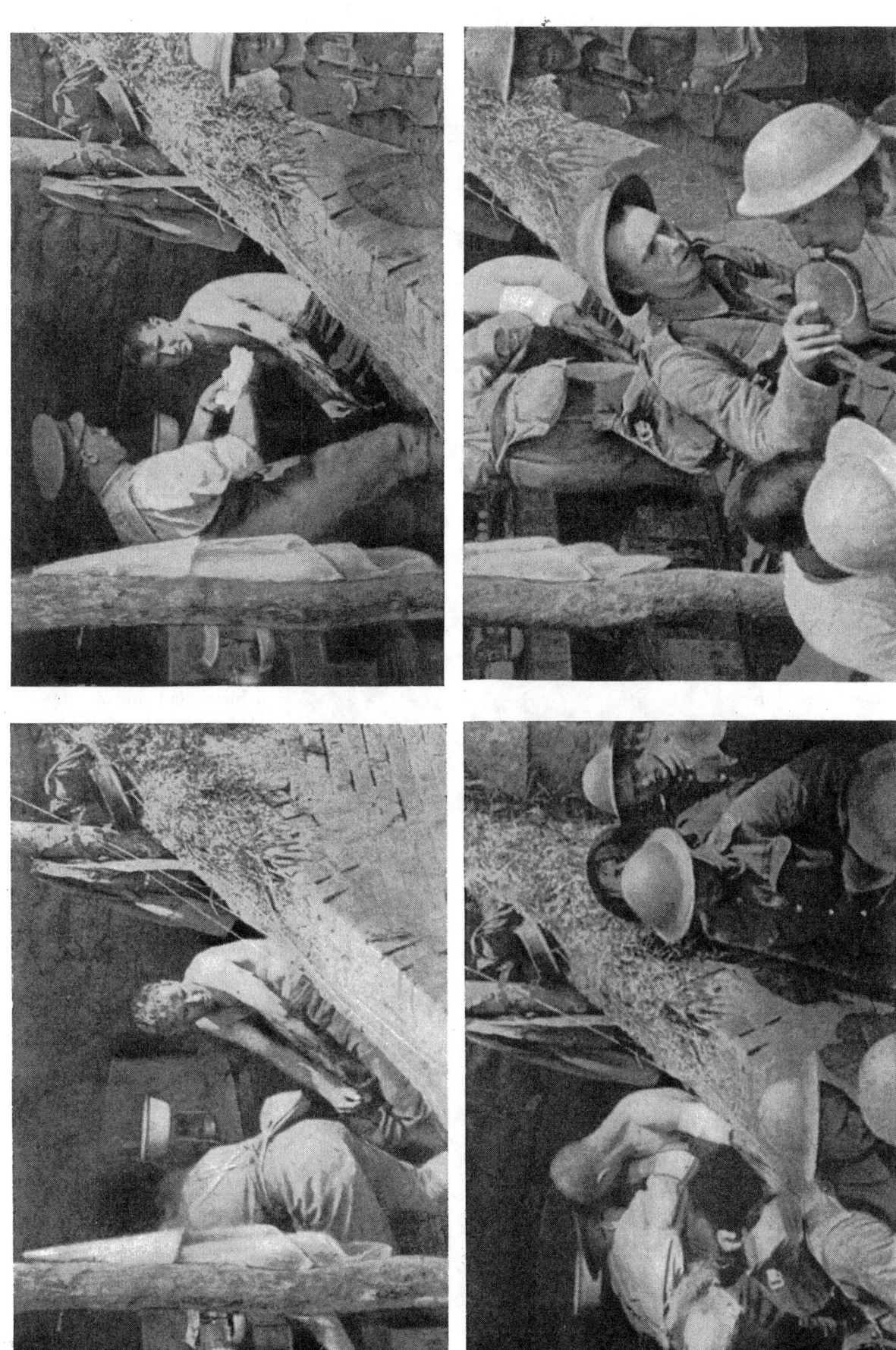

SCENES AT THE DRESSING-STATION FOR SLIGHTLY WOUNDED AT MINDEN POST.
The soldier shown in the above four illustrations has been wounded in both arms, and is having his wounds temporarily dressed.

Further scenes at Minden Post dressing-station.

On the extreme right, the Sussex and other battalions advanced from Bernafay Wood against that part of Trônes Wood to which the enemy still clung, and, though the German artillery "shelled them like hell," as one of the men expressed it, and machine-guns raked them with a withering cross-fire, forced their way forward yard by yard, carried the German trenches, and flung their defenders out of the wood. Here a remarkable incident occurred. In the north-eastern extremity of the wood were found some three hundred men of the West Kent Regiment, who, having pushed on in advance of the rest of our troops in the fighting of the 12th, had found themselves cut off and almost surrounded by the enemy. Nevertheless, for two days and two nights they had stubbornly held their ground, keeping the Germans at bay with a machine-gun. It was a really splendid achievement and worthy of a regiment which had already won so many laurels in this war.

More German prisoners being rounded-up and brought in by battle-police from No-Man's-Land.

In this last phase of the Trônes Wood conflict, the hand-to-hand fighting was of the most furious character, and in several places British and German soldiers were found lying dead close together, each pierced by the other's bayonet. Many German snipers and machine-gunners had posted themselves in trees and had been there shot, and now lay hung across branches. The whole wood was, in fact, a

Wounded soldiers leaving the dressing-station after having their wounds attended to.

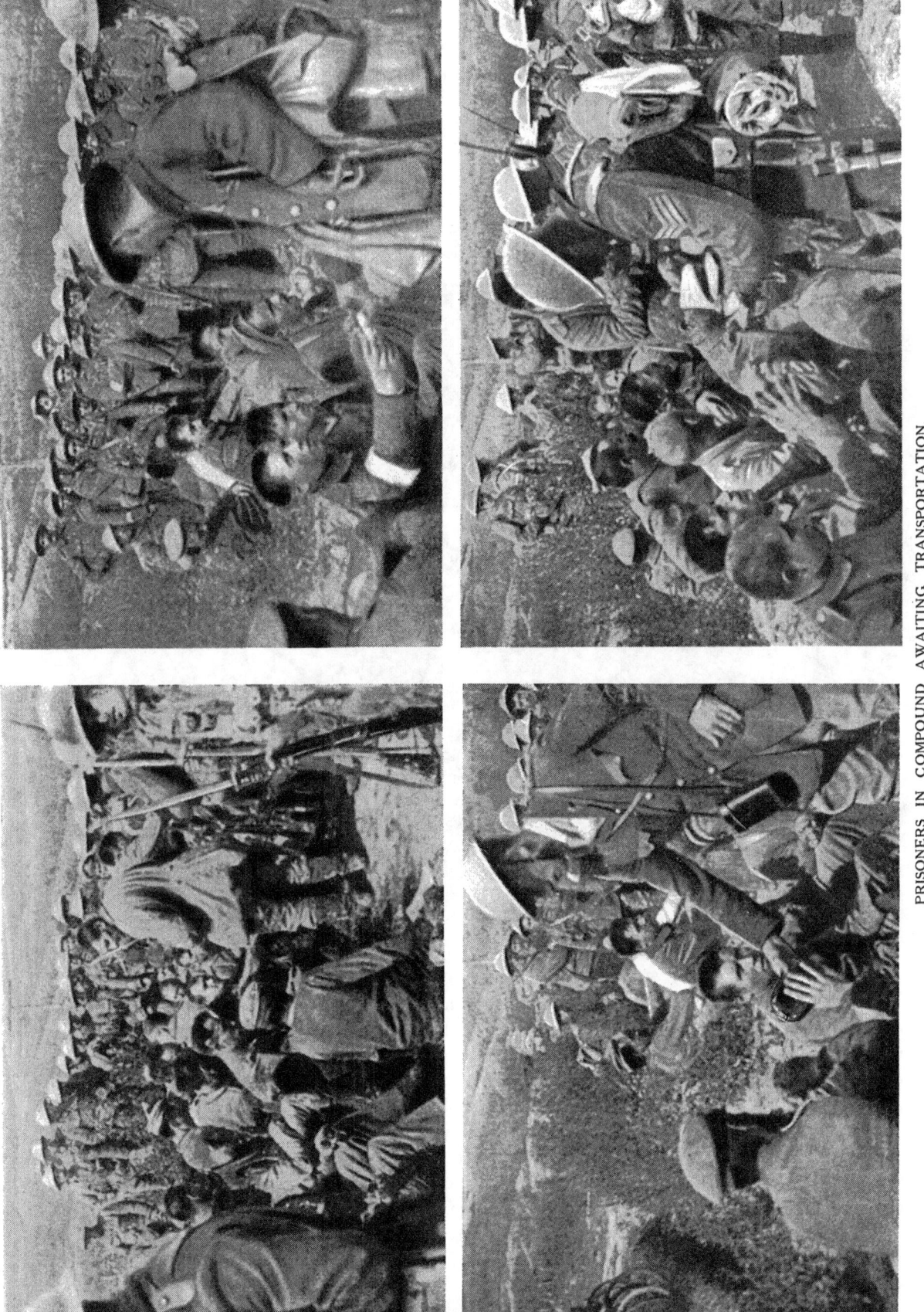

PRISONERS IN COMPOUND AWAITING TRANSPORTATION.

In the top right-hand illustration one of our men is shown handing a German prisoner cigarettes; in the bottom left-hand one a wounded German is being handed a flask; in the bottom right-hand illustration German note-books and papers of identity are being scrutinized.

charnel-house. Meanwhile, further to the left, Scottish troops belonging to famous Highland regiments were advancing near Longueval, part of which had been set on fire by our bombardment and was blazing fiercely. They had to traverse a distance of over twelve hundred yards of open ground, under heavy shell-fire and an enfilading fire from machine-guns. Many men fell, and their comrades reached the Germans' entanglements, only to find that in places they were still intact. But the Highlanders, their blood set on fire by the music of the pipes that went with them, flung themselves upon the wire, cut their way through, and swept down in a resistless torrent upon the German trenches.

Longueval was garrisoned by Prussians, and some of them fought fiercely enough, but they had no chance against the Scots, and those who resisted were quickly accounted for. From one dug-out emerged a Prussian officer, with a great axe in his hand, who called out in good English to a sergeant that he

A 75-mm. field-gun captured near Montauban.

wished to surrender. But when told to put down the axe, he changed his mind, and, instead of dropping his weapon, swung it aloft and hurled it at the sergeant's head. Fortunately, his aim was bad, and he was promptly bayoneted by the justly enraged Highlander.

In a few minutes the trenches were carried, and the kilted warriors were storming their way into Longueval village, where machine-guns were still clattering amidst the ruined houses. In one broken building, which commanded what had once been a roadway, there were no less than six of them, firing through holes in the walls; but our men rushed the place with bombs and speedily silenced them. In half an hour all resistance had ceased above ground, but below there was still a good deal of trouble. For in the cellars, where many of the Germans had taken refuge, were men who, refusing to surrender, fought like wolves at bay, and in the darkness of these places savage fighting went on for some time. At length, however, the last of these cave-men had been disposed of, and Longueval was ours.

Beyond Longueval our troops were unable to advance for a time, for the British artillery, unaware that the village had been taken, were still shelling the outskirts heavily. But presently the guns lifted,

A captured German field-gun.

A German machine-gun and an automatic rifle captured.

A captured German trench-gun.

and the impatient infantry began pushing forward into Delville Wood, some three hundred yards northeast of the village.

Westward of Longueval, the two Bazentins were carried in brilliant style. Upon Bazentin-le-Grand our heavies had flung so astonishing a weight of metal that the place had been swept almost flat, and little was left of its church and houses but heaps of bricks and twisted iron. Comparatively little resistance was encountered here, once the trenches had been carried, the Germans emerging from the cellars in which they had taken refuge, not to fight, but to surrender, and holding out their watches, their pocket-books, their helmets, anything, in fact, that they thought would ransom their lives ; and, when they had been made prisoners, readily consenting to carry back the British wounded. In one large cellar

A view of another captured German trench-mortar.

a great many of the enemy were found, suffering from wounds received during the bombardment which had not even been bandaged. Some of them would probably have bled to death if the capture of the village had been longer delayed.

Further to the left, our men fought their way through the ruined village of Bazentin-le-Petit and into the wood of that name to the west of it. Here the Germans held a strong position, more or less parallel to the Albert–Bapaume road, and at right angles to the general direction of our advance ; and severe fighting took place. Nevertheless, we succeeded in clearing the greater part of the wood, and our patrols pushed forward to the Bois des Foureaux (High Wood), which is the highest point in the neighbourhood, being some five hundred feet above sea-level.

The Germans soon showed that they had no intention of allowing us to remain in peaceable possession of the ground we had won. Their lost positions were, as usual, heavily shelled, and before the sun was up they had begun to counter-attack. Against Bazentin-le-Petit they advanced in great force and with the utmost courage and determination, and succeeded in recapturing the village. But they were immediately driven out again by a dashing attack, in which our bombers did great execution, and the whole place was once more in our hands. Two other determined counter-attacks which the enemy launched against our new positions failed to reach our trenches, being completely broken up by our fire.

About six o'clock in the evening a stirring incident occurred. For the first time since October, 1914, our cavalry were afforded an opportunity for mounted action. The troops engaged were a squadron of Dragoon Guards and another of the Deccan Horse. They had worked forward with our infantry over a stretch of ground between Bazentin Wood and Delville Wood, and had then ridden out alone on reconnaissance into the open country skirting Delville Wood. Here a machine-gun which some German

A captured German 10-cm. field-gun.

infantry had with them in a cornfield opened fire upon them. The order was immediately given to charge, and, with levelled lances, the cavalry galloped straight into the corn and rode right through the enemy, killing several of them. Then, wheeling round, they charged through them again. Some of the Germans fixed bayonets and tried to defend themselves; but the majority appeared panic-stricken, and either took to their heels or ran forward with piteous appeals for mercy, and clung to the stirrup-leathers of the horsemen. Thirty-two prisoners were taken, while about a dozen of the enemy were killed.

The victorious cavalry rode slowly on with their captives, and presently came under fire again from another field. On this occasion, however, there was no necessity for them to charge, as scarcely had the first shots been fired than an unexpected auxiliary appeared upon the scene. It was one of our aeroplanes, which came sweeping down, and, skimming very low, at no more than three hundred feet above the ground, pumped lead from its machine-gun into the astonished Germans until they scattered and made off.

A captured German trench-mortar.

A captured German field-gun.

Some machine-guns captured by our troops on the 1st of July.

This daring feat was only one of many successes gained by our airmen on this and the following day, notwithstanding that at times the weather was very unfavourable for their work. In one of our bombing raids an enemy train was derailed and a coach overturned, while in aerial combats we destroyed three Fokkers, three biplanes and a double-engined aeroplane, and forced another Fokker to land in a damaged condition.

The night was chiefly spent by the British in consolidating the ground won during the day, but with the dawn violent fighting began in the Pozières–Guillemont section of the German second line, where further important successes were gained by our troops, though, unhappily, not without heavy casualties. The struggle in the Delville Wood, north-east of Longueval, was of a particularly desperate character. This wood, which covers about a quarter of a square mile, is generally more open than Mametz and Trônes

The mascot of the Anzacs.

Woods, but the north-western part is very thick, and this the enemy had filled with snipers and machine-guns. The task of clearing the place was entrusted to the South Africans, and they accomplished it in the most gallant manner, and afterwards repulsed a strong counter-attack. Their capture of the wood was a really splendid feat of arms, for during their advance they were not only being sniped from the left by riflemen and machine-gunners at the edge of the wood, but were being enfiladed, virtually at point-blank range, by a field-gun from the neighbourhood of Guillemont to the south. Some idea of the difficulties which they had to encounter may be gathered from the following description given by an officer who was wounded on this occasion :

" The fighting at Delville was very ' hot stuff,' and we were shelled like blazes. We came through the front-line trenches up to the wood, and our instructions were to clear the place, which was strongly held by the enemy. The terrain was extremely difficult, being covered with thick undergrowth and affording plenty of cover for machine-guns. My company was the reserve company for the other South African troops, for whom matters got so hot that we were sent up to support them. Our troops in the wood signalled that the Germans were massing in force for a counter-attack. Before we got into the wood itself we ran into a large force of Boches hidden in the undergrowth. A terrific fire was opened from both sides. When I was hit it was clear that the Germans were being pushed back. Later in the day the whole wood was cleared."

North of Bazentin-le-Grand our troops penetrated into the German third line at the Bois des Foureaux, in which a detachment succeeded in securing a footing; while, further west, the whole of the Bazentin-le-Petit Wood was captured and securely held, in spite of two determined counter-attacks by the enemy. Here, amongst other prisoners, we captured the commanding officer of a Bavarian regiment with his whole staff. East of Ovillers a further advance was made, and our troops fought their way to the out-

A view of Ovillers.

skirts of Pozières. In the course of the day five heavy howitzers and four 77-mm. guns fell into our hands.

During the night, covered by the detachment which had pushed forward into the Bois des Foureaux (High Wood), our troops were engaged in strengthening our new positions, and early the following morning the Foureaux detachment received orders to withdraw into our main line, the withdrawal being carried out without interference from the enemy.

We had now reached the difficult period which invariably follows a successful offensive movement, when ground gained has to be consolidated under the savaging of the enemy's artillery; and no attempt at a further general advance was made on the 16th, while the Germans appeared to be awaiting the arrival of reinforcements before renewing their counter-attacks. The guns on both sides, however, were very active, notwithstanding that a thick mist lay over the countryside, causing what naval men call "low visibility," and rendering artillery observation difficult. The British batteries shelled High Wood, from which our troops had been withdrawn at daybreak, and pounded the enemy's lines to the north of Bazentin-le-Grand and Longueval; while the German guns retaliated upon the villages and woodlands

A little music by the Black Watch after coming back from the capture of Longueval.

Scenes behind the Anzac trenches.

we had captured and held during the past three days. All that day we continued to find large quantities of armament and other war material which had been abandoned by the enemy in the positions taken by the British; and Sir Douglas Haig reported that the captured armament collected by our troops now included five 8-inch howitzers, three 6-inch howitzers, four 6-inch guns, five other heavy guns, thirty-seven field-guns, thirty trench-howitzers, sixty-six machine-guns, and many thousands of rounds of gun ammunition of all descriptions. He added that the above was exclusive of many guns not yet brought in, and of the pieces destroyed by our artillery bombardments and abandoned by the enemy. In the same communiqué he announced that the total of unwounded German prisoners captured since July 1st was 189 officers and 10,779 non-commissioned officers and men.

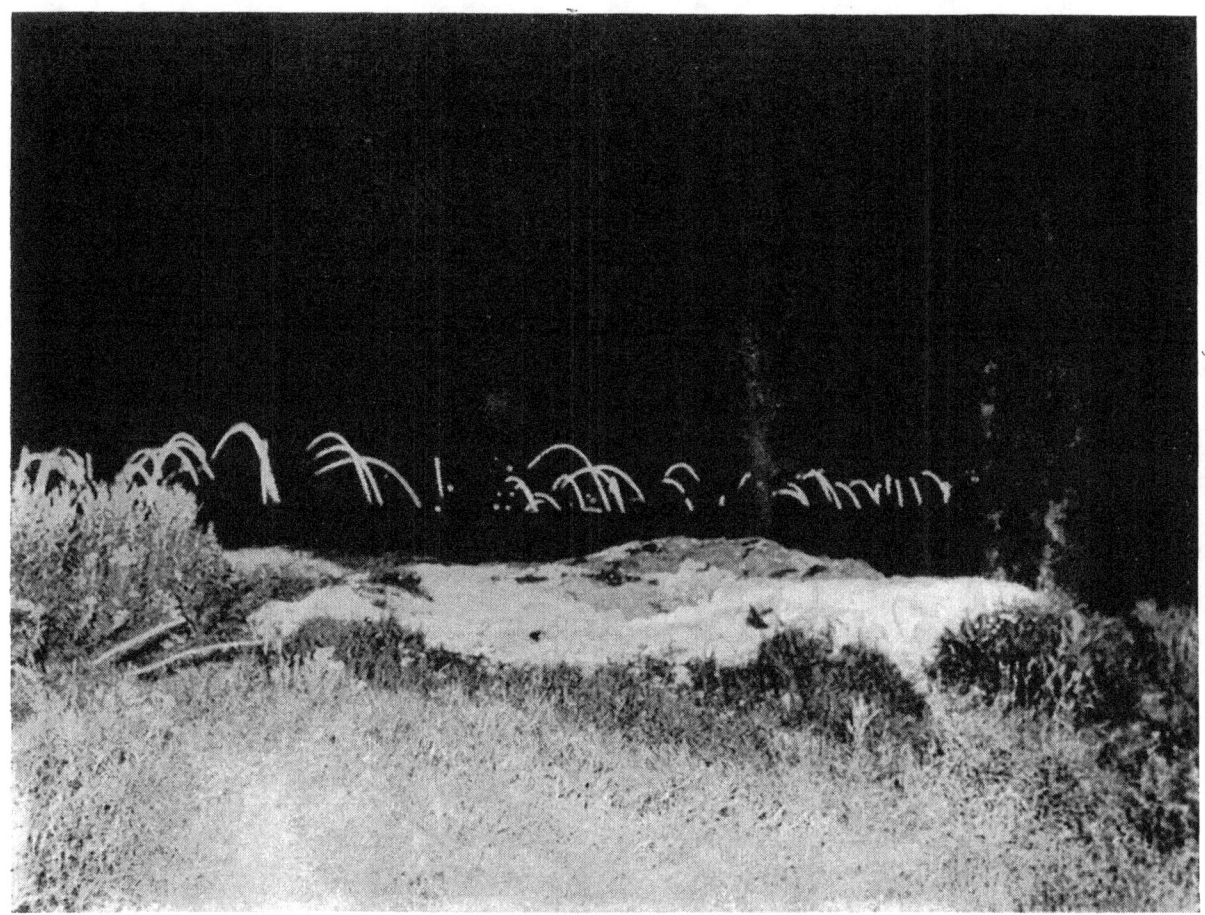

A night scene within the Australian lines.

Early on the 17th our offensive was resumed, and with splendid success. North-west of Bazentin-le-Petit Wood we stormed and captured the German second-line positions on a front of fifteen hundred yards. The large number of German dead found in this sector bore evidence to the very heavy casualties which the enemy had sustained since our advance began. East of Longueval we still further widened the gap in the enemy's second line by carrying by assault the strongly-defended position of Waterlot Farm; while, on our left flank, we captured the remaining strongholds of the enemy in Ovillers, together with the remnant of the brave garrison, and, after ten days' incessant hand-to-hand fighting of the most obstinate and murderous character, the whole village was at last in our hands.

History will not forget the struggle for the ruined village of Ovillers. Seldom has a place been attacked with more dauntless courage or defended with more stubborn resolution. Day and night since July 7th the conflict had continued, simultaneously above and below ground, and every yard had been furiously disputed. By the afternoon of the 14th the village was practically in our hands, but the work of digging out the enemy from their last subterranean strongholds presented such difficulties that it was not until three days later that all resistance was overcome.

The final assault, on the morning of the 17th, was delivered by North-Country troops who had distinguished themselves at La Boiselle at the beginning of the battle. They advanced upon the enemy from three sides, and a desperate hand-to-hand fight ensued, from house to house—or rather, from one rubbish-heap to another—and from cellar to cellar. In one of these were found twenty-five Germans, who, when made prisoners, declared that they had not tasted food for two days. Near by, our men were held up by machine-gun fire from one of the few houses which had not been entirely destroyed. An officer who had received a bullet through the arm led the attack upon the emplacements, and, when

A view in Mametz Wood.

gun and gunners had been accounted for, walked to the dressing-station, cheerily whistling "Tipperary," to have his wound attended to.

At length, about 10 a.m., the sorry remnant of the once powerful force which had garrisoned the village, now reduced to two officers and 124 men of the 3rd Prussian Guard, surrendered. They were in a hopeless position, for the fearful wall of fire which our guns had maintained to the north and east of the village had prevented supplies from reaching them, and they were weak from hunger and suffering torments from thirst. Human nature could make no longer resistance; and our troops, generously recognizing the splendid grit which their stubborn foemen had shown, formed up and presented arms as the prisoners were marched off.

An interesting little incident occurred on their way to the rear. They were in charge of a party of our men commanded by a subaltern; and one of the German officers, approaching the latter, unpinned the Iron Cross which he wore on his breast and held it out to the lieutenant. The British officer asked him what he meant. "Take it for having done what we considered to be impossible," said the German.

A German look-out post in Mametz Wood.

136 Sir Douglas Haig's Great Push

"I give it you." The lieutenant thanked him, but declined, explaining that it was not the custom of the British Army to deprive an unfortunate enemy of anything which he had won by his own valour.

Ovillers presented a horrible spectacle. Not only had it been pounded to rubbish, but the unburied dead, some of them fearfully mangled by shell-fire or bombs, lay about everywhere, and the whole place reeked of slaughter. The entrance to the village by the Bapaume road had been defended by two field-works. These had been entirely destroyed, but in their place had arisen another rampart—a rampart composed of some eight hundred corpses, piled one upon another!

A monster gun in action.

CHAPTER V

In announcing the capture of Ovillers and the other British successes gained that day, Sir Douglas Haig cited the following captured documents, which showed the very heavy casualties which the enemy had suffered in the recent fighting and the terrible effects of our artillery fire:

From a company of the 16th Bavarian Infantry Regiment:

"Severe enemy artillery fire of all calibres up to 28-cm. on company sector. Company strength, one officer, twelve men. Beg urgently speedy relief for the company. What remains of the company is so exhausted that in case of an attack by the enemy the few totally exhausted men cannot be counted on."

From another company of the same regiment to 3rd Battalion, 16th Bavarian Infantry Regiment:

"Very heavy intense enemy fire on company sector. The company has completely lost its fighting value. The men left are so exhausted that they can no longer be employed in fighting. If heavy artillery fire continues, the company will soon be entirely exterminated. Relief for the company is urgently requested."

PART V. WILL BE READY ON TUESDAY, NOVEMBER 21ST.

This part contains some wonderful panoramic views of the Battlefield of the Somme, and the illustrations include:—

- German curtain fire just outside Minden Post
- Part of the British Fire Trench wrecked by German high explosive shells a few minutes before this picture was taken
- Clearing the battlefield of snipers and hidden machine guns
- Routing Germans from dug-outs
- A big howitzer in action
- Royal Fusiliers resting after the storming of La Boiselle
- Effect of British shell fire on German trenches between Fricourt and Mametz
- The Post reaches the Devonshires during Battle
- The Toll of War. German dead on the Field of Battle
- The Manchesters' pet dog fell with his master charging Dantzig Alley
- Scenes on the Battlefield
- A Battalion of the Middlesex Regiment burying German dead
- German ammunition wagons destroyed by our bombardment
- Our men are very comfortable in the old German dug-outs
- Bringing up water pipes to supply the men in the front line with water
- A few of the captured guns and trench mortars
- "Cat o' nine tails" found in the German trenches
- An armoured car
- The crater made by a German aerial torpedo
- Troops resting in the German trenches
- View in Trones Wood
- Entrance to a German dug-out in Contalmaison
- German ammunition wagons near Mametz destroyed by our artillery fire
- Trophies captured by the Sherwood Foresters. The dog was found in a German dug-out
- A German observation post in Trones Wood
- German wounded prisoner being put on board an ambulance after treatment at the Special Field Hospital for wounded prisoners
- A big gun in action during bombardment
- Some of our giant howitzers in hiding and their shells A heavy howitzer
- A captured German Minnen Werfer (10") to throw tin canisters filled with high explosives. The barrel is constricted timber bound with galvanised iron wire
- The Regimental Barber
- British shells bursting on the German trenches
- Another photograph showing British shells bursting on the German trenches
- Some of the German Prisoners at Carnoy, just after they were captured on 14th July
- Germans cleaning some of the captured Guns and Trench Mortars
- On the horizon of this picture once stood a flourishing village—La Boiselle
- Effect of one high explosive shell on barbed wire entanglement
- The devastating effect of British shell fire. Smashed trenches and dug-outs. A mine crater 40 feet deep
- The battered German stronghold at Fricourt. Wrecked dug-outs, 20 to 30 feet under level of field. A Labour Battalion of the Duke of Cornwall's Light Infantry repair road on day following battle
- Views of the shell-shattered Village of Mametz The main street
- German dug-outs
- Some of the booty. German Trench Mortars. Battery of Field Artillery captured by the 7th Division near La Boiselle
- A welcome rest. Lancashire Fusiliers after the battle
- Assembling for a roll-call
- Royal Fusiliers cleaning-up after the successful advance
- Essex Regiment washing-up at a wayside pool. Roll-Call of the Seaforth Highlanders
- Cleaning-up Machine Guns. A cheery group of Gunners and Highlanders on the Battlefield
- Bringing up an 8-inch howitzer and placing in advance position for the next bombardment
- A "sample" of the British Army (the Worcesters) off to continue The Advance
- Whilst others less fortunate depart under escort for England

---

ORDER FORM.

To M ....
                                                                                                         BOOKSELLER OR NEWSAGENT.

Please send me Part V., and the following Parts as published, of "SIR DOUGLAS HAIG'S GREAT PUSH," for which I enclose............................

Name...

Address ....

SCALA THEATRE,

(Goodge Street Tube Station).   CHARLOTTE STREET, W.

AT THE FRONT

OFFICIAL WAR OFFICE FILMS.

Kut Relief Forces.   Salonika.   Russian Army.   French Army.   East Africa.
The King on the Somme Battle Field, &c.

THE BATTLE OF THE SOMME.

"There is no programme in London which gives so complete and vivid a description of the War on ALL FRONTS."—*Evening News.*

THE KING'S ADVICE:

SEE THE SOMME WAR FILM AND WHAT WAR MEANS.

"The public should see these pictures, that they may have some idea of what the Army is doing, and what war means."

This statement was made by the King after witnessing a programme of the Official War Office film, 'The Battle of the Somme,' which was shown by command to the King and Queen at Windsor Castle.—*Daily Express.*

Box Office, 10 to 10.   DAILY, 3 and 8.   'Phone: Gerr. 1444 & 1366.

SCALA THEATRE.

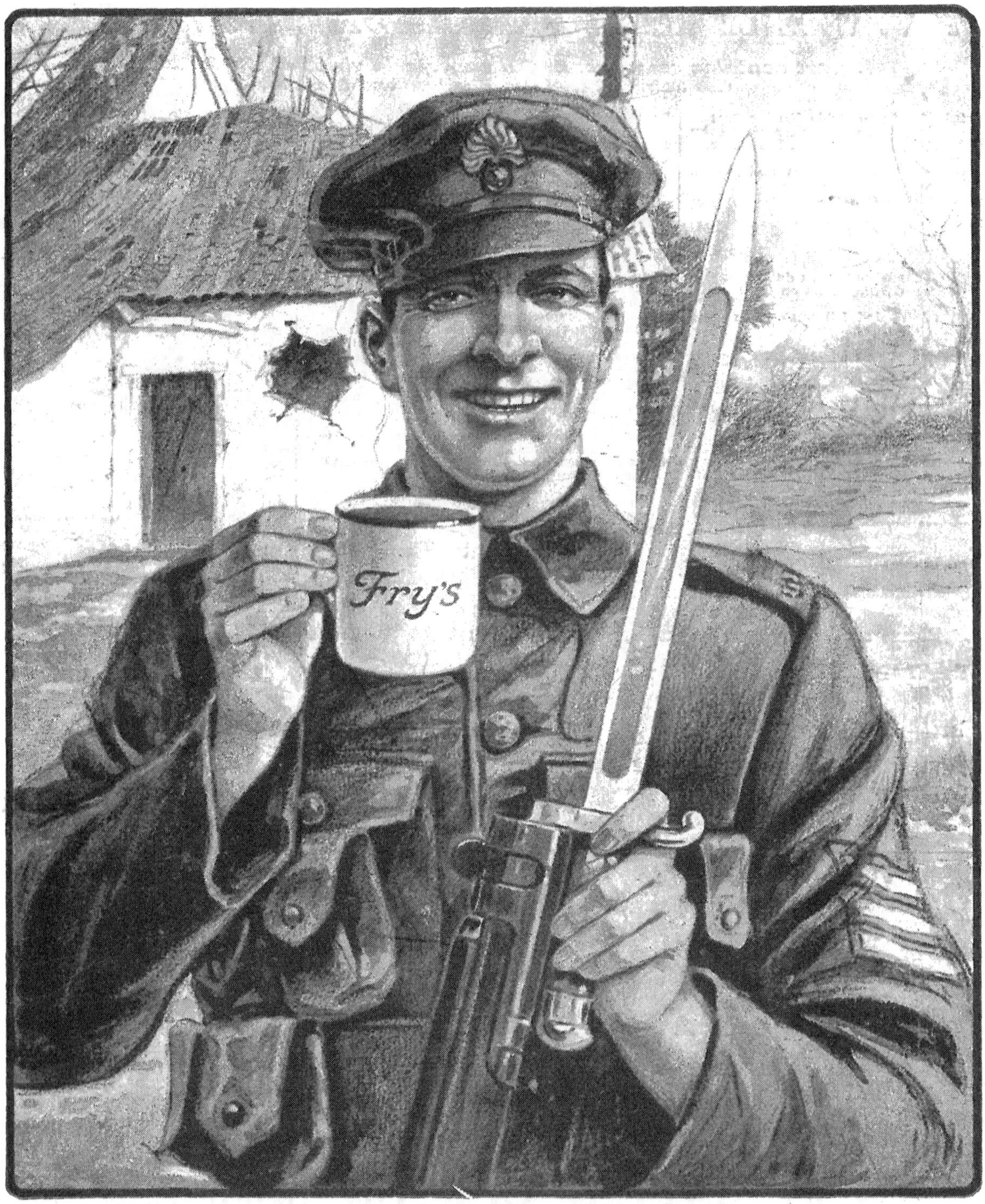

"BLIGHTY'S BEST"

Always on Active Service

PRINTED AT THE CHAPEL RIVER PRESS, KINGSTON-ON-THAMES

IN ABOUT 8 FORTNIGHTLY PARTS.　　HUTCHINSON'S NEW PART WORK　　Part VI. ready Dec. 5th. **PART V. 8d.** NET

SIR DOUGLAS HAIG'S
GREAT PUSH

THE BATTLE OF THE SOMME

A popular, pictorial and authoritative work on one of the Greatest Battles in History, illustrated by about **700 wonderful OFFICIAL PHOTOGRAPHS AND CINEMATOGRAPH FILMS** and other authentic pictures

BY ARRANGEMENT WITH THE WAR OFFICE

THE RESULT OF OUR BOMBARDMENT

GREAT VALUE FOR EIGHTPENCE

THIS PART CONTAINS 65 WONDERFUL REPRODUCTIONS OF THE FAMOUS WAR OFFICE CINEMATOGRAPH FILMS AND OFFICIAL PHOTOGRAPHS OF THE BATTLE OF THE SOMME, BEAUTIFULLY PRINTED ON THE BEST ENGLISH ART PAPER.

LONDON : HUTCHINSON & Co.

IMPORTANT.

THE GREAT NATIONAL TRIBUTE.

The ROLL OF HONOUR

AN ILLUSTRATED BIOGRAPHICAL RECORD OF **ALL** OFFICERS, NON-COMMISSIONED OFFICERS AND MEN OF HIS MAJESTY'S FORCES WHO ARE KILLED OR DIE ON ACTIVE SERVICE

NOW BEING COMPILED BY

THE MARQUIS DE RUVIGNY

Author and Editor of "The Blood Royal of Britain," "The Titled Nobility of Europe," and other works.

THE debt which the Empire owes to those who have laid down their lives in the present War must, from the very nature of things, for ever remain unpaid.

There is, however, a universal desire to keep them in remembrance, and to ensure that their names and their glorious deeds shall not be forgotten.

For this purpose, "THE ROLL OF HONOUR" is now being prepared, to place on permanent record the name of every Officer, Non-Commissioned Officer and Man of His Majesty's Forces on land or sea who is killed in action, who dies of wounds, or whose death is otherwise caused in the present War.

It may here be briefly stated that it is proposed to give, whenever obtainable, the full name, place and date of birth, parentage, biographical sketch of career, and date and place of death, with extracts from letters of Commanding Officers or Comrades relating to the action in which the Officer or Man fell, or to the particular circumstances of his death.

Many a deed of heroism is covered by the bare announcement of a name in the daily long roll of casualties. To collect and record these is the purpose of the "ROLL OF HONOUR." The names of children will also be included, so that in the years to come they may themselves read, or teach their children to read, of the glorious way their fathers died ; of those individual acts of bravery that are the chief redeeming feature of war.

Much valuable help is being given by the Authorities, by the Regiments, by Public Institutions, and the Heads of Schools, and the Publishers appeal with confidence to those who have lost relatives to assist them in the task they have undertaken by sending at once to the Editor the necessary particulars, extracts, from letters, etc.

The Editor and Publishers wish it to be distinctly understood that the insertion of any name is not in any way dependent upon the payment of any fee or of subscription to the book, and that no fee will be accepted for the insertion of any name.

A large number of portraits of Officers and Men will be included. With over 100,000 dead for the first year, it is clearly impossible to undertake that one will be given in every case, but when a portrait is supplied the Publishers will do their best to include it, and in the case of one supplied by a Subscriber, where there is no copyright fee, they guarantee that it will be reproduced.

SEND FOR A FORM to fill in particulars of your relation or friend who has been killed on active service. There is no charge, and his biography ought to be included. Unless you write probably only his name will be given,

---

To THE STANDARD ART BOOK CO. LTD.,

Publishers of "THE ROLL OF HONOUR,"

30-32, LUDGATE HILL, E.C.

EDITORIAL OFFICES:—
MARQUIS DE RUVIGNY,
"The Roll of Honour"
14-15, Hanover Chambers,
Buckingham St., Adelphi, W.C.

Please send me a form so that I may give you particulars concerning ....

.... *who was killed on active service.*

Name ....

Address ....

From 2nd Battalion to 3rd Battalion, 16th Bavarian Infantry:

"The battalion has just received orders from Lieut.-Col. Kumme that it is placed under orders of the 3rd Battalion, 16th Bavarian Regiment, as sector reserve. Battalion consists at present time of three officers, two non-commissioned officers and nineteen men."

During the night our troops made substantial progress to the north of Ovillers on a front of one thousand yards, driving the enemy from several strongly-defended points and capturing prisoners and machine guns. This advance was of considerable

Two pictures showing our men clearing the battlefield of snipers and hidden machine-guns.

importance, since it menaced from a new direction the village of Pozières, the outskirts of which troops operating east of Ovillers had reached on the 15th. On the northern part of our line, near Wytschaete, we made a successful raid into the German trenches; while opposite Cuinchy a similar attack by the enemy was checked by our fire.

The 18th brought with it a thick mist and heavy and incessant rain, which hindered the work of our airmen and converted the battleground in some parts into a sea of mud; and partly owing to these circumstances and partly owing, no doubt, to a correct judgment of the emergency ahead, there was a well-marked pause in our offensive, and the troops devoted themselves to further consolidating the ground they had won. For the British knew that the pinch was coming. For days past the Germans had been busily bringing up reinforcements and guns of every calibre, with the intention of throwing their increased weight into a tremendous counter-attack,

which was to be hurled upon us without regard to the cost. It began about 5.30 in the afternoon, when, after a tremendous bombardment of our right with "tear" shells and gas-shells, the enemy advanced in dense masses to the assault of our new positions in the vicinity of Longueval and Delville Wood, both of which places had been heavily and continuously pounded by

Routing Germans from dug-outs.

the German artillery ever since they had passed into our possession. The ground chosen for the attack showed judicious selection, since, if it proved successful, it would seriously endanger the Allied front between Longueval and Hardecourt, where the British and French lines met.

The battle raged throughout the night, and was particularly violent in Delville

Wood, in which area Sir Douglas Haig subsequently reported that the enemy had not less than thirteen battalions, drawn from four different divisions, engaged on a front of two thousand yards. The South Africans, who had carried the wood in such brilliant style on the 15th, had laboured unceasingly in the interval to consolidate their position. But digging amid a tangle of undergrowth with the ground porous as a sponge from the interminable rain of shells which the German guns poured upon it, had proved a well-nigh hopeless task; and, though they fought with the most splendid courage and tenacity, yard by yard they were forced back, and by the morning the Germans had driven deep into the wood. They had also succeeded in obtaining a footing in the northern outskirts of Longueval, despite the stubborn resistance of the Highland troops who held the village; but both these successes had been gained at the cost of very heavy losses. Elsewhere the enemy could make no headway, and three separate assaults on Waterlot Farm, a little to the south-east of Longueval, broke down completely under our fire.

Handing out letters.

In Longueval village and Delville Wood fighting of the most fierce and obstinate character continued throughout the 19th, the British guns shelling the enemy so furiously, and our infantry counter-attacking in such determined fashion, that the Germans in their turn, were obliged to give way, and by the evening most of the ground we had lost the previous night had been regained. In the course of the afternoon a large force of Germans, massing to attack Waterlot Farm from the direction of Guillemont, came under so terrible a fire from our artillery that it was very quickly dispersed.

That evening another blow was struck at the enemy in a sector far away from the scene of these operations. This

The post reaches the Devonshires during battle.

A big howitzer in action.

Royal Fusiliers resting after the storming of La Boiselle.

Effect of British shell-fire on German trenches between Fricourt and Mametz.

was on a length of about two miles of front in the country south of Armentières. For some days past our artillery had been pounding with steady insistence the entanglements and rain-softened parapets of the German first system of defences. On the 19th the bombardment became more lively, and, when evening fell, the guns lifted and put an intense barrage on the enemy's communication-trenches, which in many places were afterwards found so silted up by shell-fire as to look little more than mere scratches on the surface of the ground. Then our infantry were let loose, and, with loud cheers, advanced to the attack, the way for which had been so well prepared for them. In this attack the Australians greatly distinguished themselves. Their exploits are thus described by Captain Bean, the official Press representative with the Australian troops in France, in a despatch dated July 20th :

"Yesterday evening, after a preparatory bombardment, an Australian force attacked the German

Scenes on the battlefield.

trenches south of Armentières. The Australians on the left seized the German front line and passed beyond it to further trenches of the first system. In the centre, the Australians carried the whole of the first system and reached more or less open country.

"On the right, the troops had to cross a much wider stretch, between trenches where the Germans held a very strongly fortified salient. The Germans were ready for attack, and had managed to save a number of machine-guns from the bombardment. In spite of very brave efforts, the troops on this flank were unable to cross the ground between the trenches, and only managed to reach the German trenches at isolated points. From these they were subsequently driven out.

The Manchester's pet dog fell with his master, charging Dantzig Alley.

"This enabled the Germans to concentrate the fire of all sorts of artillery on a portion of the trenches captured. The Germans battered down their own trenches where they were occupied by our men. They also drained water from the channel down the trenches from the left flank, and the Australians there, shortly after reaching the trenches, found themselves surrounded with water rapidly rising waist-high. They endured a tremendous bombardment until early the following morning, when, after eleven hours in the captured position, the Australians retaining a small portion of the German line were ordered to retire.

"By dint of very brave work, the engineers and infantry in working-parties had managed to get communication-trenches dug completely through to the German trenches. These trenches were dug under very heavy shell-fire. This work enabled the troops to retire with a loss which was slight, when the extraordinary difficulty of the operation is considered. Among the last who returned to our trenches were eight men who said they got lost behind the German trenches and had been wandering about until daylight in the country in rear of the front line.

Wrecked dug-outs, twenty to thirty feet under level of field

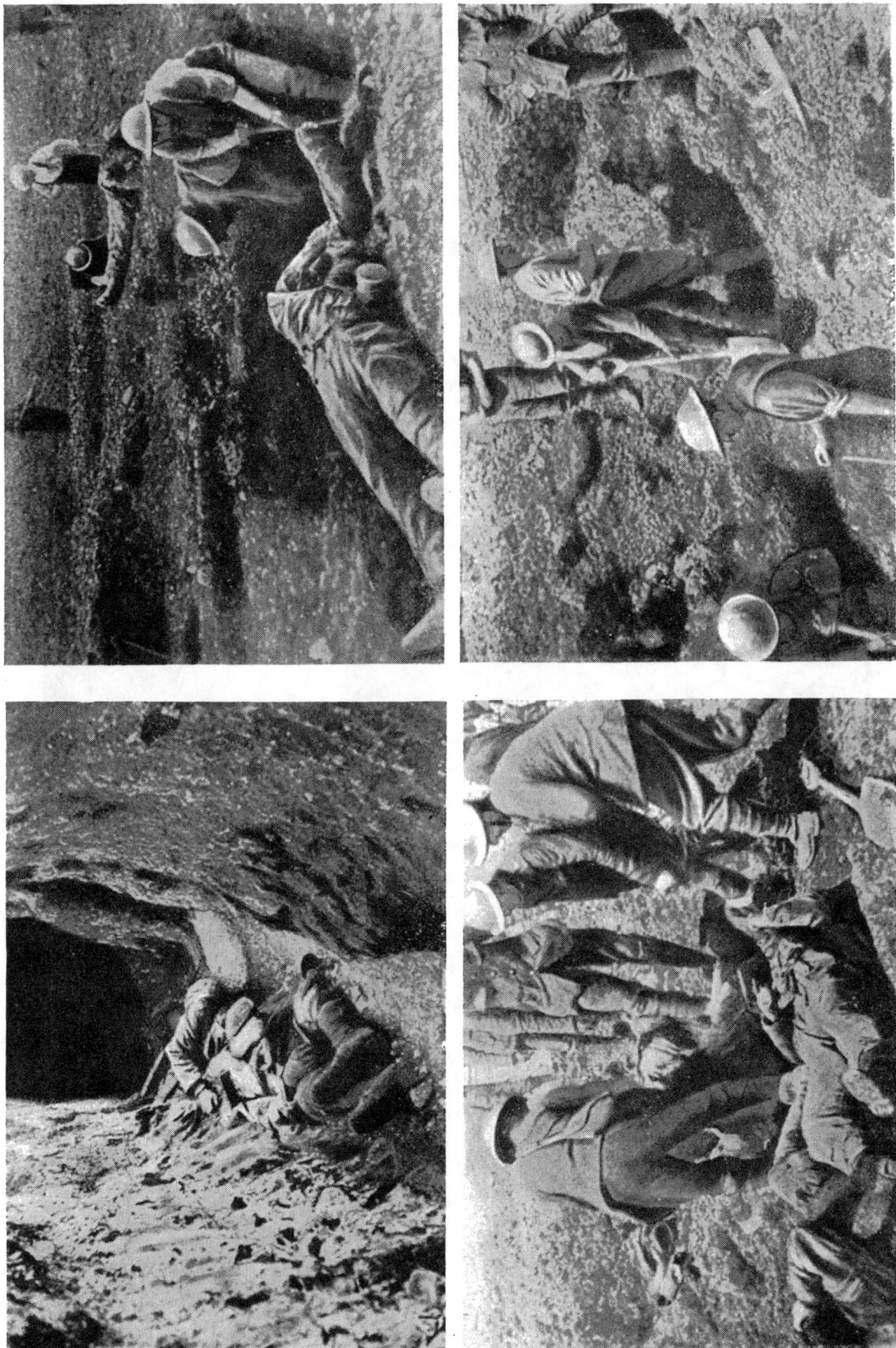

SCENES ON THE BATTLEFIELD.

The top left-hand illustration shows a captured German trench with victims of our bombardment. The other three are of a battalion of the Middlesex Regiment burying German dead.

The battered German stronghold at Fricourt.

The Battle of the Somme

A view of the battlefield showing a mine crater on the right-hand side.

"Our troops in this attack had to face shell-fire heavier and more continuous than was ever known in Gallipoli. Many of them were quite untried previously, and the manner in which they carried it through seems to have been worthy of all the traditions of Anzac. At least two hundred prisoners were captured, and several machine-guns were brought in. Many Germans were killed, and the losses amongst our troops were severe."

During the day and also during the night our bombing-aeroplanes carried out a number of successful enterprises, many tons of explosives being dropped with marked success on railway centres, among aerodromes, and at other important points. One hostile aeroplane was destroyed and several others driven to ground in a damaged condition.

At night our bombing-parties made a substantial advance east of the Leipzig Redoubt, a little to the south of Thiépval; while north of the Bazentin–Longueval line our troops continued to push forward, in spite of the most stubborn opposition, and captured a number of prisoners and a field-gun. Heavy fighting still continued in the northern outskirts of Longueval village and in Delville Wood, where we succeeded in regaining a little more ground.

In his report on the 20th Sir Douglas Haig mentioned that a captured diary belonging to a German commanding officer showed that, in the fighting on July 1st, the 6th Bavarian Regiment, which opposed us at Montauban, suffered 3,000 casualties, out of a total strength of 3,500; while another document revealed that one battalion of the 190th Regiment lost 980 men, out of 1,100, and that the other two battalions of the same regiment each lost more than half their effective strength.

Between the Leipzig Redoubt, on the west, and Delville Wood, on the east, fighting continued all that day without intermission. North of the Bazentin–Longueval line our successful advance continued, and by the evening our troops had fought their way into the Bois des Foureaux (High Wood) and driven the enemy right out of it; thus penetrating the German third line. For a few hours we remained

A mine crater forty feet deep.

A view of the shell-shattered village of Mametz.

in possession of this important position; but during the night, after an intense bombardment with gas-shells, the Germans counter-attacked furiously and succeeded in effecting an entry into the north of the wood, though they failed to dislodge us from the southern half.

During the day, our airmen, taking advantage of the fine, clear weather which now prevailed, continued their bombing operations against points of military importance, and with gratifying results. Hostile aircraft were inactive until the evening, when a good deal of fighting took place behind the German lines. One of our offensive patrols encountered eleven German machines, and, as the result of the combat which ensued, three enemy aircraft were shot down, one bursting into flames. Another encounter between four of our machines and six of the enemy's lasted for forty-five minutes. One Fokker was then shot down, and on another being badly damaged by our fire, the remaining four broke off the fight. During many other combats in the air a fifth German aeroplane was forced to the ground. Our total losses were one machine.

On the 21st, with the exception of local encounters, there was a comparative lull in the main battle area, and no change in the situation occurred. The enemy made a bombing-attack on the northern edge of our positions in the Leipzig salient, and succeeded at one point in entering our front trenches, but were at once driven out.

Our airmen were again very active and successful, six hostile aeroplanes being destroyed by them, while several others were driven to the ground in a damaged condition. One British machine was brought down by gunfire, and two were reported missing.

The artillery on both sides was very active throughout the 22nd, and in several places the British

A distant view of the shell-shattered village of Mametz.

A view of the wrecked main street of Mametz.

Wrecked German village of Mametz.

The battered German stronghold at Fricourt. On the left: our men can be seen repairing the road.

Wrecked German dug-outs.

front-line and support-trenches were heavily bombarded with gas and "tear" shells. Nothing else of importance occurred that day; but during the night the battle resumed its former intensity, and before dawn heavy fighting was in progress along all the line from Pozières to Delville Wood, and southwards from Trônes Wood in the direction of Guillemont.

About 10 p.m. our artillery began a terrific bombardment of the German trenches in the neighbourhood of Pozières, the gunners firing as fast as they could get their shells to the breech. The sky was blazing with shell-bursts and rockets, and the earth trembled. "I have never before seen such a spectacle," writes Captain Bean. "A large section of the horizon was lit up by a continuous band of quivering light." At midnight a veritable torrent of explosive was suddenly turned on to the enemy's lines in front of Pozières village, and immediately afterwards London Territorial and Australian troops were launched to the assault, the former advancing from the south-west, and the latter from the south-east.

There was a distance of something like 550 yards of shell-pitted ground to be covered between the Australian lines and the front trench of the German network of defences across the Bapaume road, which runs diagonally through Pozières village. It would have been no easy journey even in the most favourable circumstances; but amid the darkness of a very black night, and under exceptionally heavy shell and machine-gun fire, it was one of the most difficult imaginable. Nevertheless, the gallant Anzacs stumbled resolutely forward over the broken ground, going as straight through the German fire as though the bullets were raindrops. They were being shelled mostly with shrapnel; while the Londoners, on their left, advancing from the direction of Ovillers, were being greeted chiefly with high explosive. Observers could mark the precise point at which the clouds of shrapnel touched the black pillars of the high explosive. Other kinds of shells were being fired at our men. "Many of them burst high," writes Mr. Philip Gibbs, the special correspondent of the *Daily Chronicle*, "and then came down like flaming torches, with trailing feathers of flame. They were liquid-fire shells, to burn up the bodies of men—a fine devilish addition

A few of the captured trench-mortars near La Boiselle.

to all war's chemistry. 'They frightened us at first,' said a Territorial. 'It was as though the stars had suddenly dropped, all on fire. But they didn't do us much harm, and after the first scare we didn't mind them.' Other shells were dropping in a queer way. They came with a singing note, as though they had a whistle tied to them, and burst without much noise, but with a hiss like a 'dud' shell. These were of the poison-gas variety, and some of our men were made sick, but did not suffer in a deadly way, because they were quick to get beyond reach of the fumes."

The first-line trench—or what remained of it—was but lightly held, at any rate by live Germans. These were mostly machine-gunners and men with bombs, who continued to fire or hurl their missiles until the advancing troops were close to the shattered parapet. The Anzacs rushed at them with the bayonet, but they did not wait for the cold steel to reach them, some scurrying for the shelter of the German second line, while the rest threw up their hands. To the credit of the Australians, these latter, notwithstanding their tardy surrender, were made prisoners and sent back.

Some of the captured guns near La Boiselle.

could not push forward at once, as the British artillery was still shelling the ground between the enemy's first and second lines. But presently our guns lifted, and, leaving some of their number to consolidate the ground won, they swept on to the German second trench. This second line of defence was in general just beyond the tramway, which runs under the fringe of the village, and was strongly constructed, with numerous deep dug-outs, though in parts it had been almost demolished by our bombardment. It was held in force by the enemy, and our men were received with a storm of rifle and machine-gun fire. But the Australians carried it with an irresistible rush, bayoneting all who opposed them, and clearing out the dug-outs with bombs. Then, after again leaving consolidating parties to strengthen the captured position, they went forward again, stormed two more lines of trenches, and fought their way into the heart of the village, the southern portion of which was

The Australians soon in their hands. The enemy, however, still held the northern or upper part of the place, which was full of machine-guns concealed in the ruins of houses or in specially constructed emplacements.

A welcome rest: Lancashire Fusiliers after the battle.

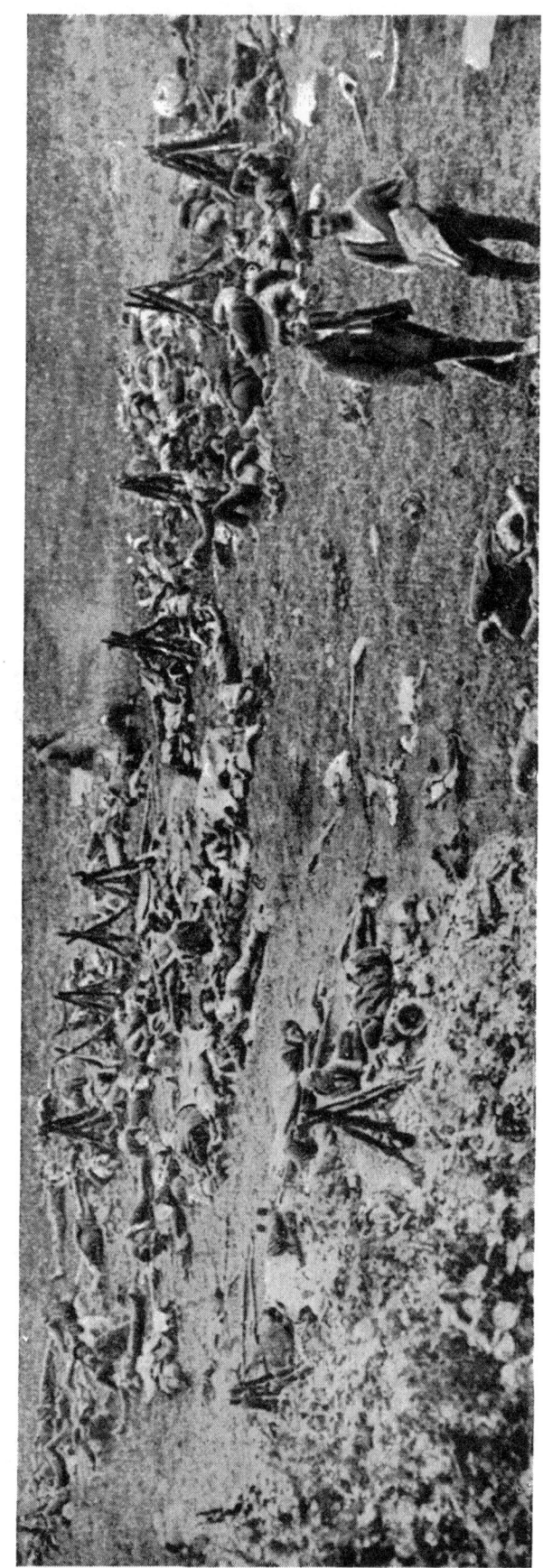

Tired out: Lancashire Fusiliers having a well-earned rest after the battle.

Lancashire Fusiliers resting after the battle.

Royal Fusiliers cleaning up after the successful advance.

But the Germans' situation was not exactly a happy one, as the Territorials, on the Anzacs' left, had fought their way gallantly forward in face of a withering fire, and had reached a point above the village, from which they threatened to outflank the enemy.

Towards midday, the Germans, who had in the interval brought up considerable reinforcements, launched a furious counter-attack against both the Londoners and the Australians, and a frightful hand-to-hand conflict ensued. "Both sides," relates one of our officers, who was wounded in the course of the conflict, "went for each other with equal fury. The Germans had evidently

Essex regiment washing up at a wayside pool.

Roll-call of the Seaforth Highlanders.

been plied with ether; they reeked of it. Our men, especially the Australians, met them with heroic tenacity. Rifles were useless in this horrible encounter —only knives, bayonets, revolvers and grenades were used. In addition, some of the Germans had long, spiked clubs. I saw one of their officers strike one of our wounded men with this brutal weapon, but he had no time to finish his job; a revolver-shot stretched him beside his victim.

"In one house a German squad, which was trying to get its machine-gun to work, was stricken down with the bayonet to the last man by a party of Australians, who broke into the ruins after them.

"I saw a thrilling duel between two officers. An English lieutenant, charging at the head of his men, found himself face to face with a Bavarian captain. He got home with a sword-stroke, but, at the same moment, received a revolver-ball in the stomach. Mastering his pain, he was able to give his adversary a deadly thrust. Unfortunately, he himself died soon afterwards."

Finally, the enemy were driven back, and by the evening we had made further progress, and nearly

Another view of the Royal Fusiliers cleaning up after the successful advance.

Examining the ammunition for machine-guns after the battle.

three-parts of the village was in our hands.

On other parts of the battle-front the fighting was equally intense, but here we were unable to gain further ground. At one time during the morning we had recaptured the whole of Longueval, but by the afternoon the enemy was once more in possession of the northern end of the village. We also twice succeeded in capturing the outskirts of Guillemont, only to be driven out again on each occasion. Between High Wood and Guillemont the Germans made repeated counter-attacks, all of which were beaten off, very heavy casualties being inflicted on the enemy by our artillery and machine-gun fire.

Apart from continuous heavy shelling by both sides, a night of comparative calm followed the severe fighting of the 23rd. But very early on the morrow, by which time further reinforcements had reached the enemy, including some units which had arrived from before Verdun, the battle was resumed all along the front from the neighbourhood of Thiépval to Guillemont. At Pozières, after a heavy cannonade, the Germans attacked with the utmost fury and determination, and succeeded in forcing the Australians back some little distance. Two hours later, however, our men launched a successful counter-attack, and, after a fierce struggle, the ground lost was regained. During the rest of the day fighting continued without intermission in the north-eastern part of the village, and we made further progress. We also gained some ground near the Bois des Foureaux (High Wood) and in the direction of Guillemont. In the course of the afternoon the Germans attempted an attack on our right flank, but it was frustrated by the fire of our artillery.

For some days past the increasing strength of the enemy's artillery,

Cleaning up machine-guns.

A cheery group of gunners.

A heavy howitzer

Some of our giant howitzers in hiding, and their shells.

and particularly of their heavy guns, had been very noticeable; and throughout the 24th the hostile bombardment of our positions was almost continuous and at times very violent. Instead of a single curtain of fire, it was remarked that, in places, the Germans let fall two and occasionally three, while they also flung a number of shells from their long-range guns on certain spots. It was largely random firing, however, for their airmen were so completely outmatched that they scarcely dared to venture beyond their own lines, and their balloons were few and remote; so that the damage inflicted was small in comparison with the amount of ammunition expended. Our own artillery was also very active, especially about Pozières. Among other heavies, the huge 15-inch howitzer "Grandmother"—beloved of our soldiers—devoted her attention to this locality. "Her great shells," writes Mr. Beach Thomas, "rattled away like a train coming from a tunnel over the heads of the Pozières troops, and at regular,

German wounded prisoners being put on board an ambulance after treatment at the special field hospital for wounded prisoners.

respectable intervals removed a rod or two of the hillside landscape where it is pointed by the windmill on the top. The tonnage of earth, stone, wire, and what-not mixture of dust and rubble from this peak clean out-towered the nearer and less dignified explosions of the many German 5.9's, which cloaked the ruins of Pozières, among which the Australians were steadily progressing."

During the night two further infantry attacks, preceded by exceptionally violent gunfire, were launched against the centre of our line. But both were broken up by the concentrated fire of our artillery, machine-guns and rifles, and at no point did the enemy succeed in reaching the British trenches, while their casualties on each occasion were very severe. In other parts of the line there was a good deal of hand-to-hand fighting, and in places our troops succeeded in working their way forward. North of Pozières we also gained ground, notwithstanding very stubborn opposition, and captured two machine-guns and some prisoners, including two battalion commanders.

Throughout the 25th there was fierce hand-to-hand and bomb fighting at various places all along our battle-front. During the afternoon the Germans attempted an infantry attack on Pozières from

the north-east, but were driven back by the fire of our artillery. North of the Ancre no incident of importance occurred. During the night a small party of the enemy raided our trenches immediately west of the Ypres–Pilkem road, but were at once driven out. Further south, after a bombardment by our artillery, a party of British troops raided the German lines. The enemy came out in front of their own wire to meet us, and a sharp hand-to-hand encounter took place, which resulted in the Germans being driven back, with the loss of some thirty killed. Our men then forced their way into the hostile trenches, in which were found many dead Germans, killed by our bombardment.

The failure of the enemy's attempt to drive us out of Pozières sealed the fate of what little of the place still remained in German possession, and by the early morning of the 26th the last defences had fallen, and, after four days and nights of the most bitter and obstinate fighting, the whole of the village was in our hands. The final assault was carried out in the most gallant manner by the Australians, covered to the westward by the London Territorials, who joined hands with them north of the village, not far from the cemetery standing on the edge of the plateau which dominates the plain of Bapaume. A Bavarian battalion which was holding the north-eastern part of Pozières met with a dreadful fate. Realizing the danger of being taken between the Territorials, who had outflanked his position, and the advancing Anzacs, its commanding officer gave the order to his men to retire, and they proceeded to fall back across the open ground which separated the village from the cemetery, a distance of some three hundred yards. As soon as the hapless Bavarians emerged into the open, their ranks were swept by a perfect deluge of shrapnel from the British batteries, with the result that the battalion was practically annihilated. Most

Conducting German prisoners to rail-head for transport to England.

Effect of one high-explosive shell on barbed-wire entanglement.

Bringing up an 8-inch howitzer and placing it in advanced position for the next bombardment.

of the survivors were made prisoners. It was a repetition on a smaller scale of the tragedy of the 3rd Division of the Prussian Guard, east of Contalmaison, during the fighting of July 7th.

The captured village, almost every building in which had been converted into a small fortress, was now nothing but a shapeless mass of débris, with its houses not only beaten to rubbish, but its very stones pounded to dust. No fewer than two hundred machine-guns are said to have been used by the enemy in the defence of the place. Most of them had been destroyed by our bombardment, and their remains lay beneath the rubbish heaps which had once been solidly built houses; but about thirty were captured by us during our various attacks, and some trench artillery also fell into our hands.

"The desperate character of the fighting at Pozières," writes a correspondent of the *Liberté*,

Bringing up an 8-inch howitzer.

"is borne out by the stories told by the wounded. In one instance, a party of Germans was surrounded in a little fort which had been constructed in the middle of the village, and held out for twelve hours against the British assault. When, after further artillery preparation, the British captured it, they found there four men alive, and, lying huddled together behind an armoured shelter, sixty dead!"

The capture of Pozières was one of the biggest achievements since our offensive began. The village stands on the edge of a plateau, and beyond it the land slopes gently down to Bapaume, seven miles to the north-east, thus making the place of great strategic importance and a vantage point for artillery. Now that it had fallen, the enemy's grip upon Thiépval, two miles to the north-west, was gravely menaced, and as soon as Hill 160, further up on the left of the Bapaume road, should be taken, that hitherto impregnable fortress would be enveloped on three sides.

A captured German divisional order issued in Contalmaison on July 11th, and cited in the British official reports on the 27th, shows the importance which the enemy attached to Pozières and other villages in their system of defence. It ran as follows:—

"Furthermore, the conversion of villages into strong points is of the greatest importance. Such villages are Pozières, Contalmaison, Bazentin-le-Petit, Bazentin-le-Grand and Longueval." With the exception of the northern outskirts of Longueval, all the villages mentioned in this order were now in British hands, thanks to the magnificent courage, tenacity and endurance of our infantry and the wonderful work of our artillery, which is stated to have fired, during one month, no fewer than five million shells in the Somme sector alone—a splendid testimony to the tireless labours of the British munition-makers.

During the forenoon of the 26th, the Territorials made a further advance to the west of Pozières, and captured two strong trenches and a number of prisoners, including five officers. With the exception of occasional artillery duels and sharp local encounters at various points, no incident of importance marked the remainder of the day. Some good work was accomplished by the Royal Flying Corps in

Seeking further laurels: The Worcesters off to continue the Great Advance.

A view in Trônes Wood.

A German observation-post in Trônes Wood.

Troops resting in German trenches.

locating the enemy's batteries and newly-constructed defences. Owing to the clouds and mist, our airmen were obliged to fly very low, and two of our machines were reported missing. Throughout the

A crater made by a German aerial torpedo.

night our artillery was very active, and we continued to press the enemy in hand-to-hand encounters at various points.

North of the line Pozières–Bazentin-le-Petit we succeeded in capturing about two hundred yards of an important German trench which had hitherto successfully resisted all our attacks.

Early on the 27th heavy fighting began to the north-east of Pozières and in the vicinity of Longueval and Delville Wood. After an intense enfilade artillery fire, in which gas and " tear " shells were largely used, the enemy succeeded in recovering possession of the whole of the trench which they had lost during the night; but our troops immediately attacked again and succeeded in regaining a footing in the southern end.

On our right, the German positions in Delville Wood—" Devil's Wood " was the highly-appropriate name which our men had now bestowed upon this horrible death-trap—were swept from end to end by

Some of the German prisoners at Carnoy just after they were captured on the 14th July.

On the horizon of this picture once stood a flourishing village, La Boiselle.

a veritable tornado of fire from our massed batteries. "I am told," writes Mr. Philip Gibbs, the special correspondent of the *Daily Chronicle*, "that our concentration of guns for this morning's bombardment secured the most intense series of barrages upon one position since the battle of Picardy began twenty-seven days ago; twice as heavy as any similar artillery attack. The bombardment began this early morning, and took line after line from south to north above the ground held by our men, in progressive blocks of fire. Our batteries over an area of several miles, from the long-range heavies to the 18-pounders far forward, flung every size of shell into this 'Devil's Wood,' and filled it with high-explosive and shrapnel, so that one great volume of smoke rose from it and covered it in a dense black pall."

So terrific was this massed bombardment that it seemed almost impossible that any Germans could be left alive, since the enemy had not had time to construct their usual elaborate system of dug-outs, and none but the strongest defences could provide shelter against such a deluge of explosives as was being poured upon the wood.

Slowly and cautiously our men began moving forward from the south behind the great barrage of our guns, which cleared the way for them, halting at intervals, while our artillery swept the ground in front of them, and then pushing on again. "It was queer to see the shells bursting in front of one," said a soldier who took part in the attack. "The line of them was just about seventy-five yards ahead of us, flinging up the ground and smashing everything. It was wonderful how the gunners kept it just ahead of us."

Meanwhile, on their left, other battalions were advancing against the northern outskirts of Longueval,

Further view of wrecked German dug-outs.

Another view of German ammunition wagons destroyed by our bombardment.

German ammunition wagons near Mametz Wood destroyed by our artillery fire.

PART VI. WILL BE READY ON TUESDAY, DECEMBER 5TH.

IT CONTAINS PICTURES OF:—

- Trophies captured by the Sherwood Foresters—The dog was found in a German dug-out
- An armoured car
- Our men are very comfortable in the old German dug-outs
- Australians parading for the trenches
- British shells bursting on the German trenches
- A few of the captured guns and trench mortars
- Germans cleaning some of the captured guns and trench mortars
- Tired out - a gunner asleep on live shells
- Some shells and men who know how to use them

- "Cat o' Nine Tails" found in the German trenches
- Bringing up water pipes to supply the men in front line with water
- Plan of German Hospital Dug-out
- Plan section of mine
- German tunnelled dug-out
- Bombardment by heavy trench mortars
- Huge mine going up
- A peep into a casualty clearing station just behind the line
- The River Hospital
- Patients coming on board a hospital barge
- An old British trench near Fricourt. This gives an idea of the number of sandbags used in trench construction

- View of a mine crater being consolidated
- Trench mortar bombs in a reserve trench ready for use
- Indian cavalry waiting to advance on 14th July
- Indian cavalry on the move, 15th July
- Working behind a smoke attack
- The centre or High Street of Guillemont after it was taken
- A smashed Bosche trench at Morval
- Motor 'buses taking the Takers of Guillemont away to rest
- Irish Brigade returning from Guillemont
- Petrol cans filled up with water ready to be taken up to the men in the trenches
- Mr. Asquith watching men adjusting fuses, etc.

ORDER FORM.

To M ....
BOOKSELLER OR NEWSAGENT.

Please send me Part VI., and the following Parts as published, of "SIR DOUGLAS HAIG'S GREAT PUSH," for which I enclose..............................

Name..

Address ....

SCALA THEATRE,

(Goodge Street Tube Station).   CHARLOTTE STREET, W.

AT THE FRONT
OFFICIAL WAR OFFICE FILMS.

Kut Relief Forces.   Salonika.   Russian Army.   French Army.   East Africa.
The King on the Somme Battle Field, &c.

THE BATTLE OF THE SOMME.

"There is no programme in London which gives so complete and vivid a description of the War on ALL FRONTS."— *Evening News.*

THE KING'S ADVICE:
SEE THE SOMME WAR FILM AND WHAT WAR MEANS.

"The public should see these pictures, that they may have some idea of what the Army is doing, and what war means."

This statment was made by the King after witnessing a programme of the Official War Office film, "The Battle of the Somme," which was shown by command to the King and Queen at Windsor Castle.—*Daily Express.*

Box Office, 10 to 10.   DAILY, 3 and 8.   'Phone: Gerr. 1444 & 1366.

SCALA THEATRE.

Nestlé's is full cream Milk

The Child's Birthright

is its mother's milk, but often that milk is absent, small in quantity, or of poor quality.

Dairy-milk is usually full of germs—more or less dangerous bacteria. It often contains preservatives or colouring matter and is otherwise adulterated.

Nestlé's Milk is full-cream—and the cream is necessary for an infant's health. Children thrive on Nestlé's Milk; it makes flesh and bone and good teeth.

**Sold by all Grocers and Stores
Cash Price 8½d. and 5d. per tin.**

Write for copy of Nestlé's "Baby Book," 1916, the most remarkable Baby Book ever issued, and for *Truth* Special Supplement on "Pure Milk Problems." Either or both sent post free on application to all readers mentioning this paper.

By Appointment   To H.M. The King.

**NESTLÉ'S,
6-8, Eastcheap,
London, E.C.**

PRINTED AT THE CHAPEL RIVER PRESS, KINGSTON-ON-THAMES.

IN ABOUT 6 FORTNIGHTLY PARTS. HUTCHINSON'S NEW PART WORK Part VII. ready Dec. 19th. PART VI. 8d. NET

SIR DOUGLAS HAIG'S
GREAT PUSH

THE BATTLE OF THE SOMME

A popular, pictorial and authoritative work on one of the Greatest Battles in History, illustrated by about **700** wonderful **OFFICIAL PHOTOGRAPHS AND CINEMATOGRAPH FILMS** and other authentic pictures

BY ARRANGEMENT WITH THE WAR OFFICE

A HOSPITAL BARGE.

GREAT VALUE FOR EIGHTPENCE

THIS PART CONTAINS **40 WONDERFUL REPRODUCTIONS** OF THE FAMOUS **WAR OFFICE CINEMATOGRAPH FILMS** AND **OFFICIAL PHOTOGRAPHS** OF THE BATTLE OF THE SOMME, BEAUTIFULLY PRINTED ON THE BEST ENGLISH ART PAPER.

LONDON : HUTCHINSON & Co.

IMPORTANT.

THE GREAT NATIONAL TRIBUTE.

The ROLL OF HONOUR

AN ILLUSTRATED BIOGRAPHICAL RECORD OF **ALL** OFFICERS, NON-COMMISSIONED OFFICERS AND MEN OF HIS MAJESTY'S FORCES WHO ARE KILLED OR DIE ON ACTIVE SERVICE

NOW BEING COMPILED BY

THE MARQUIS DE RUVIGNY

Author and Editor of "The Blood Royal of Britain," "The Titled Nobility of Europe," and other works.

THE debt which the Empire owes to those who have laid down their lives in the present War must, from the very nature of things, for ever remain unpaid.

There is, however, a universal desire to keep them in remembrance, and to ensure that their names and their glorious deeds shall not be forgotten.

For this purpose, "THE ROLL OF HONOUR" is now being prepared, to place on permanent record the name of every Officer, Non-Commissioned Officer and Man of His Majesty's Forces on land or sea who is killed in action, who dies of wounds, or whose death is otherwise caused in the present War.

It may here be briefly stated that it is proposed to give, whenever obtainable, the full name, place and date of birth, parentage, biographical sketch of career, and date and place of death, with extracts from letters of Commanding Officers or Comrades relating to the action in which the Officer or Man fell, or to the particular circumstances of his death.

Many a deed of heroism is covered by the bare announcement of a name in the daily long roll of casualties. To collect and record these is the purpose of the "ROLL OF HONOUR." The names of children will also be included, so that in the years to come they may themselves read, or teach their children to read, of the glorious way their fathers died; of those individual acts of bravery that are the chief redeeming feature of war.

Much valuable help is being given by the Authorities, by the Regiments, by Public Institutions, and the Heads of Schools, and the Publishers appeal with confidence to those who have lost relatives to assist them in the task they have undertaken by sending at once to the Editor the necessary particulars, extracts, from letters, etc.

The Editor and Publishers wish it to be distinctly understood that the insertion of any name is not in any way dependent upon the payment of any fee or of subscription to the book, and that no fee will be accepted for the insertion of any name.

A large number of portraits of Officers and Men will be included. With over 100,000 dead for the first year, it is clearly impossible to undertake that one will be given in every case, but when a portrait is supplied the Publishers will do their best to include it, and in the case of one supplied by a Subscriber, where there is no copyright fee, they guarantee that it will be reproduced.

SEND FOR A FORM to fill in particulars of your relation or friend who has been killed on active service. There is no charge, and his biography ought to be included. Unless you write probably only his name will be given.

To **THE STANDARD ART BOOK CO. LTD.,**

Publishers of "THE ROLL OF HONOUR,"

30-32, LUDGATE HILL, E.C.

EDITORIAL OFFICES:—
MARQUIS DE RUVIGNY.
"The Roll of Honour"
14-15, Hanover Chambers,
Buckingham St., Adelphi, W.C.

Please send me a form so that I may give you particulars concerning ....

.. who was killed on active service.

Name ....

Address ....

with the object of clearing out the enemy, and then joining up with their comrades moving into the wood from the south.

The latter's progress was a slow and difficult one, and they advanced in scattered groups, keeping touch, but in extended order. For in this evil place there was no clear track, and they had to make their way over ground where great shell-holes yawned at every couple of yards, and through a tangled maze of fallen trees and brushwood and the remains of barricades which had been smashed by our bombardment. And all about them lay the dead, the mutilated bodies of men who had been slain in every way known to this horrible war—by bayonet or bomb, by rifle or machine-gun bullet, or by shell-fire. For they were passing over ground which had been four times taken by the British, and four times retaken by the enemy, on each occasion after the most desperate fighting, and which had been swept

Trophies captured by the Sherwood Foresters. The dog was found in a German dug-out.

almost continuously for days by the guns of one side or the other, with the result that it had become a great graveyard of unburied dead.

As our troops advanced, they saw the most cheering of all sights—groups of the enemy in full retreat, some running away over the rising ground at the edge of the wood, while others were making use of what little protection the communication-trenches, which were generally not more than three feet deep, afforded them. The fugitives were not allowed to escape unmolested; and one of our snipers, who was in ambush just outside the wood, accounted for no fewer than ten. The majority of the enemy preferred the safer course of surrender, and handkerchiefs or white rags tied to the ends of broken branches or entrenching tools, and, in one instance, a Red Cross flag attached to the end of a stretcher, were waved frantically in token of submission from shell-craters or the remains of the shattered trenches, where they were crouching.

Little resistance was encountered in the east or north-east part of the wood. The Germans here had suffered terribly from our bombardment. The dead lay everywhere, and such dug-outs as had not been destroyed by direct hits from our shells were full of wounded lying in pools of their own blood; while on the stairways were found other wounded men, who had been endeavouring to crawl down to obtain shelter and assistance, but whose strength had apparently failed them. Some of the prisoners taken were exceptionally young and small, and wore uniforms much too big for them, their tunics coming down to their knees. They probably belonged to the 1916 class.

Before midday the whole of the wood was once more in our possession, with the exception of a strip on the north-western side, where troops belonging to the 5th Brandenburg Division, strongly entrenched and abundantly supplied with machine-guns, continued to hold us at bay.

Early in the afternoon our new positions were heavily shelled by the German guns, and a determined counter-attack launched against the left of the wood by parties of bombers, who came down saps above

An armoured car in France.

Longueval and along a communication-trench between Delville Wood and the Bois des Foureaux (High Wood). The assault, however, was repulsed with heavy loss to the enemy.

Fierce fighting continued all day in the northern part of Longueval village, and particularly in and about the Orchard, where the Germans had constructed machine-gun emplacements and a strong redoubt which our men had named "Machine-gun House." Here, behind barricades of broken bricks, fallen trees, and barbed wire, the enemy offered a most stubborn resistance, serving their machine-guns with murderous effect. Bombing parties, led on in the most gallant manner by our officers, made repeated attacks upon this hornets' nest, and eventually succeeded in capturing or knocking out several of the machine-guns which had given most trouble; and by the end of the day a good deal of ground had been gained.

Our aircraft again did good service, and in the neighbourhood of Bapaume two hostile aeroplanes were destroyed by one of our aerial patrols.

The enemy's guns shelled our new positions fiercely during the night, and there were heavy artillery duels in various sectors of the battle area. Near Neuve Chapelle small parties of Germans succeeded

Our men are very comfortable in the old German dug-outs.

British shells bursting on the German trenches.

in entering our front trenches at two points, but were at once driven out by a counter-attack, leaving a few wounded in our hands. North-east of Souchez and at several other points our artillery shelled the enemy's front-line and communication trenches.

Soon after dawn our guns began to concentrate their fire upon the northern part of Longueval and the strip of Delville Wood which was still in possession of the enemy. At the same time, the German batteries started shelling the British positions in the wood and village, the double bombardment steadily increasing in violence until the uproar was indescribable. For some three hours the guns on both sides continued to rage, and then the British artillery became momentarily silent, as our infantry advanced to the attack.

Fierce was the struggle in both village and wood. In the former, though we made considerable

Australians parading for the trenches.

progress, midday still found the enemy clinging stubbornly to a few strongholds; but in the wood the Brandenburgers, after severe fighting, were driven from their remaining positions, leaving three officers and 158 men as prisoners in our hands.

Scarcely had our men started to consolidate the ground which they had fought so valiantly to regain than they were called upon to repel a heavy counter-attack. This was successfully beaten off, only to be followed, at a short interval, by another and even more determined onslaught, which, however, shared the fate of the first. In both of these fruitless assaults the German casualties were very severe.

Encouraged by the success of their comrades in Delville Wood, by the evening our troops in Longueval had succeeded in capturing the last of the enemy's strongholds, and with them a number of prisoners. Thus every yard of both wood and village was once more in our hands.

CHAPTER VI

It is doubtful if in the whole course of the war on the Western front any place of similar size has been the scene of such terrible slaughter or of so colossal an expenditure of ammunition as Delville Wood.

"The wood, including the north of Longueval," writes Mr. Beach Thomas, " has certainly swallowed over 100,000 shells, besides much ' small stuff,' and machine-guns have seldom ceased to rattle. Think of some pretty English copse about one hundred and fifty acres large, and imagine its beauty before and its terror afterwards; its sides, ' those cloisters of a sanctuary,' dug and pitted, its foliage scorched

Bringing up water-pipes to supply the men in the front line with water.

and beaten to the ground, its trees ripped and felled, every yard trodden and retrodden, and every other yard pitted till the roots are an entanglement.

" If I could tell every atom of the ruin and convey the sense of it, as seen by men fighting in a din audible twenty miles away, I should still not have touched the meaning of the battlefield. It is not ' the beauty's ruin,' but ' the life's defeat ' which makes the wood what it is. The faces of the prisoners we took there are witness of what it means to live awhile in a wood of the dead."

In the vicinity of Pozières hand-to-hand fighting continued throughout the day, but elsewhere on the battle-front nothing of importance occurred. Our airmen were very active; three enemy aeroplanes were destroyed by them, and a kite-balloon was seen to fall in flames.

The British had still to struggle hard to retain possession of Delville Wood, for during the night the enemy made two more desperate attempts to recapture it. Gathering some half-mile away and advancing

Germans cleaning some of the captured guns and trench-mortars.

Some shells and men who know how to use them.

Tired out: A gunner asleep on live shells.

along two communication trenches and through the long grass, they twice drove a great ram of men against our defences in the north-eastern part of the wood. On one occasion, a few Germans succeeded in breaking into a small section of trench; but they were promptly disposed of by bayonet or bomb, and both attacks were beaten back, the enemy losing heavily both in the advance and the retreat.

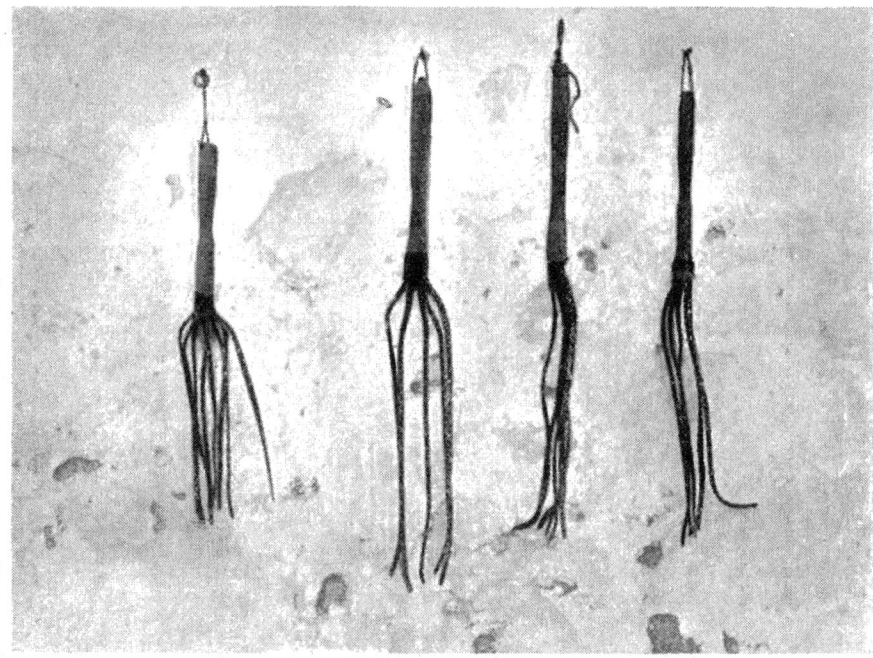

Cat-o'-nine-tails found in the German trenches.

North and east of Pozières and in the neighbourhood of the Bois des Foureaux (High Wood) the hand-to-hand struggle continued without intermission, and we made progress in all three places, despite the most violent opposition.

On the 29th, except for minor local actions and some heavy artillery fire on both sides, nothing of importance occurred on the Somme front. On other parts of the British line there was the usual trench-warfare activity, and one of our patrols entered the enemy's trenches at Puits 14 *bis* and killed several Germans. The enemy exploded a mine at Neuville St. Vaast, and one at the Hairpin Crater, without doing us any damage or causing any casualties. Our airmen were again very aggressive and successful, three hostile aeroplanes being destroyed and several others forced to land in a damaged condition.

During the night the British artillery heavily bombarded the enemy's trenches and reserve areas between the Ancre and the Somme. In the course of this bombardment a hostile ammunition depôt near Courcelette (one and a half miles north-east of Pozières) was exploded by our fire. Parties of Canadian infantry raided the German trenches in two places south of Ypres, and the Royal Munster Fusiliers carried out a similar enterprise in the Loos salient. In both cases severe casualties

THE CONNECTING PASSAGE OF A DUG-OUT.
The larger dug-outs are entered through a steel door. After descending a thirty-foot wooden staircase, one finds spacious rooms, in which floors, walls and roofs are closely boarded. The connecting passages are finished in the same way, and another staircase leads to a similar group of rooms.

were inflicted upon the enemy. Near the Hohenzollern Redoubt the Germans took the offensive and attempted two raids. One of these attacks was met by so withering a fire that it failed to get further than our wire; in the other, the enemy succeeded in entering our front trench, but were immediately driven out again.

Early on the morning of the 30th, in co-operation with the French on our right flank, the offensive was resumed on a front of about six miles, extending from east of Delville Wood to the Somme. It was a very hot day, with a scorching sun, but a curious haze hung about the countryside, as thick at times as a November mist, which rendered artillery observation very difficult for anything like long-range firing. In spite of this, our guns managed to maintain a heavy bombardment of the enemy's lines in support of our troops, who had to advance over very broken ground.

Petrol cans filled up with water ready to be taken up to the men in the trenches.

The chief work of the day was the cleaning up of trenches south-east of Trônes Wood and north-west of Guillemont across the old German second line, during which we were exposed to a hot machine-gun fire from ruined houses in Guillemont and over the edge of the valley running south-east of the village. Nevertheless, good progress was made here, and also east of Waterlot Farm, and further south about Maltzorn Farm. In all these areas there was some heavy fighting, in which the enemy sustained severe casualties, while about 250 prisoners fell into our hands.

The great heat severely tested the physical endurance of our troops, and those who had been so imprudent as to empty their water-bottles early in the day suffered cruelly from thirst. The wounded, particularly those lying in places beyond the quick reach of stretcher-bearers, of course suffered infinitely more. "It was fair awfu' to hear them crying," said a Highlander. "It was 'Water! Water! For Christ's sake—water!' till their voices died away." The stretcher-bearers worked magnificently under very heavy fire to get these men in, several of them being shot down whilst doing so; and a number of

GERMAN BARBED-WIRE ENTANGLEMENTS.

This differs from the Allies' barbed-wire entanglements by the fact that the wire is supported with iron, as will be seen in the illustration. Also the sandbags in the German entanglements are not so visible as in the Allies'. The German parapet makes more show of rough clay or chalk.

ALLIES' BARBED-WIRE ENTANGLEMENTS.

As stated above, the fact that the Allies' barbed wire is supported by wooden stakes, and their parapet is strengthened by rows of sandbags, distinguishes it from a German barbed-wire entanglement.

This shows a tunnelled corridor which runs straight forward for anything up to fifty yards, out of which open various rooms and passages on each side.

A view in the officers' quarters of the dug-outs. They are very comfortable, and, as shown in the illustration, contain in some instances full-length mirrors and cushioned arm-chairs.

This illustration shows the main entrance, through a steel door, to one of the German trench houses. Outside the front door you will observe a perforated sheet of metal to serve for a door-mat or scraper.

our brave fellows crawled to where their stricken comrades lay, and, in spite of their own thirst, gave them the last drops of their water. A splendid act of generosity is related of a young soldier belonging to a Yorkshire regiment, who, though wounded himself, gave the little water that was left in his bottle to a wounded German who was lying near him.

For the first time for many days there was no infantry fighting in the neighbourhood of Pozières, where our troops were employed in consolidating the ground gained the previous week, while the Germans confined themselves to shelling our positions.

The night was spent in strengthening the positions won during the day, the enemy making no attempt to counter-attack. On the plateau north of Bazentin-le-Petit there were some local encounters, as a result of which we advanced our posts at certain points.

No infantry fighting took place on the 31st, though the guns on either side did not cease their activity. The Royal Flying Corps was in a very aggressive mood, several bombing-raids being carried out, in the course of which seven tons of bombs were dropped on the enemy's communications and billets. In one case, a train was blown up, and in another an ammunition depôt was set on fire, and a hostile aeroplane on the ground was destroyed. Many aerial combats took place, and several German machines were driven to the ground in a damaged condition. Three of our aeroplanes were reported missing.

The night was uneventful, save for heavy artillery fire on both sides, and no change in the general situation marked the following day. North of Bazentin-le-Petit an attack on our positions was

These staircases, passages and rooms are lined throughout with wood, and are as fully strengthened with it as the entrance staircase.

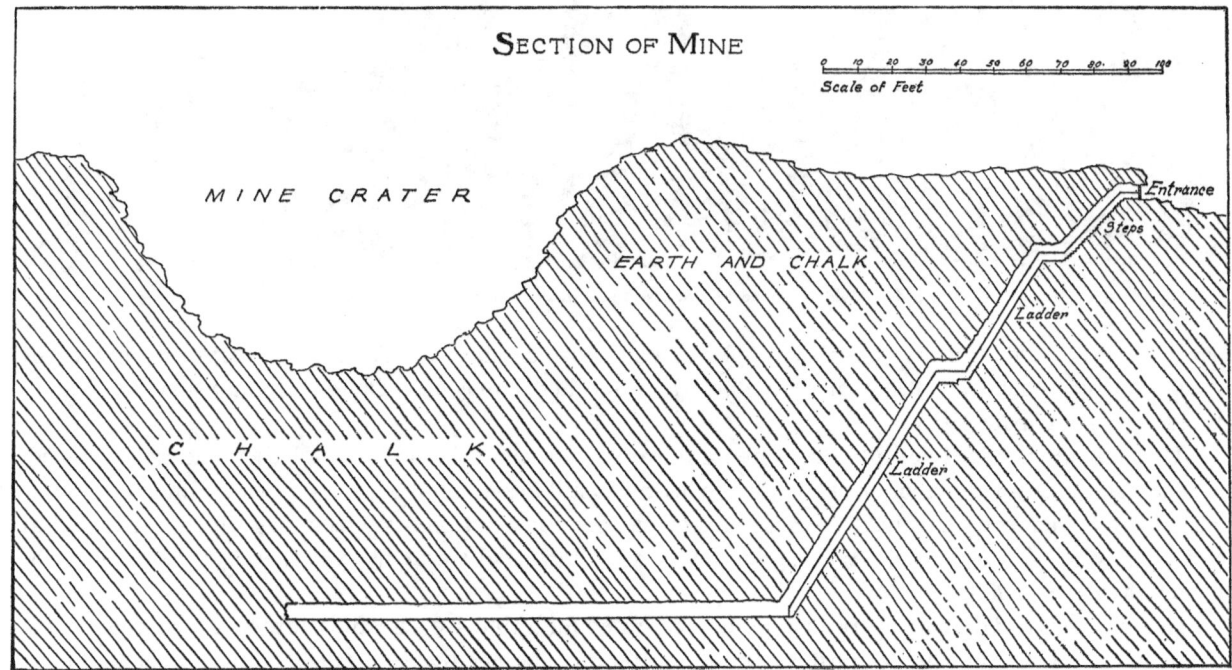

This illustration shows a section of the mine which the Germans blew up under the base of the old crater at the moment of the advance in July.

successfully repulsed. Soon after darkness fell the Germans launched a counter-attack against our new trenches west of the Bois des Foureaux (High Wood) ; but it was completely broken up by our artillery. During the night we made some further progress in the hostile trenches east of Pozières, where sharp close-quarter fighting between small detachments took place.

On August 2nd the German artillery indulged in a heavy bombardment of Trônes Wood, and the British exploded a big mine at Courcelette, north-east of Pozières. Otherwise, the day was comparatively quiet.

In his report that evening Sir Douglas Haig announced that during the past twenty-four hours our artillery, in co-operation with the Royal Flying Corps, had destroyed seven German gun emplacements and six ammunition depôts near Grandcourt, and further gun emplacements in other

The nights begin to get cold, so the men don their winter clothes.

parts of the front. A few hostile aeroplanes had crossed our lines for a short distance, only to be speedily driven back, one being brought down and another damaged. The enemy appeared anxious to avoid aerial combat.

Throughout the night our infantry were hard at work consolidating the ground they had lately gained. This was not only a very laborious task, for the heat was still intense, but at times an exceedingly gruesome one, since it frequently involved the necessity of digging out dead bodies which were in the way, and at certain places, such as Ovillers, the dug-outs were so full of dead Germans that there was nothing to be done but to seal them up.

In Delville Wood digging operations were interrupted for a time by a hostile counter-attack, four strong detachments being launched against us simultaneously. The enemy were allowed to approach to close range before a shot was fired, when a withering blast from rifles and machine-guns burst upon them, driving

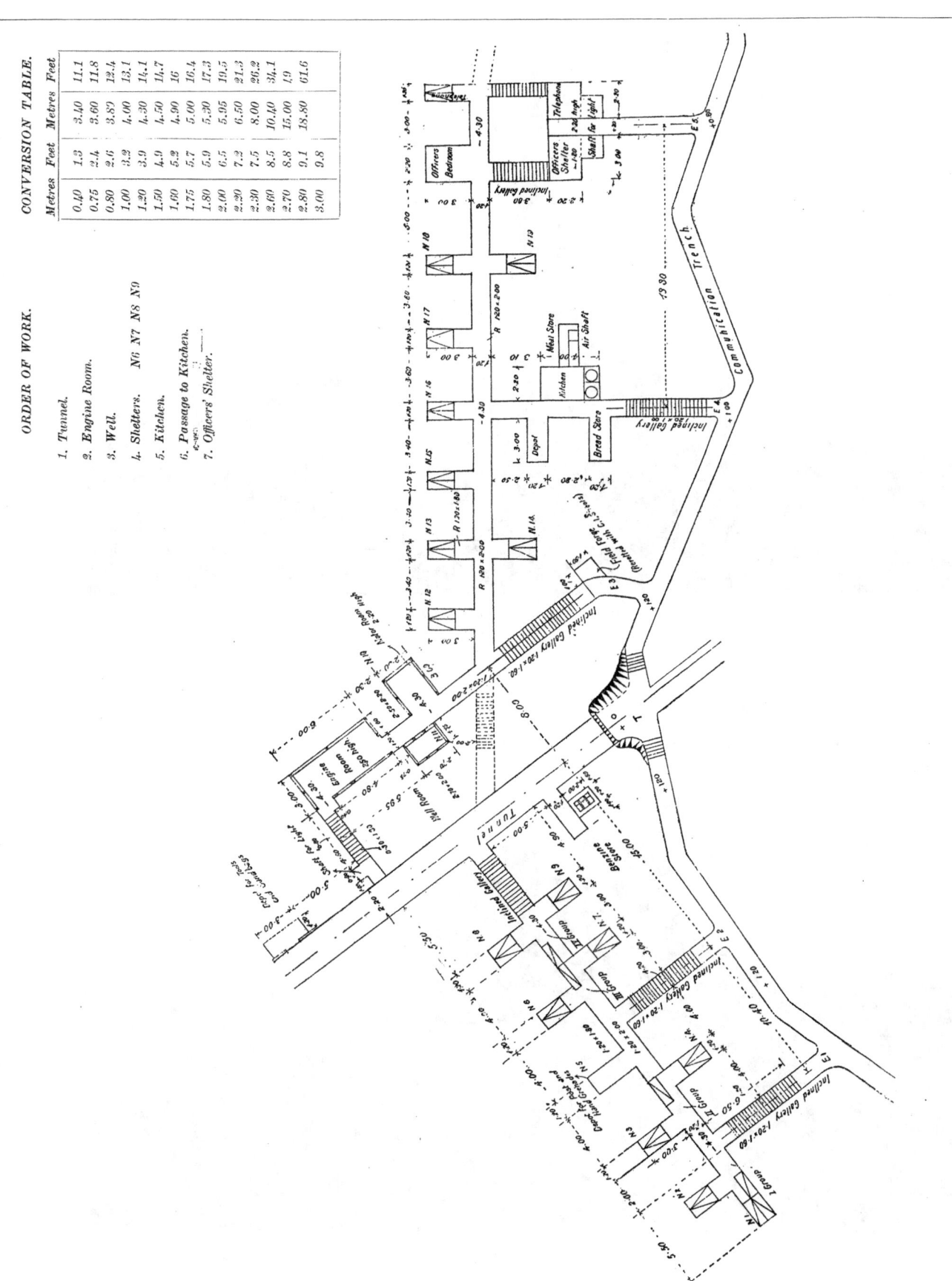

A GERMAN TUNNELLED DUG-OUT.

The German front in the west is like one huge straggling village, the houses of which are all underground. They are on one or two floors, built to official designs, drawn out in section and plan. They contain kitchens, provision and munition store-rooms, a well, a forge riveted with sheets of cast iron, an engine-room and a motor-room. Many of the captured dug-outs were thus lighted by electricity,

Bombardment by heavy trench-mortars.

A huge mine going up.

them back in disorder, with heavy loss. In one place some fifty Germans were caught in mass formation by our machine-gun fire and practically wiped out.

Our guns were, as usual, very active, while from sunset to dawn, when its fire slackened, the German artillery retaliated briskly along our front from Maltzhorn Farm to Longueval, and also on the woods of Mametz, Fricourt and Bécourt, and the village of Pozières. Near Souchez the enemy exploded a small mine, which, however, caused no casualties and little damage.

Except for a successful bombing attack north of Bazentin-le-Petit, which gained us some ground, hostilities on the morrow were chiefly confined to the guns. Our heavies bombarded a German *fortin* between Pozières and Thiépval, which they speedily rendered untenable ; and the garrison, while hurriedly retiring across the open, came under our field-gun fire and suffered severely. Throughout the day the

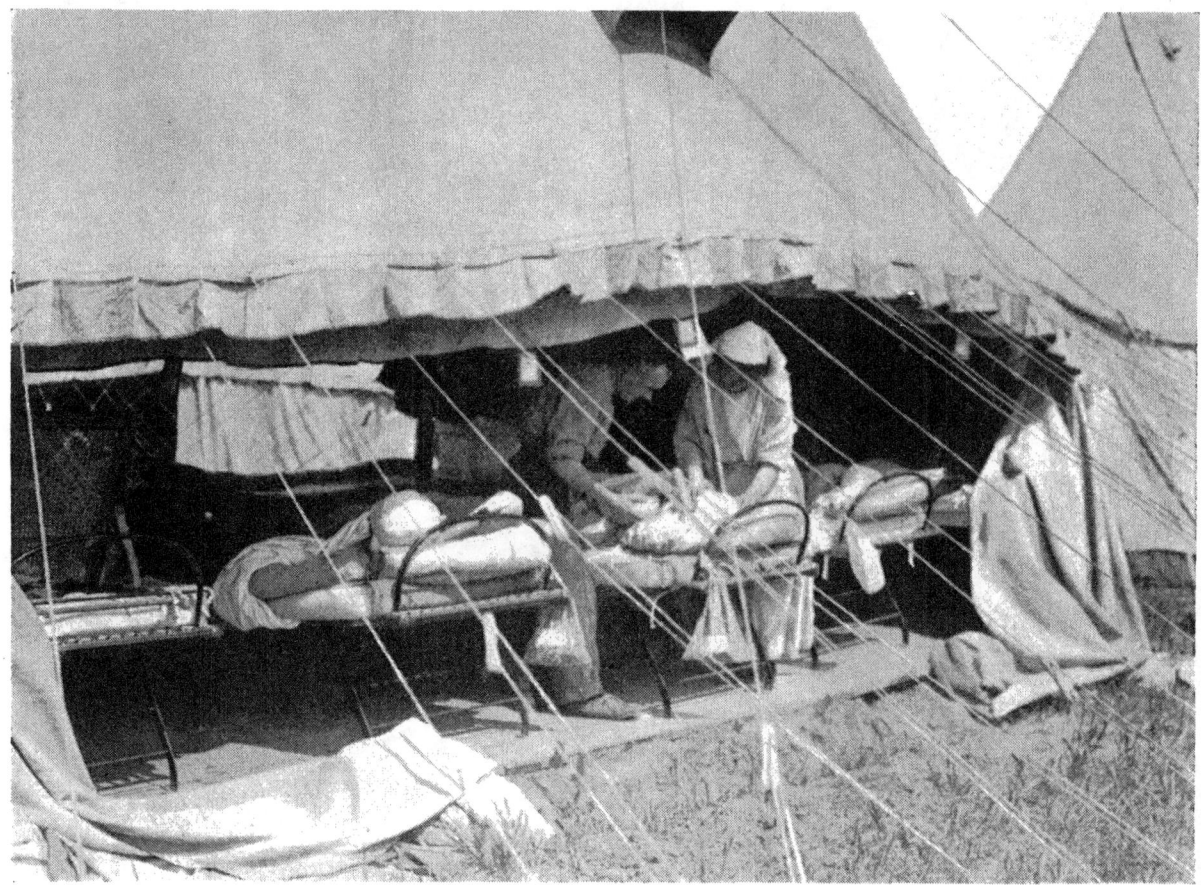

A peep into a casualty clearing-station just behind the line.

enemy's artillery maintained a barrage west and south-west of Pozières, and shelled Longueval, Mametz and Caterpillar Wood intermittently. Further north the Germans shelled the villages near Arras and Armentières, and dropped bombs on the outskirts of some villages without doing any damage. In the Givenchy district we bombarded the enemy's lines near Hulluch ; while in the Loos salient there was considerable trench activity on both sides. Two enemy aeroplanes were brought down in the northern section of our line, one of which appeared to be of a new pattern ; but, on the other hand, three of our machines were brought down by gunfire.

During the night there was some heavy shelling by both sides on various portions of the front, and, as the result of a minor operation, we gained some ground west of Pozières and took over one hundred prisoners. All round the captured trenches, in which our men found themselves in very close touch with the enemy, a large number of German dead were lying. In other minor operations north of Bazentin-le-Petit and north-west of Delville Wood we captured a few prisoners. A raiding-party destroyed an enemy's mine-shaft east of Loos; and near the Ypres–Commines road we exploded a small mine in the German lines and occupied the crater.

The 4th was a quiet day, so far as the infantry were concerned, though the artillery was busy enough. The enemy's guns maintained a barrage south of Pozières nearly all day, and also directed their attention to the southern portion of Mametz Wood. Near St. Eloi the Germans exploded a small mine, which only damaged their own wire, and fired another near Auchy, on their own side of the crater, which seemed to indicate some nervousness amongst their miners. A patrol of four of our aeroplanes engaged seven hostile machines in a fight which lasted forty-five minutes. Three of the enemy's aeroplanes were driven down, and two of ours were reported missing.

Although during the last few days the British had done a good deal of successful nibbling at the enemy's

The river hospital.

defences, there had been no attempt at a resumption of our offensive on anything approaching an important scale since July 30th. The Germans, however, had been allowed no opportunity of recuperating their nerves, shattered by the appalling strain of the past months, for day and night the British bombardment continued, our long-range guns, aided by the wonderful work of our aviators, reaching out far behind their lines and shelling their billets and rest-camps and ammunition depôts; while in the trenches there was no safety anywhere for the harassed Hun save in the deepest dug-outs.

In the German second line along the Pozières plateau these dug-outs were about all that was left of their original trenches—those trenches upon the construction of which so many months of labour and so much ingenuity had been expended. The rest was a wavy line of hummocky and tumbled earth; and it was against these broken defences that about nine o'clock on the evening of the 4th we rudely disillusioned those of the enemy who had been flattering themselves that our offensive had come to a standstill by launching a determined assault.

Patients being taken on board/a hospital/barge.

Motor 'buses taking the Takers of Guillemont away to rest.

The Battle of the Somme

The troops taking part in this movement were the Australians and Kent, Surrey and Sussex battalions of the New Army. The Australians worked up to the right, the English to the left. The enemy were anticipating the attack, and when our men scaled our parapet and began to cross the 500 yards of No Man's Land which separated the British and German trenches, they found themselves, in the words of an officer who took part in the operation, "in the middle of a Brock's benefit." That is to say, the Germans were sending up distress signals to their guns and flinging coloured lights over to our lines to illuminate the advancing troops. These lights when they fell flared up with vivid red and green fires, and the enemy's machine-guns at once began to play upon the figures thus revealed. But, notwithstanding

View of a mine crater being consolidated.

the risk they were running, several of our men gallantly rushed forward into the illumination and kicked out the burning canisters.

In spite of some fierce machine-gun fire, our troops reached the German lines with comparatively few casualties. Our officers, with splendid coolness and courage, stood against the uncut sections of the enemy's wire, shouting to their men to move to the right or left, wherever the way was clear; and when the din was too great for their voices to be heard, they used their whistles, as though inviting the Germans to shoot at them. Great bravery was shown by a young lieutenant and a party of bombers belonging to the Kents, who rushed on ahead so rapidly as to risk death from our own barrage, and by the effectiveness of their work contributed not a little to demoralize the enemy in that quarter.

Once our troops were upon them the Germans showed little disposition to oppose their advance. In several places, indeed, the enemy did not wait for the British to reach the wreck of earth which had once been trenches, but, emerging from the dug-outs in which they had been sheltering from our bombardment, came forward to meet them with hands held up. Most of them were utterly nerve-shattered—beaten and broken creatures without an ounce of fight left in them, their one desire being to escape from what the unceasing rain of shells had rendered little better than a death-trap. Their surrender was accepted, and they were sent back to our trenches under guard, while our troops went on to clear out the dug-outs and to deal with those who had the courage to defend themselves. Here and there some sharp fighting took place with bomb and bayonet, and trouble was experienced from machine-guns in isolated redoubts behind the enemy's lines. But, on the whole, the resistance was very feeble, and in half an hour the Kents and Surreys had carried the positions aimed at on the Bapaume road, while the Australians, with the Sussex men on their left, overran several lines of trenches, carried a large work situated where the Thiépval road crosses the Mouquet stream, and triumphantly continued their advance east of the Leipzig Redoubt in the direction of Thiépval.

Over four hundred prisoners were taken, while the enemy's casualties were very heavy. The greater part were caused by our bombardment, and in one spot a whole machine-gun company were found lying dead around their guns.

The prisoners were chiefly of the 17th and 18th Divisions of the 9th Reserve Corps, with miscellaneous drafts from various Ersatz, or reserve, battalions, most of them men with families, who had been sent into the field very much against their will and were rejoiced at the prospect of being removed from the danger-zone. Before, however, they could breathe freely again, the 500 yards or so of No Man's Land which lay between the captured trenches and the British lines had to be negotiated; and this journey, which German shells and machine-gun bullets rendered somewhat hazardous, was one which certain of the prisoners evinced a marked disinclination to undertake. The task of getting them across was, in consequence, not wanting in touches of comedy.

Trench-mortar bombs in a reserve trench ready for use.

"One of the prisoners," writes Mr. Philip Gibbs, the special correspondent of the *Daily Chronicle*, " was a forward observing officer, a Prussian giant well over six feet high and enormously stout, and he was put in charge of a little Kentish man standing five-feet-one in his socks. The German giant was very frightened at the machine-gun fire of his own people which was whipping over the ground, and he went back crouching in a bear-like way, prodded from behind by the wee man in khaki. This sight, illuminated by the flares, was seen by the men left behind in our own trenches, and they stood up on their parapets, laughing and cheering wildly."

Indian cavalry waiting to advance on 14th July.

Indian cavalry on the move, 15th of July.

The Battle of the Somme

Including the German trenches we had just captured, we had during the last two days pushed forward our line north and west of Pozières from 400 to 600 yards over a front of about 6,000 yards; and the new part of the enemy's line now in our possession, together with the part captured on July 14th, made up a distance of nearly 10,000 yards.

Before the night was over our troops were called upon to repel three separate counter-attacks. The Germans advanced with real courage and determination; but they had to meet more than an infantry busy with the task of consolidating the ground which had been won. For our gunners were ready for them, and they marched straight into a murderous barrage of shells, both heavy and light, which crumpled up each attack long before it reached our trenches and drove the enemy back in disorder, with heavy loss.

Working behind a smoke attack.

Except for some mining activity in the neighbourhood of Souchez and Loos, no incident of any importance occurred on the British front during the night.

On the 5th, the Germans confined themselves to shelling our new positions on the Pozières ridge and did not attempt any further counter-attacks. Our own artillery bombarded Courcelette and Miraumont, causing heavy explosions in both places. Ten gun emplacements and three ammunition stores were destroyed. The enemy made an attempt to seize a crater near Souchez, but were repulsed with bombs. There was artillery activity between Hooge and St. Eloi, and in this area the Germans exploded a small mine, but no movement followed. The enemy's aeroplanes appeared very anxious to avoid the British aviators, and eight of their machines scattered when engaged by three of ours.

The German artillery was very active during the night, shelling various areas on and behind our front between the Ancre and the Somme. North-east of Arras an amusing incident occurred. The enemy's guns suddenly started shelling No Man's Land very heavily, and maintained the barrage for about a quarter of an hour, which must have entailed a great waste of ammunition. It subsequently appeared that the Germans in the trenches, alarmed by one of our patrols, had been under the impression that we were about to attack and had accordingly signalled to their guns for support. A little further progress was made by us in the Bois des Foureaux (High Wood). Otherwise, there was no change in the situation.

Early on the morning of the 6th, after a heavy artillery preparation, two furious counter-attacks were launched against our new positions north-west of Pozières. The British, however, rose to the occasion. An Australian battalion occupying the advanced trenches to the left of the Bapaume road, on the edge of the plateau, held on heroically under a terrible cannonade, followed by a succession of assaults by three Bavarian and Saxon regiments. Their losses were considerable, but they gave time for the line to be strengthened and the position of Hill 160 and the Pozières mill to be saved.

In one of these counter-attacks, by the use of liquid fire, the Germans succeeded in temporarily forcing

The centre or High Street of Guillemont after it was taken.

us back along one of the trenches we had captured; but later we recovered all but some forty yards of the ground thus lost. In the other, the enemy were caught in a dreadfully effective barrage from our guns and repulsed with heavy casualties.

An army order found on some of the German prisoners explained in part the fierceness of the enemy's counter-attacks. It was signed by General von Below and was as follows:

"At any price the Pozières plateau (Hill 160) must be recovered, for, if it remains in the hands of the British, it will give them an important advantage.

"Troops which first reach the plateau must hold on until reinforced, whatever their losses.

"Any officer or man who fails to resist to the death on the ground won will be immediately court-martialled."

During the afternoon our troops carried with the bayonet two lines of the enemy's trenches east of Pozières and advanced some two hundred yards in the direction of Martinpuich. There was considerable

A smashed Boche trench at Morval.

Australians returning from the trenches with their mascot.

artillery activity in the vicinity of Carency and Loos; while to the south of St. Eloi we raided the enemy's trenches and caused many casualties. The fine, clear weather enabled some very useful work to be carried out by our heavy guns in co-operation with our aeroplanes, and several German gun emplacements were destroyed.

During the night we made a successful raid on the enemy's trenches east of Neuville St. Vaast. Southeast of Bois-Grenier the Germans endeavoured to raid ours, but were driven back with loss. Their artillery continued to bombard our trenches between the Ancre and the Somme, both on the front line and back areas, and several small counter-attacks were made on our positions east of Pozières, all of which were repulsed with more or less heavy casualties.

Between 4 and 5 a.m. on the 7th, after an intense bombardment of our new lines north and north-east

Irish Brigade returning from Guillemont.

of Pozières, the enemy delivered two determined attacks, and in one or two places succeeded in entering our trenches. But they were speedily driven out again, leaving some prisoners in our hands, while their casualties were heavy. Two further strong attacks made just before nine o'clock met with exactly similar results.

Soon after 4 p.m. the Germans advanced against us once more; but their effort on this occasion was a feeble one, and was easily repulsed, more prisoners being captured.

A singular feature about the men sent forward to these attacks was that, while some of them, notably the bombers who headed the assaults, came on with great bravery, others seemed to have little stomach for the fight, and showed at a distance as ready a disposition to surrender as had their comrades in the trenches we had lately captured. "At one juncture," writes Mr. Beach Thomas, "some four hundred Germans, who had been driven forward to a counter-attack, offered to surrender. They came forward in good order, with hands properly up, till they were quite close to our trenches, when a panic seized them and they dashed away like minnows before a pike. Well, before any of them had reached their own lines the German shrapnel opened on them from the flank. The British shrapnel also opened on the area, and a dozen machine-guns got down to work. Of the four hundred a few wounded men crept away into a coppice. They were the only possible survivors."

There was some liveliness during the day in other sectors. In front of Souchez the enemy exploded a mine, and a few minutes later several parties of Germans entered our trenches over the crater. They were, however, immediately driven out with bombs. At Zwarteleen another small mine was sprung by the enemy, but with no effect. In the neighbourhood of Béthune, the La Bassée Canal and Loos the

An old British trench near Fricourt. This gives an idea of the number of sandbags used in trench construction.

German artillery was very active. The result in casualties and damage was negligible. The British guns retaliated vigorously.

The enemy's airmen were, for once in a while, in an aggressive mood, and a squadron of ten aeroplanes endeavoured to cross our lines on a bombing expedition. They were cut off by one of our offensive patrols of four machines, whereupon they scattered and returned with all speed, pursued by our patrols. Two of the hostile aeroplanes had to make forced descents behind their own lines.

During the night our troops resumed the offensive in places east of Trônes Wood, and heavy fighting began in the outskirts of Guillemont, near the station. On the eastern part of the Leipzig Redoubt the enemy attempted a bomb attack on our lines; but it was easily repulsed. North of Roclincourt we successfully raided the German trenches at two points and blew up some dug-outs.

After their five fruitless attempts against our positions north and east of Pozières, the enemy during the night and the early part of the following day did not attempt any further infantry attacks, but maintained a heavy bombardment on this part of our front and on other portions of the battle area. In the

Mr. Asquith watching men adjusting fuses.

course of the afternoon and evening, however, they delivered another succession of assaults against our trenches north-west of Pozières, in which *flammenwerfer*, or flame-jets, were again employed.

The *flammenwerfer* is a somewhat clumsy form of "frightfulness." It requires two men to work it, one having the reservoir strapped to his back, while the other pumps out the long spray of flame, which has a range of some twenty-five yards. It frequently happens, however, particularly in attacks by daylight, that the *flammenwerfer* men are all picked off before they get near enough to do any damage. Thus, in a previous counter-attack, eight of these flame-throwers were brought against the trenches held by the Sussex men; but the sixteen Germans in charge of them were all shot down without being able to discharge a single spray.

In all the enemy delivered four attacks. Three of them failed completely, but in the other they succeeded in occupying fifty yards of our trenches.

General Birdwood meets some of the Australians in a wood after the battle.

Fighting continued all day near Guillemont station. South-west of the village we advanced our line about four hundred yards. The enemy shelled Longueval, the Bois des Foureaux (High Wood) and Pozières heavily, and also the vicinity of Mametz. Elsewhere it was a quiet day, except for some artillery activity in the Loos salient and north of Hulluch.

Between the Ancre and the Somme the night was not marked by any incident of importance, but in the Ypres salient it was a very lively one. From 10 p.m. until midnight the enemy heavily bombarded our trenches between the Bellewaarde Lake and the Yser Canal, and discharged gas on a broad front. The gas had little effect, and some partial attacks which followed failed to reach our lines.

In the early part of the 9th we made some further progress north of Pozières by bombing along the enemy's trenches, and captured twenty-five prisoners. Throughout the day the German artillery industriously "plastered" the Pozières ridge with all manner of shells, phosphorus shells figuring amongst them. For many months the enemy had been using shrapnel bedded in phosphorus powder, presumably

PART VII. WILL BE READY ON TUESDAY, DECEMBER 19TH

IT CONTAINS PICTURES OF:—

King Albert of Belgium introducing his Generals to King George.
German Prisoners arriving at a Divisional cage in motor lorries.
Photograph showing, left to right: General Joffre, President Poincare, King George, General Foch and General Haig.
Australian troops cheering the King.
The King is carrying a bouquet presented to him by a little girl.
The King in a gun-pit.
The King passing between two mine craters near Mametz.
The King on the Battlefield with Sir Henry Rawlinson and General Congreve.
The King meets the matron of a hospital.
The King outside a German dug-out.

The King attends Church Service among his troops.
The King conversing with wounded officers.
The King in a captured German trench.
Sorting the packs of dead and wounded for letters, etc., to send to relations.
A German machine gun emplacement smashed up by our artillery.
Royal Engineers on the march.
Gun captured in Mametz Wood.
Captured German howitzer photographed on the Battlefield.
Tommy's cookhouse near Thiepval.
Scene at the burial of some of our men behind the line.
View in Pozieres.

Everything is so well arranged in this advance that Tommies can get their water from the main just behind the front line.
Scene at an aerodrome.
Putting up a water-trough for the cavalry.
Preparing for winter in the trenches.
View of Mametz.
Making a road through captured ground.
An observation balloon and its nurse in a pit.
Men of the R.F.C. bringing up a nurse balloon.
Irish Brigade returning from Guillemont.
Once the railway station at Guillemont.
Stretcher-bearers and dressing station at Guillemont.
Respirator drill for the Guards near the Somme.

ORDER FORM.

To M..
BOOKSELLER OR NEWSAGENT.

Please send me Part VII. and the following Parts as published of "SIR DOUGLAS HAIG'S GREAT PUSH," for which I enclose...........................

Name..

Address..

SCALA THEATRE,

(Goodge Street Tube Station).   CHARLOTTE STREET, W.

AT THE FRONT

OFFICIAL WAR OFFICE FILMS.

Kut Relief Forces.   Salonika.   Russian Army.   French Army.   East Africa.
The King on the Somme Battle Field, &c.

THE BATTLE OF THE SOMME.

"There is no programme in London which gives so complete and vivid a description of the War on ALL FRONTS."—*Evening News.*

THE KING'S ADVICE:

SEE THE SOMME WAR FILM AND WHAT WAR MEANS.

"The public should see these pictures, that they may have some idea of what the Army is doing, and what war means."

This statement was made by the King after witnessing a programme of the Official War Office film, "The Battle of the Somme," which was shown by command to the King and Queen at Windsor Castle.—*Daily Express.*

Box Office, 10 to 10.   DAILY, 3 and 8.   'Phone: Gerr. 1444 & 1366.

SCALA THEATRE.

A big Economy

THE EVERYDAY MILK

Ideal Milk is simply the richest and purest cows' milk concentrated till it is as thick as cream. Only the excess moisture is removed. Nothing is added. *Guaranteed* absolutely pure. No Sugar. No preservatives. With Milk at present price "Ideal" means a big Economy in the home.

IDEAL MILK

Diluted—for every purpose of fresh Milk
Undiluted—for every purpose of fresh Cream
except "IT WON'T WHIP"

**Sold by all Grocers and Stores
Cash Price 7½d. and 4d. per tin**

AS SUPPLIED TO THE NAVY AND ARMY

PRINTED AT THE CHAPEL RIVER PRESS, KINGSTON-ON-THAMES.

IN ABOUT 8 FORTNIGHTLY PARTS.   HUTCHINSON'S NEW PART WORK   Part VIII. ready Jan. 2nd.   PART VII. 8d. NET

SIR DOUGLAS HAIG'S
GREAT PUSH

THE BATTLE OF THE SOMME

A popular, pictorial and authoritative work on one of the Greatest Battles in History, illustrated by about **700** *wonderful* **OFFICIAL PHOTOGRAPHS AND CINEMATOGRAPH FILMS** *and other authentic pictures*

BY ARRANGEMENT WITH THE WAR OFFICE

RESPIRATOR DRILL

GREAT VALUE FOR EIGHTPENCE

THIS PART CONTAINS **33 WONDERFUL REPRODUCTIONS** OF THE FAMOUS **WAR OFFICE CINEMATOGRAPH FILMS** AND **OFFICIAL PHOTOGRAPHS** OF THE BATTLE OF THE SOMME, BEAUTIFULLY PRINTED ON THE BEST ENGLISH ART PAPER.

LONDON : HUTCHINSON & Co.

New Christmas Gift Books.

THE ELEPHANT
By AGNES HERBERT
With 9 Coloured and Black and White Illustrations
By WINIFRED AUSTIN

6/- NET

WINNING THE V.C. IN THE GREAT WAR
With 57 Paintings by well-known Artists

5/-

RENÉ BULL'S
NEW COLOUR-BOOK
'CARMEN'
By PROSPER MERRIMÉ
IS UNQUESTIONABLY THE MOST
BEAUTIFUL GIFT-BOOK
PUBLISHED THIS YEAR.

With 16 Plates in colour
74 Illustrations in line, and Decorations, End Papers and Cover Design
In one large handsome volume, gilt and gilt top, boxed, 21/- net
Edition de luxe, signed by artist, bound in parchment and limited to 100, 42/- net

'NEATH VERDUN
From AUGUST to SEPTEMBER, 1914.

6/-

AN ARTIST IN THE RIVIERA
With 30 fine mounted Plates in Colour, by
WALTER TYNDALE, R.I.

15/- NET

London: HUTCHINSON & CO.

with the object of making the wound inflicted by the bullet slow to heal; but the employment of phosphorus as a direct weapon in itself appeared to be a new departure in chemical warfare. The phosphorus burns the flesh, making an ugly wound. These phosphorus shells were chiefly directed at a small area east of the Bapaume road, and were mingled with a considerable number of gas shells.

In the midst of all this " strafing " with shrapnel, high explosive, stinking gases, chemical powders and so forth, our troops continued to make progress, and by the evening the Australians, advancing in their usual dashing style, had wrested from the enemy a valuable rectangle of trench north-west of Pozières and advanced our line 200 yards on a frontage of 600 yards.

King Albert of Belgium introducing his Generals to King George.

During the day our aircraft were very active and rendered most valuable service. As a result of their effective co-operation with our artillery, several German guns were destroyed and some magazines blown up. A train was set on fire by bombs dropped from our aeroplanes. The enemy's aircraft were unusually active, but appeared anxious to avoid combat. Nevertheless, a number of aerial encounters took place, and several of the German machines were driven down in hostile territory. Three of ours failed to return to the British lines.

The night was generally quiet along our front, except for heavy hostile shelling of our lines southeast of Trônes Wood. North-west of Pozières we made further progress, gaining all our local objectives and capturing seventy-two prisoners. South of Arras we raided an enemy's sap and inflicted several casualties; while a similar attempt by the enemy against our trenches north-west of Hulluch met with no success. South of Loos the enemy exploded a mine, but without effect.

There was no change in the situation during the 10th. Some parties of the enemy advanced against our lines south of Martinpuich, but the effective fire of our trench-mortars and machine-guns prevented any attack from developing. Our airmen were active and continued bombing operations against the enemy's billets and other points of military importance.

During the night the enemy opened heavy machine-gun and rifle fire on our trenches in the Bois des Foureaux (High Wood), followed by artillery barrage on the back areas. This was obviously intended to prepare the way for an infantry attack in force; but the British guns retaliated vigorously and caused the Germans to alter their plans, since no hostile movement developed. North of Bazentin-le-Petit we made further progress, capturing a short length of trenches and inflicting considerable loss on the enemy. Near Neuville St. Vaast we exploded a mine and occupied the crater with but little opposition; while south of Ypres we successfully raided a ruined farm in the enemy's lines.

German prisoners arriving at a divisional cage in motor lorries.

Towards six o'clock the following morning the enemy made a determined counter-attack on the trenches we had just captured north of Bazentin-le-Petit. But our men held their ground, and the attack was beaten back, with further heavy loss to the enemy. North-west of Pozières we advanced our line slightly in certain places. Otherwise, the day witnessed no change in the situation.

The British official reports on the 11th announced that, in addition to numerous daily raids, long-distance raids had recently been carried out by the Royal Flying Corps against the following objectives: the Zeppelin sheds at Brussels; railway sidings at Mons; railway sidings and airship sheds at Namur; Busigny railway station (twice); Courtrai railway station (twice). In all, sixty-eight machines had taken part in these raids, of which only two had failed to return.

In the evening the enemy renewed their efforts to recapture the trenches we had wrested from them on the Pozières ridge, against which they launched a strong infantry attack, supported by heavy artillery fire. Our own artillery was prepared for it, however, and the guns were registered on the line across

THE KING IN FRANCE.

The illustration, from left to right, shows General Joffre, President Poincaré, King George, General Foch and General Haig.

Australian troops cheering the King.

which the hostile troops would advance; and, as soon as the Germans, who had been concentrated in a gully, emerged into the open, a dreadful storm of shrapnel and high-explosive descended upon them, while, as they drew nearer, our machine-guns and trench-mortars opened upon them with murderous effect. Before half the distance was traversed the ground was carpeted with dead and wounded men; but, with the courage of despair, the survivors still struggled on, until, realizing the hopelessness of the attempt, they turned and endeavoured to regain their own lines. Comparatively few succeeded, however, and their losses must have been terrible.

During the night we carried out three successful raids on the enemy's trenches: one south-west of La Folie Farm on the Vimy ridge; another opposite Calonne, and the third east of Armentières, in which a machine-gun and some prisoners were taken and many casualties inflicted on the enemy. The Germans attempted a raid near the Hohenzollern Redoubt, which was repulsed with loss by our infantry, several

The King is carrying a bouquet which was presented to him by a little girl.

prisoners belonging to a Bavarian regiment being taken. We fired three mines north of Neuve Chapelle and also south of the quarries to the north-west of Hulluch. The enemy made no attempt to occupy the craters; while, on the other hand, we occupied the lip of one made by a mine which the Germans had exploded near Cabaret Rouge. South-east of Guillemont, the enemy made a bomb-attack on a part of our trenches, but it was driven back.

The 13th was marked by further progress in the Pozières area. North-west of the village we advanced our line between three and four hundred yards on a front of nearly a mile, our casualties being light, in spite of a heavy barrage by the enemy's artillery. North of Pozières the Germans were observed by one of our airmen concentrating in large numbers behind Mounault Farm. He immediately communicated with our artillery, and so effective a fire was directed upon the enemy that they scattered wildly in all directions, and the projected attack was abandoned. In the same neighbourhood a working party of 200 Germans was surprised by our machine-guns and lost heavily. Along the remainder of the front the enemy's guns indulged in a heavy bombardment of some of the villages behind our lines, but there was no infantry fighting. On our right flank, except for some heavy shelling of our front trenches and some minor encounters with hostile detachments near Delville Wood, nothing of importance occurred.

The Royal Flying Corps was in a very enterprising mood, and, in addition to much successful work in co-operation with our artillery and infantry and several short bombing-raids, including three separate attacks on a hostile aerodrome, carried out another long-distance raid, in which great damage was done to some railway works and sidings. Hostile aircraft, though fairly active, sought to avoid combat. One of them, however, was driven down, while one of our machines failed to return to the British lines.

At night the enemy delivered a counter-attack against the trenches we had captured from them during the day to the north-west of Pozières, and succeeded in securing a footing in a portion of them. South of the Ypres salient we carried out a successful raid without any loss ourselves. There was further mining

The King in a gun-pit.

activity on the northern part of our line. At the Bluff, north of the Ypres–Comines Canal, we forced an entry into a German gallery, and, after exploration, blew in a considerable length. We also successfully exploded a mine near Cordonnerie.

The 14th passed without any change in the situation. West of Pozières a successful bombing-attack resulted in the capture of a machine-gun and some prisoners. The enemy exploded a mine west of La Folie Farm, which did little damage. The German guns were active, their fire being more particularly directed on Mametz Wood and Pozières, and also on Arras and our trenches north of the Verstraat–Wytschaete road.

At night a party of our men forced their way into the enemy's trenches near Mouquet Farm, returning to our lines with eleven prisoners. A feinted raid on the German trenches south of Armentières caused much commotion in the enemy's lines, of which our artillery took full advantage. North-west of Hulluch, the Germans exploded a small mine, but we promptly occupied the crater. North-west of Pozières we

The King passing between two mine craters near Mametz.

The King on the battlefield with Sir Henry Rawlinson and General Congreve.

continued to make progress, and by noon on the 15th were once more in possession of nearly the whole of the trenches retaken by the enemy two days previously.

During the remainder of the day hostilities were chiefly confined to the guns. The enemy maintained a heavy barrage all along that part of our line which ran south of Mouquet Farm (called by our men "Moo-cow" Farm or "Mucky" Farm, according to their whim) to below Thiépval village and wood. Our own guns were busy with the farm, and, further off, with Courcelette, while now and again one of our heavies sent a huge shell crashing into Thiépval.

Thiépval was steadily being reduced to the condition of Ovillers, Pozières, and other unfortunate villages in the vicinity. "It is a ghastly-looking place," writes Mr. Philip Gibbs, who had a good view of it that day from an artillery observation-post, "with its stripped trees like withered limbs, and a ruined church above a row of apple-trees, which stand a little separate from the village. Above is a cemetery, with broken tomb-stones and shell-craters among its graves. Beyond, on a road running northwards, is a tall crucifix with the figure of Christ looking down upon all this death."

Strongly garrisoned though Thiépval was, no sign of human life was to be seen in the village. The Germans were hiding in their dug-outs, with the exception of those on duty in the trenches, and of the latter not a man dared to raise his head above the parapet.

The King meets the matron of a hospital.

CHAPTER VII

IN the evening, in conjunction with the French advance on Maurepas, we pushed forward our line both west and south-west of Guillemont. West of the Bois des Foureaux (High Wood) we captured some 300 yards of hostile trench about the same distance in front of our line. East of Mouquet Farm a German attack was nipped in the bud by the effective fire of our machine-guns. West of Vimy we exploded a mine and occupied the crater with only slight opposition. South of Loos both sides blew *camouflets*, the enemy's causing us neither casualties nor damage.

During the night and early hours of the morning the enemy delivered yet another series of determined counter-attacks on our trenches north-west of Pozières, on a broad front and with considerable forces.

Six lines of German infantry advanced to the assault, but in no case did they succeed in entering our lines, being received with so withering a fire from our artillery and machine-guns that they were utterly routed, with very heavy losses.

Throughout the 17th there was considerable artillery activity on the British right. North-west of Bazentin-le-Petit we captured about 100 yards of trench from the enemy; and a counter-attack delivered by the Germans from Martinpuich was repulsed and some prisoners captured. Our aircraft were active, and the enemy's billets at various places were successfully bombed. As the result of an aerial combat, a German machine was brought down in flames in our trenches, and two other machines were brought down by our " Archies," as the anti-aircraft guns are called.

During the night the German artillery showed increased activity and indulged in some heavy bursts

The King outside a German dug-out.

of shelling. North-west of Bazentin-le-Petit, by means of a small local enterprise, we gained further ground. The enemy's trenches in this area were found to have been greatly damaged by our shell-fire and to be full of their dead. Another counter-attack by the Germans from Martinpuich shared the fate of that delivered on the previous day.

Early in the afternoon of the 18th, after an artillery preparation of the utmost violence, we again took the offensive on an important scale, the operations extending from Thiépval to our extreme right, south of Guillemont, a distance of about eleven miles. The advance was attended with splendid success. From the Bois des Foureaux (High Wood) to the point when we joined up with the French we pushed forward our line over a front of more than two miles for a distance varying between 200 and 600 yards, and by the evening were in possession of the western outskirts of Guillemont, including the railway-station and the quarry, a point of considerable military importance, and a line thence northwards to midway between

The King attends church service among his troops.

The King conversing with wounded officers.

Delville Wood and Ginchy, while the orchards north of Longueval were also in our hands. Between High Wood and the Albert–Bapaume road we captured some hundreds of yards of hostile trenches. East and south of Mouquet Farm we advanced our line by some 300 yards; while between Ovillers and Thiépval we pushed forward on a front of over half a mile, capturing the ridge south-east of and overlooking Thiépval and the northern slopes of the high ground north of Pozières, from which we obtained an extensive view to the east and north-east.

A most gallant piece of work was accomplished south of the Leipzig Redoubt by some Territorial troops, who attacked a maze of German trenches, carried them by assault, and linked up with the redoubt itself, which, it will be remembered, had been in our hands since the fighting of July 7th, thus securing a still closer grip at the throat of the Thiépval garrison. Another fine achievement was that

The King in a captured German trench.

of a battalion of the Warwicks between Pozières and Thiépval. They had to force their way between machine-gun posts and scramble over ground which continuous shell-fire had transformed into a billowy sea of earth with deep pits at the bottom of each billow; and when the German trenches were reached to clear out an underground system of galleries, where numbers of the enemy were waiting with bombs and every kind of weapon. At one point, on the right, the advance was held up by a German *fortin*, from which came a stream of machine-gun bullets. So fierce was the fire that the men were ordered to lie down to wait until our own machine-guns could get to work. The officer in command of a heavy battery which had been supporting them telephoned to inquire whether his guns should shell the place. But this offer the colonel of the Warwicks refused, since his men were so close to the redoubt that the slightest shortage in the flight of a shell might have been attended with disastrous results; and it seemed as though nothing could stop that deadly squirt of bullets, when on a sudden it ceased, as quickly as water that is turned off at a tap, and a white flag fluttered up. Then, as our troops entered the place, from a dug-out which they supposed might be giving shelter to a score or so of men emerged a whole company of Germans, all unwounded, with the exception of half a dozen men who were carried on stretchers. Their leader, a gigantic Hun wearing a steel casque, appeared quite at his ease, and was laughing and joking merrily with his brother officers as he came forward.

The occupants, however, of some of the other dug-outs in the trenches captured by the Warwicks were made of sterner stuff and resisted stubbornly, even to the death. Outside one of them a sentry was posted, who, as our men approached, shouted a warning to his comrades below. They came up the

Sorting the packs of dead and wounded for letters, etc., to send to relations.

stairway in a swarm, and a ferocious conflict ensued, which ended only when the last German had been despatched.

Many acts of great individual gallantry were performed by the Warwicks. At one place, a sergeant sprang on to the parados of the trench and single-handed kept a machine-gun team away from their weapon until assistance arrived, thereby undoubtedly saving the lives of many of his comrades. At another, a company officer, held up at a barricade, called for a rifle, and, with two men to reload for him, kept up a brisk fire at the German machine-gunners on the further side, while bombers behind him flung grenades over his head.

To defend the northern slopes of the high ground north of Pozières, the enemy had with feverish haste constructed a new line of trenches; but our heavies had battered the parapets to pieces, and they had no chance of holding them against our advancing infantry. Australian, English and Scottish troops shared the honour of carrying this all-important position, the Scots capturing the trenches opposite Martinpuich, which lies some 500 yards on the further side of the ridge.

A German machine-gun emplacement smashed up by our artillery.

Royal Engineers on the march.

The Battle of the Somme

"It is not long ago, as the calendar counts time," wrote Mr. Philip Gibbs on August 25th, "though a lifetime ago for many thousands of men who have fought along the road to Martinpuich, since that village with a queer name seemed as unattainable as any dream city. No man of ours, except our flying men, had ever seen it, for it lies just below the Pozières ridge, and before the battle opened on July 1st the ridge itself was a high and distant barrier defended by great strongholds like Fricourt and Mametz and Contalmaison, and by all those woods which could be captured, as every soldier knew, only by desperate fighting. Now, after the greatest battle in British history—a series of battles rather in one great and continuous attack—we have gained that ridge above Pozières and the windmill, and look down the slopes beyond.

"There, only 500 yards away, across No Man's Land lies Martinpuich, as I saw it myself to-day from our front-line trench, surprised that one could see so close into its ruins. To my left, as I stood out in

Gun captured in Mametz Wood.

the open above the trenches, was the windmill for which the Australians fought—the conical base of it being all that is left as a memorial of the heroism which gained this ground—and behind it was Pozières, which is linked also, for ever, with the memory of those boys from the Overseas Dominion who gave a treasure of life to take it.

"The way to Martinpuich is truly 'The Street of Adventure' for hundreds of thousands of our men who have fought their way over the ground about it since that first day of July, which was the beginning of the great adventure. . . . It is a road of immortality. Alas! also of great death, as one sees all along the way past Fricourt and Contalmaison over ground dotted with new-made graves, where white wooden crosses stick up above the mounds of earth, everywhere, amidst the torn tree-stumps, and very thickly between the upheaval of those fields flung into chaos by gunfire, and clustering thickly about piles of broken brickwork which are still called by their old village-names."

Our advance on the right, in conjunction with that of the French, was also very successful. At

Guillemont, there was fierce fighting with bomb and bayonet for possession of the deep quarry, which lies just within the precincts of the village, between South Midland troops and the powerful German garrison who held the place. It was a grim struggle, but the Midlanders triumphed, and the whole of the garrison was either killed or made prisoners.

In the centre, less ground was gained, for here the German defences were in places too formidable to be taken at a rush. A singular incident occurred between Delville Wood and High Wood, where there ran a sunken road, strongly fortified and held. Here we did little more than ascertain the strength of the position; but at a point where the road flattened out some English troops succeeded in capturing a trench which had been battered to pieces by our gunfire and was full of dead. Some of the Germans

Captured German howitzer photographed on the battlefield.

who had survived the bombardment remained and fought to the death; but the majority bolted for the rear before our men were within striking distance.

It was impossible, however, to hold the ground we had gained, for the troops on the right and left had been held up by the sunken road, and the enemy, after raking the position with machine-guns from a sandbagged redoubt on the edge of High Wood and from a sap on the left, despatched two strong parties of bombers up the trench, one on either flank. Our men, having used up all their own bombs and those of the enemy which they had found in the captured trench, had no alternative but to retire, which they began to do just as dusk was falling. And then a strange thing happened. The two parties of German bombers, swarming up on either side, mistook one another in the fading light for the enemy, and engaged in a furious battle of bombs, in which both must have suffered pretty severely before the mistake was discovered.

It was also in the High Wood area that the unusual sight was witnessed of a hostile aeroplane brought down by one of our machine-guns in the trenches. " Apparently, the pilot, who circled round courageously

Tommy's cookhouse near Thiépval.

Scene at the burial of some of our men behind the line.

enough," writes Mr. Beach Thomas, " wished to pick up the signals sent by our advancing troops in the wood, and, perhaps, attempt to send false signals to our guns. But he flew just too low. As he crossed the line, a half-round of shots from a Lewis gun finished his course. A little flash of fire was seen on the plane. It shook, appeared to make a back somersault, then tilted as violently forward, crumpled up, and crashed on to the German lines in High Wood."

In the course of the advance we discovered that the fertile imagination of the Hun had evolved two new devices in devilry. One of these inventions was a man-trap, which he placed just outside his parapet or in one of the shell-craters with which No Man's Land was now so thickly covered that the rim of one frequently touched and sometimes intersected that of another. As soon as one of our men set foot in this trap, it closed upon his leg with a tremendous snap, and brought him down like a log. The second device

View in Pozières.

was a bomb which stood on four little legs and looked very much like a tortoise. These " tortoises " were so contrived that they exploded at a touch and severely punished the inquisitive.

During that day and the early part of the next close upon 800 prisoners were passed back. They were for the most part fine men both in physique and training, belonging to the best Prussian regiments, such as the 29th, taken north of Pozières, and the 123rd and 127th, some of whom had surrendered to us at Guillemont. Among them were men who spoke English fluently, having been waiters, barbers, and so forth in England before the war, and one even used English slang to express the utter weariness of himself and his comrades. " We are fed up," said he. " We couldn't stick it any longer." The ceaseless stream of shells which our artillery had been hurling over their lines, smashing their parapets to pieces, blowing in their dug-outs and scattering death and mutilation all about them, and the fierce assaults of our infantry which followed the bombardment, had unnerved these men, so that they no longer had any stomach for fighting.

During the evening several determined counter-attacks were launched against the positions we had captured. Near Thiépval the enemy advanced in great force, but the assault was completely broken up by the fire of our artillery and machine-guns. On the extreme right, another formidable concentration of troops in the neighbourhood of Ginchy was observed and reported by one of our aeroplanes, which was hovering over the German lines, and orders were given to put the heavies on to them and to follow with shrapnel from the field-guns. The enemy began to advance in four waves; our guns opened fire, and presently came a message from the aeroplane: " O.K. The first two waves are wiped out. The others are scuttling."

During the 19th our troops were chiefly occupied in consolidating the ground won; but north-east of

Scene at an aerodrome.

Pozières we made further progress on both sides of the Pozières–Bapaume road, and advanced our line for some three hundred yards north-east of the Windmill.

It was in this area that the Germans suffered, perhaps, their very heaviest losses, in a counter-attack which was met with such a devastating storm of shell and machine-gun fire that the successive waves of men were mown down like corn and appeared to vanish away. Altogether, their casualties since the offensive began on the previous afternoon must have been beyond measure, the number of severely wounded alone, to judge by the activity of their stretcher-bearers, whom we humanely permitted to work unmolested, being very great.

In spite of low clouds, our aircraft performed much useful work in connection with our advanced infantry. One of our aeroplanes came down to a low altitude and opened machine-gun fire very effectively on the German infantry in their front-line trenches, and also on hostile reinforcements coming up the communication-trenches.

Everything is so well arranged in this advance that Tommies can get their water from the main just behind the front line.

Putting up a water trough for the cavalry.

A view of Mametz.

The Battle of the Somme

Preparing for winter in the trenches.

At certain points on our front between the Ancre and the Somme there were local bombing encounters during the night; but the enemy made no serious attempt to recover the ground he had lost. At other parts of the line we carried out successful raids, capturing a machine-gun and other war material and inflicting numerous casualties on the enemy.

About midday on the 20th the enemy delivered a strong attack on the new lines which we had established for about half a mile on the western corner of High Wood. At some points he succeeded in entering our trenches, but was soon driven out again by our infantry. Subsequent attacks broke down under our artillery fire. North of Bazentin-le-Petit we captured a further section of the enemy's trenches. The German artillery was very active all along the front, High Wood, Hamel and Mailly being shelled with particular severity. Elsewhere nothing of importance occurred.

During the night we effectively shelled portions of the German line, while the enemy bombarded our trenches in the vicinity of Pozières and Contalmaison and the area north-east of it, using gas-shells freely. Mr. Philip Gibbs, who passed through Contalmaison on the following day, states that the stench caused by these gas-shells was still prowling about, " stealing out of crannies and shell-holes with faint, sickly whiffs as though from rotten eggs."

North-west of Hulluch and east of Le Plantin the enemy attempted to raid our trenches, but only succeeded in penetrating them at one point, from which he was quickly driven out again. In the neighbourhood of Givenchy the Germans exploded a mine near one of our forward saps, but without causing

Making a road through captured ground.

any casualties; and we promptly occupied the crater and used it as a defensive post. Further north, we liberated gas with success against the enemy's trenches at two places.

About 1.30 in the morning, after heavy artillery preparation, the Germans made three bombing attacks on High Wood, all of which, however, were easily repulsed. North-west of High Wood some of our covering patrols had to withdraw before strong detachments of the enemy; but these detachments were effectively checked by fire from our positions west of the wood. In the course of the afternoon, the Germans attempted an attack on a small scale near Mouquet Farm, which was immediately driven back. The artillery on both sides was active, and at times very violent. Ours was very effective, and inflicted severe damage on the enemy's trenches south of Thiépval. A conflagration was caused in one of the enemy's batteries, which burned fiercely for some time. South of Loos, as a result of a successful mine, we much improved our local position.

In addition to much useful work in co-operation with our artillery, our aircraft successfully bombed the enemy's billets at various places. The German aeroplanes showed rather more enterprise than usual, and some ventured over our lines. A hostile balloon was forced to descend by our gunfire.

An observation balloon and its nurse in a pit.

Men of the R.F.C. bringing up a nurse balloon.

During the evening, as the result of a dashing piece of work by some English troops, following in the wake of a furious bombardment, which made an utter chaos of a section of the German trenches, we gained further ground in the Leipzig salient and advanced our positions to within 1,000 yards of Thiépval. The enemy's losses were very severe, as our guns caught them during a relief, while a number of Germans who, on the approach of the British infantry, made a bolt for the rear, plunged straight into a heavy barrage which our artillery was flinging across the ground behind their trenches and were destroyed almost to a man. Over 100 prisoners were taken, amongst whom was an ex-waiter of the Savoy Hotel, who appeared much relieved that his part in the war was at an end, and declared that Verdun, from which he had just come, was a heaven compared to the Picardy battlefields.

We also made considerable progress in the Pozières area, where, advancing on a front of half a mile,

How a German trench between Guinchy and Guillemont looked after our infantry had taken it.

we established ourselves at the road-junction just outside Mouquet Farm, and pushed forward along the right of the Pozières–Miraumont road.

On the 22nd, between Martinpuich and Bazentin, Scottish troops captured a further hundred yards of hostile trench, and a successful raid was made on the German lines south of Guillemont, in which village the enemy's garrison still maintained an obstinate resistance, though their casualties from our artillery bombardments must have been very heavy.

During the day the immense advantage we had gained in having, by the capture of the Pozières ridge, enabled our guns to be turned on to the German positions on the further slopes with direct observation of results was shown when our artillery registered something like twenty-five hits on the enemy's batteries.

The situation of the Germans in the Courcelette area, which was swept continuously by our shell-fire, must have been almost unendurable. It was bad enough a fortnight earlier, to judge from the following letter, written on August 10th by an officer of the 133rd Infantry Regiment :—

"The relief yesterday is incredible. The route taken—Ligny–Warlincourt–Pys–Courcelette—on the way to the trenches, was very dangerous. . . . Heavy shells fell right and left of the road. Mounted troops, cars, field-kitchens, infantry in column of route, were all enveloped in an impenetrable cloud of dust. The last stage consisted of troops in single file crouching on the slopes beside the road, with shells bursting overhead. From Courcelette we relieved across the open. If the enemy had only noticed that, what a target he would have had ! . . . The hundreds of dead bodies make the air unendurable, and there are flies in thousands. . . . We have no dug-outs. We dig a hole in the side of a shell-hole and lie and get rheumatism. We get nothing to eat or drink. . . . The ceaseless roar of the guns is driving us mad. Many of the men are knocked up. The company-commander thinks we were breathing gas yesterday, which slowly decomposes the blood, and there is an end of one. What a variety of different ways one can lose one's life in this place ! . . ."

The rain which fell during the greater part of the day interfered with aerial work, but towards evening the weather cleared, and the enemy's aircraft began to display unwonted enterprise. They had reason

A view of what was once the railway station of Guillemont.

to regret their temerity, as they were at once attacked by our aeroplanes, which destroyed at least four hostile machines, drove down a number of others in a damaged condition, and pursued others back to their aerodromes. All this was accomplished without any casualties on our side, while an important reconnaissance and several bombing-raids were also successfully carried out.

At 9 p.m. the Germans launched a determined counter-attack against our new trenches south of Thiépval, in which they succeeded in gaining a footing, only to be driven out immediately. About an hour after midnight they made a second attempt, but it broke down completely under our fire. In both these attacks the enemy's losses were very heavy.

On the following day we resumed our offensive in this sector and captured a further 200 yards of German trench, by which success we straightened our lines and improved our positions. The enemy's artillery, which was showing a good deal of activity and had during the night shelled High Wood and Bazentin-le-Petit, was silenced in three different areas by the counter-battery work of our heavy guns, which appeared to be very effective.

During the night there was heavy fighting on our extreme right, where the enemy made strenuous efforts to regain their lost ground between Guillemont Station and the Quarry. After an intense

Stretcher-bearers and a dressing-station at Guillemont.

Respirator drill for the Guards near the Somme.

PART VIII. WILL BE READY ON TUESDAY, JAN. 2ND, 1917.

IT CONTAINS THE FOLLOWING ILLUSTRATIONS:—

- Australians drawing water for the guns' crews. Working a heavy gun is thirsty work
- Once the main road of Guillemont.
- An advanced dressing station. A Red Cross flag is affixed to the tree.
- Cavalry on the march.
- Ammunition pack horses going up to the front during the battle of the 15th Sept.
- Cavalry on the march near the Somme.
- A British graveyard, a smashed railway track, German ammunition left in their retreat, and a transport waggon going up to the front line.
- Battlefield signposts.
- View of Thiepval.
- A broken down ambulance in the battlefield.
- A view in Delville Wood.
- A view of Flers.
- View of Flers—The Main Street.
- One of the roads of Flers.
- Taking up boarding for bottom of trenches.
- Red Cross men carrying wounded over the top of the trench in Thiepval village.
- Comfort! An officer's dug-out with his washing-stand and his bedding out to air or dry.
- Australians cheer the King.
- A model place for watering horses.
- A few plum puddings that Fritz will soon receive.
- Trench mortar ammunition.
- Travelling water butts.
- Infantry waiting to advance.
- Infantry waiting to advance on the 25th.
- Waiting to attack on the 25th.
- A scene of desolation—once a village.
- A bombing party off to the attack.
- View of Morval which we captured on the 25th.
- General view of Morval which we captured on the 25th.
- The entrance of a captured German dug-out.
- Ruins of Combles.
- View of Combles.
- Some of the large ammunition left when the Huns had to clear out of Morval.
- One of the Boche gun emplacements at Combles. Note the great baulks of timber
- Combles - Main Street.
- View of Square at Combles.

ORDER FORM.

To M..
BOOKSELLER OR NEWSAGENT.

Please send me Part VIII. and the following Parts as published of "SIR DOUGLAS HAIG'S GREAT PUSH," for which I enclose................................

Name..

Address..

SCALA THEATRE,

(Goodge Street Tube Station). CHARLOTTE STREET, W.

AT THE FRONT

OFFICIAL WAR OFFICE FILMS.

Kut Relief Forces.   Salonika.   Russian Army.   French Army.   East Africa.
The King on the Somme Battle Field, &c.

THE BATTLE OF THE SOMME.

"There is no programme in London which gives so complete and vivid a description of the War on ALL FRONTS."— *Evening News.*

THE KING'S ADVICE:

SEE THE SOMME WAR FILM AND WHAT WAR MEANS.

"The public should see these pictures, that they may have some idea of what the Army is doing, and what war means."

This statement was made by the King after witnessing a programme of the Official War Office film, "The Battle of the Somme," which was shown by command to the King and Queen at Windsor Castle.—*Daily Express.*

Box Office, 10 to 10.   DAILY, 3 and 8.   'Phone: Gerr. 1444 & 1366.

SCALA THEATRE.

Made in a Moment

"MILKMAID" MILK-COCOA

The Cocoa with the Milk-Chocolate Flavour. The most delicious, most nourishing and most economical Cocoa you can buy. Neither Milk nor Sugar needed—you simply add boiling water.

SOLD BY ALL GROCERS AND STORES

IN ABOUT 12 FORTNIGHTLY PARTS.   HUTCHINSON'S NEW PART WORK   Part IX. ready Jan. 16th. PART VIII. 8d. NET

SIR DOUGLAS HAIG'S
GREAT PUSH

THE BATTLE OF THE SOMME

A popular, pictorial and authoritative work on one of the Greatest Battles in History, illustrated by about **700** *wonderful* **OFFICIAL PHOTOGRAPHS AND CINEMATOGRAPH FILMS** *and other authentic pictures*

BY ARRANGEMENT WITH THE WAR OFFICE

WAITING TO ATTACK

GREAT VALUE FOR EIGHTPENCE

THIS PART CONTAINS **35 WONDERFUL REPRODUCTIONS** OF THE FAMOUS **WAR OFFICE CINEMATOGRAPH FILMS** AND **OFFICIAL PHOTOGRAPHS** OF THE BATTLE OF THE SOMME, BEAUTIFULLY PRINTED ON THE BEST ENGLISH ART PAPER.

LONDON : HUTCHINSON & Co.

A Beautiful Cookery Book FREE

Simply as an extra inducement to purchase "Cookery and Domestic Management" we are giving to every purchaser a handsome 187 page book entitled "Dainty Entrées." This contains 187 recipes for every kind of entrée. A well-known chef said of "Dainty Entrées," "If ever I was at a loss for an entrée this is the book to which I would turn for assistance, for I could be sure of finding something more than dainty."

Bound in cloth, with a full index, with particularly clear directions, "Dainty Entrées" is worth at least 5/-, and should be in every housewife's hands.

COOKERY and DOMESTIC MANAGEMENT.

Here is an opportunity for every housewife not only to economise in her housekeeping accounts, but to provide her table with far more appetising and dainty dishes then ever before.

This happy combination can be effected solely by her purchasing the most wonderful and comprehensive work by Katharine Mellish, entitled "Cookery and Domestic Management," which will be sent on receipt of 2/6 only.

This work, which is published in two volumes, was written by a lady of acknowledged repute as an expert on domestic economy. It is the most extraordinary work ever published, and every one of its 1,000 pages is a revelation as to what can be effected in the kitchen, not only at the minimum of cost, but with the maximum nourishment and appetising flavour.

IT SAVES ITS COST IN A FEW WEEKS.

No housewife with a copy of "Cookery and Domestic Management" can fail to realise what a labour-saving, cost-cutting production it is. 1,000 Recipes for dainty dishes, illustrated by 56 Beautifully Coloured Plates, 441 Photographs of finished dishes, a comprehensive index, and the cost of every menu worked down to the lowest minimum, so that there can be no failures and no spoiled dishes.

WHAT ONE LADY SAID ABOUT IT: "SOLVED ALL MY PROBLEMS."

"In the early days of my married life my cooking was the despair of both myself and my husband. I bought all the well-known and popular cookery books, took lessons and employed cooks, but all to no avail. Either the books used the most expensive methods or the dishes I turned out 'strictly to directions' were more than enough for my small table. In either case the result was the same—another miserable failure, a cross and miserable husband. Mellish's 'Cookery and Domestic Management' solved all my problems, and now I am never at a loss for a dainty, inexpensive dish."

How to obtain the 2 Volumes and the Free Book.

"Cookery and Domestic Management" will be sent to any address on receipt of 2/6 deposit, and both volumes, beautifully bound, printed in large and clear type in simple language, will be found to be worth their weight in gold. Their cost will be saved in a few weeks by the economy effected, and not only will there be an improved housekeeping account, but the cooking will be greatly enhanced, and dishes hitherto impossible will be added to the menu. Meals will be looked forward to, and the happy housewife will receive nothing but praise and commendation for the dainty meals she achieves.

Do not hesitate to send the first deposit of 2/6 for the 3 beautiful volumes. Just at the moment, when prices are high and every penny counts, it amounts to a duty for every housewife to economise, and only by having "Cookery and Domestic Management" always at hand can she ever hope to make such economies as will make any appreciable difference in the weekly accounts. Whatever it is she would like to know about—how to cook any joint, vegetable, sweet, fish, or to use up any portions from one meal for another—there it is clearly shown in "Cookery and Domestic Management."

Write soon, because there are only limited numbers of the book in circulation, the cost of production being too high to allow of a large number to be sold at the price at which it is offered.

STANDARD ART BOOK Co. Ltd.,

(Dept. D 3), 30-32, Ludgate Hill, London, E.C.

SPECIAL COUPON

To THE STANDARD ART BOOK CO. LTD. (Dept. D 3), 30-32, Ludgate Hill, London, E.C.

I enclose 2/6, please send me carriage paid "MELLISH'S COOKERY AND HOUSEHOLD MANAGEMENT" and the FREE Copy of "Dainty Entrées." If I like the work I agree to pay the balance by small monthly instalments of 3/-; should I not be entirely satisfied I will return the two volumes within two days, when you will return me my 2/6.

Name.................... Address.................... Occupation....................

bombardment of our trenches, which began about 7 p.m., they delivered a strong infantry attack, which was pressed with such determination that in places it reached our parapet. A fierce struggle ensued, which ended in the enemy being repulsed at every point. Their losses were very severe. At 12.30 a.m. our trenches were again heavily shelled, but no infantry attack developed. North of Bazentin-le-Petit a hostile bombing attack against our new trenches was easily repelled, as was an attempted raid further north, in the vicinity of the Hohenzollern Redoubt, which had been preceded by a heavy bombardment. On the other hand, we successfully raided the enemy's lines north-west of La Bassée.

In the afternoon of the 24th a splendid success was achieved south of Thiépval, where we captured a line of trenches extending across the Leipzig salient for a distance of 700 yards, and so strong that they might well have been thought impregnable to assault and to threaten certain destruction to the assailants.

Drawing water for the guns' crews. Working a heavy gun is thirsty work.

But no defences however formidable and however strongly held are proof against the courage and tenacity of our splendid lads, backed as they now are by the devastating power of a great mass of artillery. Throughout the morning our heavies steadily pounded the enemy's positions, until all in a moment, with a suddenness which one who was present compares to that of a near clap of thunder succeeding occasional low and distant growlings, the bombardment swelled into one mighty and continuous roar which seemed to split the heavens, as hundreds of great guns began to belch forth their message of death in the direction of the row of broken, leafless apple-trees which marked the spot where had once stood a thriving village, and just below which the enemy's trenches lay.

The huge shells came screaming through the air in flocks, throwing up long, swirling pyramids of dust as they burst amidst the enemy's defences, which were speedily enveloped in a dense pall of smoke. " I had just fixed my glass on a certain German strong point," writes Mr. Beach Thomas, " when a great shell hit it full. A black and sepia rush of foul smoke shot up into the shape of a sweep's brush, out-topping all other explosions by many yards. Then from the edges of this toadstool of smoke solid things began to drop : black oblongs and rhomboids and shapeless lumps. What they were, mortal or material, I do not know, nor what created the immensity of this explosion. Thiépval itself was like a forest fire, in which the fumes and smoke had taken the colour of the autumnal leaves—' yellow and black and pale and hectic red.' "

The moment for the infantry to go forward to the attack was at hand, and presently out of our frontline trenches scrambled long lines of men—Wiltshire and Worcestershire men, who had already won fame, the former in the fighting around Pozières, the latter in the attack on Contalmaison. For a moment or two they waited until all had got up into their alignment, and then started to cross the four or five hundred

Once the main road of Guillemont.

yards of rising ground which lay between them and the enemy's lines. From these lines a rocket had just gone up as a signal to the German guns; and in less than half a minute shells began to fall rapidly—great shells which tore up the solid earth as though it had been cardboard and covered No Man's Land with clouds of smoke, and shrapnel which burst above the heads of the advancing troops with orange flashes and rained bullets down upon them. Here and there a shell took toll of a cluster, but nothing could stay the advance of those long lines of English lads, and on and up they went, disappearing for a while in the smoke of shell-bursts, falling into shell-craters and scrambling out again, dodging this way or that as the shriek of a shell warned them of its near approach, flinging themselves down to avoid the flying splinters, but always managing to keep in touch with each other, until at last they reached the top of the slope and sprang down into the German trenches. Some, however, did not do so, but ran along the parapets of the trenches, hurling bombs amongst their occupants as they ran.

An advanced dressing-station. A Red Cross flag is affixed to the tree.

Cavalry on the march.

For a time the fighting was fierce, but two other waves of our men pushed gallantly forward through the German barrage to the support of their comrades; and in half an hour all resistance was at end, and almost the last of the defences which barred our way to the southern entrance of the village-fortress was in our hands.

There were many thrilling incidents in the struggle in the trenches, and several deeds of great individual gallantry were performed by our troops. One stretch of trench on the right was held by Prussian Guards, who had stored a great quantity of bombs there, with which they defended themselves desperately and threatened to hold up the attack in this quarter. But a company-officer of the Worcesters, seizing a rifle, brought down five of them in quick succession, although while he was firing he was in imminent risk of being blown to pieces by the grenades which the enemy were hurling at him. At the same time, a sergeant ran along the outside of the trench, bombing its occupants most effectively, and a young machine-gunner fixed his Lewis gun on the parapet and poured down a stream of bullets upon the Prussians. This obliged them to seek cover, and soon the trenches on either side of them were carried, and they were surrounded and obliged to surrender.

On the left, where the Wiltshires attacked, there was some fierce bayonet fighting and bombing, on ground already thickly strewn with the enemy's dead, killed by our bombardment. Our men were much

Ammunition pack-horses going up to the front during the battle of the 15th of Sepetmber.

annoyed by snipers concealed in shell-holes, until a sergeant coolly walked out into the open and shot no fewer than twelve of them. Here, as on the right, the Prussian Guards fought with great courage and only surrendered when further resistance was hopeless. It was remarked that the equipment of both officers and men was brand new, which showed that they had only just been sent into the trenches.

The enemy's barrage between our trenches and the ground just gained still continued, so that the passage of the wounded and prisoners to the rear was a most hazardous undertaking. Nevertheless, a number of our lightly wounded men did not hesitate to run the gauntlet of fire in order to get their injuries attended to, and, what is more, succeeded in accomplishing it in safety, though some of them experienced almost miraculous escapes.

" It was with a sense of horrible fascination," writes Mr. Philip Gibbs, " that I watched the adventures of these men, separately. One of them would jump down from the sky-line, and come at a quick run down the slope. Then suddenly he would stop and stand in an indecisive way, as though wondering what route to take to avoid the clusters of shell-bursts spurting up below him. He would decide sometimes on a circuitous route, and start running again in a zigzag way, altering his direction sharply when a shell crashed close to him. I could see that he was out of breath. He would halt and stand as though listening to the tumult about him, then come on very slowly. I wanted to call out to him, ' This way, old man ! . . . Quick ! ' But no voice would have carried through that world in uproar. Then perhaps he would stumble and fall, and lie as though dead. But presently I would see him crawl on to hands and knees, stand up, run again. He would reach our line of trenches and jump down, or fling himself down. Some cover at last, thank God! So it happened with man after man, and each journey was the adventure of a man trying to dodge death. It was horrible to see."

Much heavy fighting took place during the night and early hours of the morning on the northern and eastern edges of Delville Wood, in which some fine work was accomplished by English and Scottish battalions. A hurricane bombardment by our guns which preceded the advance of these troops was countered by an intense barrage from the enemy. But our men, pushing forward with unflinching courage, advanced our line several hundred yards and captured nearly 300 prisoners and several machine-guns.

The hottest work was on the eastern edge of the wood, where fighting went on without intermission for twelve hours. The enemy in this quarter had constructed their defences with considerable ingenuity, old gun-emplacements and dug-outs being connected by deep trenches, so as to form a very formidable

Cavalry on the march near the Somme.

line. The strong points were only carried after desperate fighting, the defenders having been stimulated or bullied to the most stubborn resistance. Sentries were even found tied to their posts, and, one, forcibly faithful to the death, was headless when our troops reached his trench. There were many fierce bombing duels, in one of which one of our sergeants caught German bombs before they burst and flung them back again. A feature of the fighting was the effective manner in which our men used their machine-guns to silence those of the enemy; and the employment of these murderous weapons as engines of attack has seldom been more cleverly exploited. "The deed that perhaps stands out most conspicuously," writes Mr. Beach Thomas, "is the duel one of our machine-gunners fought against an emplaced gunner of the enemy. He was the last of his group, but had managed to wriggle forward within twenty yards or so of the strong point they were attacking, and there secure cover in a shell-hole. From this hole he engaged in single combat with the German, and knocked him out just as his ammunition began to fail. Another isolated gunner, whose drums were exhausted, managed to save his gun and carry it back for more ammunition." The expenditure of machine-gun ammunition on this occasion was enormous. On the northern edge of the wood alone, where the enemy trenches were "watered" by continuous streams of bullets, nearly a million are said to have been fired.

A British graveyard, a smashed railway track, German ammunition left in their retreat, and a transport wagon going up to the front line.

Battlefield signposts.

View of Thiépval.

During the 25th we joined up, on our extreme right, with the French, who had made important progress the previous day through Maurepas; while south of Thiépval further ground was gained by means of bombing attacks.

In the course of the day our aeroplanes carried out two bombing raids against some of the principal railway-sidings on the German lines of communication. Several trains were hit and considerable damage caused to the enemy's rolling-stock. Other points of military importance were also bombed. Hostile aeroplanes generally avoided combat, but there were, nevertheless, a number of engagements, in which several of the enemy's machines were damaged and driven down. One of our own machines was brought down by gunfire.

About seven o'clock that evening the German guns began a heavy bombardment of our first-line trenches

A broken-down ambulance on the battlefield.

along the greater portion of our front south of the Ancre, which continued at intervals until early the following morning. Under cover of their artillery fire the enemy attacked our positions west of Guillemont, between the quarries and the Montauban–Guillemont road; but at no point did they succeed in reaching our lines, and were repulsed with loss.

But the heaviest shelling and the fiercest fighting took place at the other extremity of the battle-line, in the Thiépval sector, where the enemy had lately been effecting a great concentration of guns of every calibre to oppose our progress and to support their counter-attacks. About 7 p.m. this mass of artillery concentrated a terrific fire upon our new trenches south of the village, which continued for half an hour, when picked troops of the Prussian Guard were launched to the attack. The finest troops in the Kaiser's armies, however, could make no impression on the steadfastness of the defence. The Prussian Guards are good, but not good enough—not equal to the stuff of which the Wiltshires and Worcesters are composed.

They were worn out, these English lads. They had charged and fought and dug until every fibre in their bodies craved for rest. And they had just been mercilessly hammered. But the English county regiments have an even greater reputation in defence than in attack, and can always be relied upon to " stick it out," no matter how heavy the odds against them. They " stuck it out " now with dogged gallantry, and, though the attack was pressed with the utmost determination, it was everywhere repulsed, with heavy loss to the enemy. Seldom was the motto, " What we have we hold," better observed. The stand that evening was, if it be possible, an even finer achievement than the charge on the preceding day, and well deserved the tribute paid to it in the official communiqué of August 26th :—

" The success of our defence is largely due to the steadiness and determined gallantry of Wiltshire and

A view in Delville Wood.

Worcestershire men, who, in spite of being subjected to a very heavy bombardment, steadily maintained their positions and repulsed the determined assault of the enemy."

Just before the Prussian Guard advanced to the attack, and while the enemy's bombardment was at its height, one of the most remarkable incidents in the war occurred. A runner, one of several, it would appear, who had heroically endeavoured to make their way through the tremendous barrage which the German artillery was maintaining between our newly-won trenches and our old line, only to perish in the attempt, was sent back with an important message. He passed through the first stage of the ordeal unscathed, delivered his message, and started on his return journey. But in the brief space which had elapsed since he last passed over the ground shells had fallen in such profusion that the landscape was quite changed, and old trenches which had served him as signposts were battered into confusing pits and paths. The result was that he lost his sense of direction, and stumbled about amid the smoke and the shell-craters, until at last he came upon a trench which, to his amazement, he found to be occupied, not by his own comrades, but by the enemy—tall Prussian Guards, crowded together under a frieze of bayonet, evidently

View of Flers.

View of Flers: The main street.

One of the roads of Flers.

Taking up boarding for bottom of trenches.

awaiting the signal for the assault. Happily, he contrived to get away unobserved and to reach our own trenches in safety. Not a moment was lost in reporting his experience to our artillery, and " in three shakes," as an officer of the Wiltshires expressed it, " our heavies were smashing the German lines to glory."

CHAPTER VIII

THE same night we resumed offensive operations in the vicinity of Mouquet Farm, and made further progress, both on the east side of the farmstead and also to the south-west, where we captured another

Red Cross men carrying wounded over the top of the trench in Thiépval village.

400 yards of the enemy's trenches along the Courcelette–Thiépval road. On the northern part of our line we exploded two mines opposite Auchy and occupied the craters.

On the 26th fighting continued round Mouquet Farm, while in the evening we nibbled off a further slice of the enemy's line north of Bazentin-le-Petit ; but on the rest of the front hostilities were mainly confined to the artillery. The Germans bombarded Mametz Wood and Delville Wood, and were also very active in the Ypres salient and other northern sectors. The British artillery retaliated vigorously, and our counter-batteries engaged many of the enemy's gun positions, some of which were destroyed and others damaged.

Throughout the day our aircraft were very aggressive and carried out a number of attacks on points of military importance behind the enemy's lines, dropping in all about five tons of bombs. A hostile machine was brought down, and at least one other forced to descend in a damaged condition. In the evening eight of our aeroplanes were overtaken by a heavy storm, and five of them did not return to our lines.

Bad weather interfered to some extent with our operations during the next twenty-four hours, but we gained ground north-west of Ginchy. There was a good deal of heavy shelling by both sides, the enemy's fire south of the Ancre being directed mainly against our support-trenches, more especially north of Longueval, while further north the Germans bombarded Béthune. Our guns retaliated on railway-stations and barracks used by the enemy, some of whose bomb-stores were blown up by our fire. There was considerable subterranean activity on the Flanders front, both sides exploding mines.

The weather was again unfavourable on the 28th, but, in spite of this, we made some progress east of Delville Wood and carried out some minor successful enterprises in the neighbourhood of Mouquet Farm. The artillery, however, continued to hold the centre of the stage, and our long-range guns made matters very unpleasant indeed for the enemy's troops and traffic in various places between Bapaume and Mirau-

Comfort! An officer's dug-out, with his washing-stand and his bedding out to air or dry.

mont; while the German guns, which had shelled Delville Wood and our trenches north of Pozières heavily during the night, devoted most of their attention to the ground between Pozières and Thiépval Wood. Several aeroplane encounters took place, and four of the enemy's machines were accounted for, two being destroyed and two badly damaged. Two of our machines were reported missing.

During the night and the early part of the following day we captured a German barricade between Delville Wood and High Wood, and there was some bombing among the shell-craters on the way to Ginchy, which resulted in our strengthening our hold on the ground between that village and the western outskirts of Guillemont. South-east of Thiépval we also made progress. During the afternoon violent storms, accompanied by claps of thunder which completely drowned the sound of the guns, converted the battle-field into a swamp and practically suspended operations.

In his report on the 29th Sir Douglas Haig stated that since July 1st the British had captured 266 officers, 15,203 other ranks, 86 guns and 160 machine-guns, besides other war material.

Australians cheer the King.

A model place for watering horses.

During the night two half-hearted attempts by the enemy to advance against our trenches in the vicinity of Guillemont were easily frustrated by our fire. A patrol of Australians entered and reconnoitred what remained of Mouquet Farm—a few rubbish-heaps among the shell-craters—and captured some prisoners, but most of the Germans were shot down by their own comrades' machine-guns as they were being brought back to the British lines. Near Neuville St. Vaast we carried out a successful raid on the enemy's trenches.

On the 30th, in spite of adverse weather conditions, there was a good deal of activity between the Ancre and the Somme, and south of Martinpuich we extended our lines and captured 2 officers and 124 men belonging to a Bavarian regiment. The Bavarians occupied a trench, known as the "Intermediate Trench," about 300 yards long, though, notwithstanding its imposing name, it was really only a muddy

A few plum-puddings that Fritz will soon receive : Trench-mortar ammunition.

ditch, which afforded them but scant protection. Our machine-guns enfiladed it, and the artillery put a barrage behind it, thus cutting off all hope of escape, and soon a white flag fluttered up; and, with this emblem in his hand, a tall officer came over to our lines and offered to surrender. His offer was accepted, and the defenders came trooping out. They were in a woeful plight, covered with mud, drenched to the skin and half-starved, and appeared only too thankful to have done with the intolerable hardships which they had been suffering.

On the 31st we discharged gas against the enemy's trenches over a broad front near Arras, and also near Armentières, in both instances with satisfactory results. South of the Ancre, with the exception of an attempted attack upon our trenches in the vicinity of High Wood, which did not develop, owing to our machine-gun fire, nothing of importance occurred during the day. But during the evening the Germans delivered a series of determined counter-attacks against our trenches between Ginchy and High Wood, on a front of some 3,000 yards. These counter-attacks were preceded by an intense bombardment on the front assailed and on each side of it, and were made in considerable force   In all, five were delivered, four of which were completely repulsed, while at the fifth attempt the enemy only succeeded in penetrating two small sections of our advanced trench line. In these assaults, the Germans, in addition to being met everywhere with a withering rifle-fire, came at various places under a concentrated fire from our trench-mortars and massed machine-guns, and at others were very heavily shelled by our artillery while in close formation; and their casualties were very severe.

September 1st was marked by considerable artillery activity on the northern part of our line, and from the Ypres salient we discharged gas against the enemy's trenches with considerable effect. Between the Ancre and the Somme the day was uneventful.

Travelling water-butts.

During the night we successfully bombed the enemy out of the small area which they had just re-captured at so high a price, and re-established our line.

The 2nd dawned with a cloudless sky, and the ruined villages and shattered woods along the battle-front were once more bathed in sunshine. It was an ideal day for the gunners, and they made the most of it. Guided admirably by our flying-men, our great guns pounded the German positions hour after hour, their heaviest fire being directed upon the enemy's lines between Thiépval and High Wood, whence great columns of smoke and earth were continually ascending into the air. The Germans, though, owing to the inferiority of their airmen, they were for the most part constrained to fire by the map, retaliated vigorously, particularly upon the ground between Mametz Wood and the Bazentins, and discharged a great quantity of gas-shells; but our bombardment was unmistakably the heavier, as well as the better directed.

With the exception of a few bombing encounters, no infantry action took place that day; but on the 3rd another important forward movement was undertaken and carried out with splendid success.

Transport men cleaning their harness at a pond after the wet weather.

Infantry waiting to advance on the 25th of September.

On the left, we attacked the German lines north and south of the Ancre and captured Mouquet Farm and a considerable section of ground to the east of it. On the right, in conjunction with the French, who, advancing in irresistible fashion from the south, linked up with us near Angle Wood, we captured Guillemont, with the ground to the north of it running into Ginchy, the last real point of observation possessed by the enemy on the ridge we had set out to conquer. With the capture of Guillemont and of the ground beyond it, the whole of the German second line, which we had broken in parts on the great day of July 14th, passed into our hands.

The northern and southern attacks were not delivered simultaneously, the former being launched about 5 a.m., while the latter did not begin until nine o'clock. Both were preceded by an artillery preparation which continued for several hours, and the violence of which baffles all description. One quite small section of trench in the Guillemont area was bombarded with the following varieties of shell: 15-inch, 12-inch, 8-inch and 6-inch, to say nothing of smaller species, which followed one another in a

Waiting to attack on the 25th of September.

ceaseless stream for upwards of an hour. As the biggest of these projectiles weighs something like 1,400 lbs., the weight of metal and explosive lavished there may be imagined.

On the left, our attack was delivered just as the first faint glimmer of the dawn had lightened the sky. All along the line, extending for some distance on both sides of the Ancre, our men reached the German trenches, which had been battered into shapeless ruin by our bombardment and were full of dead, with comparatively few casualties. South of the river English troops forced their way into and through the enemy's first and second lines, bayoneting all the Germans who tried to oppose them and clearing the ground of snipers and hidden machine-guns. But they were fiercely enfiladed by other machine-guns from across the river, while a mass of artillery was quickly concentrated upon them. They held on with stubborn courage to the ground they had won, and checked and severely punished a determined German counter-attack. But the shell-fire was too heavy for mortal man to endure, and they were forced to withdraw to our original line.

The Australians, in their advance against Mouquet Farm, which was held by the 1st Regiment of the Prussian Guard Reserve, were more fortunate. They knew the position well, having already, it will be remembered, penetrated the ruins of the farm by a strong patrol, and they were confident of success.

It proved, however, a more formidable undertaking than perhaps they had bargained for. They had to scramble over some 200 yards of ground which constant bombardments had transformed into a mass of shell-holes, some of them so full of mud and water that when they plunged in, it reached to their arm-pits and they had hard work to extricate themselves; and, when they had successfully negotiated these obstacles, to drive the enemy, not out of trenches, since these had been long obliterated, but from lines of shell-craters, where machine-guns had been fixed and bombs stored.

It was a task of extraordinary difficulty, and the fighting quickly resolved itself into a series of separate encounters between small parties of Australians and small parties of Prussians, and sometimes into duels between men who bombed or sniped one another from the cover of craters. But eventually, after a stubborn conflict, the men from Overseas got the better of their antagonists, and, pushing forward,

A scene of desolation : once a village.

captured the farm, or rather the site where it had once stood, and advanced over 200 yards beyond it, when they started to consolidate the ground they had won and held on grimly, despite a severe " strafing " from the enemy's artillery.

It was on the south, however, that our most important successes were gained. Here Guillemont, which had been converted into a fortress as strong as any yet built by German engineers, with a chain of dug-outs so deep and so solidly constructed that many of them had defied even our heaviest shells stretching along the southern side of what had once been a village, was stormed in magnificent style. The Irish —Munsters, Dublins, and Irish Fusiliers—who attacked on the left and in the centre, were the heroes of the occasion. On the signal to advance being given, they dashed forward, with their pipes playing them on, in a headlong, irresistible rush, and even if the Germans opposed to them had been three times as numerous as they were, the result would have been the same. The English troops who fought on their

A bombing party off to the attack.

View of Morval, which we captured on the 25th of September.

right declared that they had never seen anything like that Irish charge. " It was like a human avalanche," said one of them. On they rushed, cheering wildly, straight through the tremendous barrage of the German artillery, stormed the first, second, and third lines of the enemy's trenches, sweeping away all resistance, and never halted until they had advanced some distance beyond the village.

It was an astonishing feat of arms, its only fault being that the rapidity of their advance prevented the Irishmen from safeguarding the ground behind them, and from some of the German dug-outs which they had neglected to clear men emerged as soon as the Irish whirlwind had passed over their heads and began sniping our gallant fellows from the rear. Happily, they were unable to do much mischief, as the colonel of an English battalion which was advancing on the right promptly diverted several platoons

General view of Morval, which we captured on the 25th of September.

in their direction, which soon accounted for the Germans who had ventured above ground and routed their compatriots out of their hiding-places.

These English lads on the right showed, in a different way, courage as splendid as their Irish comrades, and when a short halt was called to wait for the barrage of our guns to lift, lighted their cigarettes and began smoking calmly, with shells bursting all about them ; and then went forward again with their rifles slung, as though marching on a field-day.

After the dug-outs in Guillemont had been cleared of the enemy and our supports had come up, the British troops advanced their line to a sunken road some 500 yards beyond the village, the farther bank of which they proceeded to " organize," so as to obtain some cover from the heavy fire which the German artillery very quickly opened on the captured position. They did not succeed, however, in holding their ground, except at the cost of a good many casualties, and just before they were relieved and sent back to the support-lines six men were killed in a heap by a single shell. These poor fellows were buried a little later by a gallant corporal of their battalion, who volunteered to go back for the purpose, and went under heavy shell-fire to perform this last service for his comrades.

The success of our attack on Guillemont was mainly due to the effect of our shell-fire upon the defenders, for not only did it work frightful havoc amongst them, but demoralized the majority of the survivors to such a degree that they were too dazed and exhausted to offer any effective resistance, and when our infantry advanced, they encountered but little machine-gun fire. In the village and all the approaches to it the dead lay everywhere, and the sunken road was in places almost impassable, owing to the bodies which littered it. Many of them were quite naked, all their clothes having been stripped off by the blasting force of high explosives. Some must have been robbed of life, not by any metal fragment, but by the enormous concussion of the air, for there was no sign of a wound upon them.

"Those who were given the work of clearing the subterranean parts of the village," writes Mr. Beach Thomas "found yet more indelible proofs of the power of explosives. Heavy concrete roofings were broken through by our shells. One ample dug-out could scarcely be entered for the number of bodies. It contained forty-three men. All but three were dead. One only was unwounded; and he—shattered in nerve and pitifully obsequious for his life—insisted on handing up a succession of trophies and souvenirs taken from his dead companions. Imagine this lifted pair of hands, offering from the black steps of the tomb, and through the swarms of flies and the reek of battle, all this store of pilfered gewgaws and homely toys!"

The entrance of a captured German dug-out.

Of the German garrison of 2,000 men hardly any appear to have escaped, those who were not killed or wounded falling into our hands. Nearly all the prisoners, who numbered some 600, were in a pitiable condition, as, owing to the violence of our bombardment, no rations had reached them for three days, and they were weak with hunger. The spirit not only of the majority of the men, but even of some of their officers, appeared to be utterly broken; and in one place two of them clung about the necks of our own officers, crying for mercy; while in another a German officer fell on his knees, with bowed head and uplifted hands, in an attitude of prayer.

Ruins of Combles.

View of Combles.

Meanwhile, on our extreme right, near our point of junction with the French, obstinate fighting had been in progress for the possession of Falfemont Farm and a little solitary copse of naked trees called Wedge Wood, which were connected by a strongly organized system of earth defences. Here our advance was held up, or rather we were obliged to settle down to a slow bombing attack up trenches on either side; and it was not until late in the afternoon that we made any substantial progress.

At noon the left wing of our southern attack, moving eastwards at a slight angle to the troops who were storming Guillemont, penetrated into Ginchy, and at one time practically the whole of the village was in our hands. But, owing to fierce artillery-fire and heavy counter-attacks, we were compelled to

Some of the large ammunition left when the Huns had to clear out of Morval.

fall back, though we retained our hold on part of the village, and during the night repulsed several determined assaults on our new position.

Throughout the battle our aircraft rendered splendid service in co-operation with our artillery and infantry. The enemy's aeroplanes showed great activity, and fighting in the air was continuous. Our airmen, however, easily asserted their superiority, and the Germans were forced to remain some miles in rear of their own line, and their efforts to interrupt aerial observation failed entirely. As the result of the many combats which took place, three hostile machines were brought down, and many others were forced to descend in a damaged condition; while two British machines were reported missing. One of our aeroplanes destroyed a hostile kite-balloon, and on two occasions our aviators opened fire with their machine-guns on the enemy's troops on the ground.

Most of the shell-fire which our troops had to face during their advance came from heavy long-range guns, the enemy having withdrawn their field-batteries to a safer distance before our attack was delivered.

Prior to our advance, the Germans opened an intense bombardment of our trenches in Trônes Wood with " five-point-nines," which was maintained for many hours. " Some of our men behind the front lines," writes Mr. Philip Gibbs, " had escapes from death which seem like miracles. One young officer I know received an invitation to tea at a dug-out a few hundred yards, I reckon, from his own hole in the earth, where he lay with two comrades. It was a pleasant and friendly idea, that cup of tea, but he decided against it when he heard the awful crash of shells outside. Later, a message came that he must go on a matter of business. It was his duty to go, and so he went as fast as possible. A moment or two after reaching the other dug-out, there was the tinkle of a telephone-bell, and he heard that both his comrades had been killed by the direct hit of a five-point-nine. He went back with a soldier to see if there was any hope for his friends—one of them might be wounded only—and as he went a shell exploded a

One of the Boche gun-emplacements at Combles. Note the great baulks of timber.

yard or two away; the man by his side was killed, and his shoulder was splashed with the man's blood, but he was left unscathed."

On the morning of the 4th, the enemy delivered a counter-attack on our newly-won position in the vicinity of Mouquet Farm; but it was easily repulsed by the Australians. On our right, in the course of the afternoon, we captured Wedge Wood and gained ground to the north of Falfemont Farm. Two determined counter-attacks delivered by the Prussian Guard from Leuze Wood on the ridge above Falfemont Farm were broken up by our machine-gun fire.

During the night we made further important progress in the Guillemont area, and, despite stubborn resistance on the part of the enemy and an unceasing deluge of rain, which filled the shell-holes with water and greatly increased the difficulties of the advance, pushed forward some 1,500 yards east of the village and obtained a footing in Leuze Wood. Further south, after severe fighting, we captured the whole of the enemy's strong system of defence on a front of 1,000 yards in and around Falfemont Farm.

Combles: Main street.

View of Square at Combles

PART IX. WILL BE READY ON TUESDAY, JAN. 16TH, 1917.

IT CONTAINS THE FOLLOWING ILLUSTRATIONS:—

Clearing up a battlefield after an advance.
Laying a railroad as we advance.
Indian cavalry despatch riders.
Big guns ready to move up.
A mishap to a despatch rider's bike.
One of our many light railways.
Swinging a big gun round to haul up into position.
Taking up a big gun with a 12-horse team and the help of the gun crew.
How our artillery dealt with a German battery at Martinpuich.
Cab, Sir! Found in a captured village.
Moving day in a captured village.
A shelter made under the pontoons.
A light railway engine made out of the parts of a discarded motor car.

Taking up medical stores.
Motor machine guns taking cover in a sunken road.
A parade of the wounded walking cases.
A light railway taking up its own rails to lay as we advance.
The church bells of Montauben.
The military cemetery, showing the grave of Colonel Fuch's, of the Russian Imperial General Staff, who was killed recently while attached to the British Armies in France.
Where the British line joins up with the French.
The two batteries have a tug of war.
A South African at home.
The mail arrives.

A scene in one of the German trenches in front of Guillemont, showing the havoc wrought by the British bombardment.
Wounded men waiting to be taken away to the clearing station.
Transport men cleaning up their harness at a pond after the wet weather.
Stretcher-bearers on their way out near Guinchy to bring back the wounded.
Scene near Guillemont. An armoured motor car.
Scene on the battlefield near Courcelette.
How bad water is guarded.
A large German shell which did not explode. By the side of it is one of the smaller brand, commonly called a whizz-bang

ORDER FORM.

To M..
                                                                                              BOOKSELLER OR NEWSAGENT.

Please send me Part IX. and the following Parts as published of "SIR DOUGLAS HAIG'S GREAT PUSH," for which I enclose..............................

Name..

Address..

SCALA THEATRE,

(Goodge Street Tube Station).   CHARLOTTE STREET, W.

AT THE FRONT

OFFICIAL WAR OFFICE FILMS.

Kut Relief Forces.   Salonika.   Russian Army.   French Army.   East Africa.
The King on the Somme Battle Field, &c.

THE BATTLE OF THE SOMME.

"There is no programme in London which gives so complete and vivid a description of the War on ALL FRONTS."—*Evening News.*

THE KING'S ADVICE:

SEE THE SOMME WAR FILM AND WHAT WAR MEANS.

"The public should see these pictures, that they may have some idea of what the Army is doing, and what war means."

This statement was made by the King after witnessing a programme of the Official War Office film, "The Battle of the Somme," which was shown by command to the King and Queen at Windsor Castle.—*Daily Express.*

Box Office, 10 to 10.   DAILY, 3 and 8.   'Phone: Gerr. 1444 & 1366.

SCALA THEATRE.

FOR THE MEN WHO DO THINGS!

At the Headquarters of the Forces where the Campaign is planned and momentous questions decided, there is ceaseless activity, day and night. During the War great use has been made of Cocoa and Chocolate, the natural ingredients of which make them "A Perfect Food" which repels fatigue and adds largely to powers of endurance, both physical and mental.

CONTRACTORS TO H.M. NAVY AND ARMY.

Fry's Pure Breakfast Cocoa

PRINTED AT THE CHAPEL RIVER PRESS, KINGSTON-ON-THAMES.

IN ABOUT 12 FORTNIGHTLY PARTS.   HUTCHINSON'S NEW PART WORK   Part X. ready Jan. 30th. PART IX. 8d. NET

SIR DOUGLAS HAIG'S
GREAT PUSH

THE BATTLE OF THE SOMME

A popular, pictorial and authoritative work on one of the Greatest Battles in History, illustrated by about **700** *wonderful* **OFFICIAL PHOTOGRAPHS AND CINEMATOGRAPH FILMS** *and other authentic pictures*

BY ARRANGEMENT WITH THE WAR OFFICE

SEARCHING GERMAN PRISONERS

GREAT VALUE FOR EIGHTPENCE

THIS PART CONTAINS **33 WONDERFUL REPRODUCTIONS** OF THE FAMOUS **WAR OFFICE CINEMATOGRAPH FILMS** AND **OFFICIAL PHOTOGRAPHS** OF THE BATTLE OF THE SOMME, BEAUTIFULLY PRINTED ON THE BEST ENGLISH ART PAPER.

LONDON : HUTCHINSON & Co.

NOW IN PREPARATION.

The V.C. and D.S.O.

"THE V.C. AND D.S.O." will be a complete and authentic record of the men and deeds that have earned these distinctions since their foundation. It is being compiled from the official records, as published in the *London Gazette* and in the dispatches, supplemented, wherever possible, by contemporary accounts in the Press, and from letters written by Commanding Officers or others who had cognisance of the acts for which the honours were awarded.

The need for such a publication is obvious. The deeds which have won such recognition are the finest episodes in British military history, and their perpetuation, in as complete a form as possible, is the aim of the editors. The assistance and co-operation of all those directly interested, the holders of the honours themselves, or their immediate relatives, are earnestly requested to that end.

"THE V.C. AND D.S.O." will be not only a record of the deeds themselves, but will be a who's who of those who performed them, military and brief biographical details being included.

Publication will take place as soon as possible after the issue of the final awards on the termination of the War.

It is proposed to include a Regimental Index in which will appear under each regiment the number of V.C.'s and D.S.O.'s awarded.

Many portraits will be given, and in the case of subscribers, where a portrait, upon which no fee is payable to the photographer is supplied, the publishers guarantee to include it.

The work will be complete in two large handsome volumes, of which Volume I. will be issued shortly, and Volume II. at the end of hostilities—as soon as possible after the final list of honours in connection with the War has been gazetted.

The price of the set of two volumes of the ordinary edition will be Two Guineas net. There will also be a special edition (limited to 200 copies numbered and signed) richly bound, price Five Guineas net. Copies of this special edition will, where desired, be stamped with the Regimental Crest.

The first edition published will be for subscribers only, and orders limited to the number of one thousand will now be accepted.

The EDITOR of "The V.C. and D.S.O.," THE STANDARD ART BOOK Co. Ltd., 30-32, Ludgate Hill, E.C.

NOW IN PREPARATION.

The V.C. and M.C.

"THE V.C. AND M.C." will be a complete and authentic record of the men and deeds that have earned these distinctions since their foundation. It is being compiled from the official records, as published in the *London Gazette* and in the dispatches, supplemented, wherever possible, by contemporary accounts in the Press, and from letters written by Commanding Officers or others who had cognisance of the acts for which the honours were awarded.

The need for such a publication is obvious. The deeds which have won such recognition are the finest episodes in British military history, and their perpetuation, in as complete a form as possible, is the aim of the editors. The assistance and co-operation of all those directly interested, the holders of the honours themselves, or their immediate relatives, are earnestly requested to that end.

"THE V.C. AND M.C." will be not only a record of the deeds themselves, but will be a who's who of those who performed them, military and brief biographical details being included.

Publication will take place as soon as possible after the issue of the final awards on the termination of the War.

It is proposed to include a Regimental Index in which will appear under each regiment the number of V.C.'s and M.C.'s awarded.

Many portraits will be given, and in the case of subscribers, where a portrait, upon which no fee is payable to the photographer is supplied, the publishers guarantee to include it.

The work will be complete in two large handsome volumes, of which Volume I. will be issued shortly, and Volume II. at the end of hostilities—as soon as possible after the final list of honours in connection with the War has been gazetted.

The price of the set of two volumes of the ordinary edition will be Two Guineas net. There will also be a special edition (limited to 200 copies numbered and signed) richly bound, price Five Guineas net. Copies of this special edition will, where desired, be stamped with the Regimental Crest.

The first edition published will be for subscribers only, and orders limited to the number of one thousand will now be accepted.

The EDITOR of "The V.C. and M.C.," THE STANDARD ART BOOK Co. Ltd, 30-32, Ludgate Hill, E.C.

This latter success was in a great measure due to the pluck and initiative of West Country troops, who, when the attack which they had been ordered to make on Falfemont Farm from the south was checked by a withering machine-gun fire, worked their way westwards, and, joining other bodies of men advancing from the sunken road beyond Guillemont, crept round the slope of the ground that goes up to Leuze Wood and contrived to outflank the position.

On the 5th, despite heavy shelling from the German guns and indifferent weather conditions, we continued to push forward, and by the evening were in possession of the greater part of Leuze Wood, and of all the ground between Leuze Wood and Falfemont Farm and between the wood and Ginchy.

On the northern part of our line our artillery was very active, and bombarded the German positions in the vicinity of the Hohenzollern Redoubt, opposite Givenchy, and south of Neuve Chapelle, while our heavy guns effectively shelled the enemy's hutments in Polygon Wood, east of Ypres, which had been the scene of much desperate fighting during the great battle of October and November, 1914.

Clearing up a battlefield after an advance.

During the day our aeroplanes co-operated with their usual success with the artillery. One of our patrols, consisting of four machines, encountered and drove off a hostile patrol of thirteen aeroplanes.

During the night we drove the enemy from the small section of Leuze Wood to which he still clung, and by the morning the whole of the place was in our hands. Fighting continued throughout the day between the wood and Combles village and at Ginchy. The artillery of both sides was very active north of Pozières and in the neighbourhood of Mouquet Farm. A large party of Germans emerging from Courcelette was caught by our artillery fire and scattered, and, in addition, our guns dispersed a number of the enemy's working parties. In the afternoon portions of our front in the neighbourhood of Thiépval were heavily shelled. Further north we carried out a successful bombardment of the German lines north of Arras and between the La Bassée Canal and Richebourg l'Avoué.

The Royal Flying Corps was in a very aggressive mood. An important railway-junction on the enemy's lines of communication was bombed and great damage caused to the station and rolling-stock. Many other points of military importance were attacked, including an aerodrome, where our airmen destroyed a machine on the ground and damaged another. A number of combats in the air took place, which resulted in three hostile machines being wrecked and four others damaged; and some very useful work was done from low altitudes, locating the positions reached by our troops. Two of our machines failed to return to our lines.

At night the enemy made a heavy counter-attack against our position in Leuze Wood and, pressing forward with great courage and determination, succeeded in reaching our trenches. But, after fierce hand-to-hand fighting, the Germans were repulsed, leaving some twenty of their number prisoners in our hands, including two officers.

The 7th was marked by very heavy shelling by the artillery on both sides. Assisted by aerial observations, our counter-battery work was very effective between the Ancre and the Somme, and a number of the enemy's gun-emplacements were destroyed. East and south-east of Ginchy, in which fighting continued all day, our guns repeatedly dispersed the enemy's working-parties, and between Souchez and the La Bassée Canal our artillery and trench-mortars bombarded the German lines continuously. Our bombing aeroplanes attacked no fewer than ten of the enemy's aerodromes, upon which they inflicted considerable damage, and a British airman directed artillery-fire on a hostile machine which had landed behind its own

Laying a railroad as we advance.

lines, with the result that it was set on fire and destroyed. In the evening the enemy shelled Armentières, and during the night we successfully raided the German trenches south-east of Givenchy and near Richebourg l'Avoué, inflicting severe casualties.

During the night there was some sharp hand-to-hand fighting in High Wood, where we captured a trench, together with a score of prisoners belonging to a Bavarian battalion. The enemy's artillery shelled our trenches north of Pozières and in the neighbourhood of Mouquet Farm rather heavily, but a small hostile infantry attack in this sector was easily repulsed. A detachment of the enemy which attempted to advance from Courcelette was stopped by our fire. On the northern part of our front several successful raids were carried out.

Towards five o'clock in the afternoon of the 9th, after a severe bombardment of the enemy's positions, we resumed the offensive on a front of six thousand yards from High Wood to Leuze Wood and also north of Pozières. East of High Wood we advanced three hundred yards on a five hundred yards' front, while in the Pozières area we gained a further six hundred yards of German trench and inflicted heavy casualties on the enemy, who were caught by artillery fire while massing for a counter-attack.

Indian cavalry despatch-rider coming back from Flers.

Big guns ready to move up.

The Battle of the Somme

But the outstanding success of the day was the capture of Ginchy, the last observation post of high tactical value left to the enemy on our battle-front. As at Guillemont, the chief honours of the fighting rested with the Irish, who charged northwards against the western half of the village.

Since their brilliant feat of arms on the 4th the Irish had been experiencing a very hard time, and had lain for five days under heavy shell-fire, without sleep or hot food, and with a very inadequate supply of water. But the hour of the assault found their spirit unbroken, and every man eager to get to grips with the enemy once more.

Over the parapet they went in four waves, in open order, with about fifty yards between each wave, and with shouts of " Go on, Munsters ! " " Go on, Dublins ! " " Now then, Irish Rifles ! " pushed across

A mishap to a despatch-rider's bike.

the six hundred yards of No Man's Land at such a pace that in eight minutes from the start the troops on the left had carried the first German trenches and dug-outs.

On the right, the Irish were held up by a trio of well-placed machine-guns which swept the ground with a perfect squall of bullets, beneath which many brave fellows dropped, while, at the same time, they were being industriously sniped by marksmen who had crept out into shell-craters. But, happily, a party of our men, by a really brilliant little piece of tactical work, executed an encircling movement which obliged the German gun-teams to retire hurriedly to some battered trenches three hundred yards in the rear, where they presented an easy target to the trench-mortars attached to one of the Irish battalions, and were very quickly knocked out. This enabled the right wing to advance and link up with the left, and they then pushed on together through the village, the Irish Rifles being left to hold the ground that had been won, while their comrades dashed forward.

Near the centre of the village, cunningly concealed amid the ruins of an old farm, was another machine-gun, which was served with deadly accuracy. But again the situation was saved by the trench-mortar men, whose little engines directed a storm of high explosives upon the farm, which speedily disposed of both gun and gunners.

The northern half of the village was full of snipers and ordinary riflemen concealed in all manner of places. Here the Germans had built concreted and tunnelled chambers, with loopholes level with the ground, and through these they kept up a sharp fire. But the Irish addressed themselves to the task of routing out the enemy from their hiding-places both above and below ground with fierce energy and a reckless disregard of danger; and, though there was some savage hand-to-hand fighting amid the shell-craters and down in the dug-outs, where many Germans—Bavarians of the 19th Division—resisted until the bayonet did its deadly work, it was soon over. Indeed, within ten minutes of entering the village the Dublins had reached the northern end of the place, and their patrols were feeling out into the open country beyond.

The situation of the victorious Irishmen was, however, a critical one, for so rapid had been their

One of our many light railways.

advance, that the troops attacking between Ginchy and Delville Wood, who had to make their way over very difficult ground, had been unable to keep pace with them. In consequence, their left flank was "in the air," open and undefended, and disaster might easily have followed, had not a young sapper officer from Dublin, who came up in one of the later waves, perceived the danger. Without the loss of a moment he set about collecting men, who only just in time got a trench dug at the threatened spot towards Delville Wood.

The position on the extreme right was for a time equally perilous, as the troops who were to have supported that flank had also not yet made good their ground; and the achievement of the Irish Brigade of capturing a hostile front of nine hundred yards to the depth of nearly a mile with no supporting troops on either flank is one which it would be difficult to praise too highly. It was a feat of arms which deserves to be told not in bare prose, but in heroic verse, for it must be borne in mind that the splendid fellows who charged like a whirlwind through Ginchy were not fresh troops, but men who had been in the fighting-line for many days, and whose powers of endurance had been subjected to the severest possible test.

Swinging a big gun round to haul up into position.

Taking up a big gun with a twelve-horse team and the help of the gun crew.

"When they came out of the battle this morning," writes Mr. Philip Gibbs, in a despatch to the *Daily Chronicle* dated September 10th, "they were weary and spent, and they had left many good comrades behind them; but the spirit of war sustained them, and they came marching steadily with their heads held high. It was one of the most moving things I have ever seen in this war.

"A great painter would have found here a subject to thrill his soul, that long trail of Irish regiments, some of them reduced by their losses, and with but few officers to lead them, coming across a stretch of barren country strewn with the wreckage of two years' bombardment, and crowded with the turmoil of the present fighting. Behind them arose the black curtain of smoke across the battlefield, through which there came the enormous noise of the unending gun-fire, and around them were some of our own batteries hard at work with great hammer strokes, as their shells went on their way to the enemy's lines;

How our artillery dealt with a German battery at Martinpuich.

but ahead of them walked an Irish piper, playing them home to the harvest fields of peace with a lament for those who will never come back.

"A Brigadier came riding over the fields to meet them. It was the first time he had seen them together since the early dawn of to-day, when they were still fighting beyond the ruins of Ginchy. He stood, a solitary figure, by the side of the track down which his men came, and there was a great tenderness in the eyes of this Brigadier as he watched them pass and called out to them—words of thanks and words of good cheer, and turned to me now and then to say how splendid they had been.

"'Eyes right!' shouted the officers or sergeants who were leading their companies, and the General said, 'Carry on there,' and 'Well done—you did gloriously!' 'Bravo, Dublins!... You did well, damned well, Munsters, my lads!'

"The men's eyes brightened at the sight of him, and they squared up and grinned under German caps and German helmets.

"'Hullo, Greene!' called out the Brigadier to a very tall fellow tramping in the outside file. 'Glad to see you're all right. And a big target, too!'

"The music of the Irish pipes went cutting down the valley, and I watched the men out of sight with something stirring at my heart."

A few of the Irish were veterans who had served during the early months of the war, and two of the Munsters who had fallen had fought all through it from Mons. Many had been in Gallipoli, and one of them declared that the taking of Ginchy was the "hottest" thing he had seen since the Suvla Bay fighting in August, 1915. But whether old Regulars or men of the New Army, all alike had borne themselves like paladins.

Among many stories which might be related to show the fighting spirit of these Irish troops is that of

"Cab, sir!" Found in a captured village.

three servants of the Brigade Staff, who, to their profound chagrin, had been prevented by their duties from taking part in the capture of Guillemont. They were determined, however, that come what might, they would not be left out at Ginchy, and, since there seemed but little chance of them being granted permission to join the fighting-line, they took French leave. One of them, before taking his departure for the trenches, left the following note on his master's table: "As I could not be at Guillemont, I am going to Ginchy. I hope to be back again, so please excuse."

Ginchy had proved a hard nut to crack. The defences were of surprising strength, when we consider the colossal weight of metal and explosive that fell on the village, and the garrison had been so abundantly furnished with provisions, even to comparative luxuries like bottles of ginger-beer and stores of fruit, that the difficulty of bringing up fresh supplies created by our bombardment did not entail any serious shortage of food, as had been the case at Guillemont. A great number of heavy guns, too, had been

Moving-day in a captured village.

A scene on the battlefield near Ginchy.

massed behind the village, and every piece of ground that our troops gained in their advance upon the place had to be consolidated in the face of a violent bombardment.

All this showed the great importance which the Germans attached to the possession of the village, and a further proof was afforded by the fierceness and determination of the counter-attacks launched against our new positions. In one of these the enemy succeeded in reaching our trenches, but, after furious hand-to-hand fighting, they were beaten back, leaving four officers and over one hundred men prisoners in our hands.

Throughout the fighting, both in the Ginchy area and further north, our airmen rendered most valuable service, closely following the progress of our attacks and at times swooping down and opening

A light railway engine made out of the parts of a discarded motor-car.

fire on the enemy with their machine-guns. Many aerial combats took place, in which three German machines were destroyed and others driven down in a damaged condition.

It may here be observed that, to judge from letters found on German prisoners, comparison of the rival air services, very much to the disadvantage of their own, appears to be a common subject of talk in the enemy's trenches. "The airmen," writes one German, "sit covered with medals in the best restaurants and grow fat; but, as for flying, they never think of going near Mr. Englishman." "The Englishmen," says another, "come so low you have to take care the propeller doesn't hit your head." "You can't move by day, or they see you, and perhaps shoot at you." "Some day they'll come and take us out by the scruff of the neck." "Our hero airmen are never to be seen," and so forth. The writers are, of course, very unfair to their own men; but there can be no question that the loss of the offensive in the air has supremely depressed the German Army and increased its reluctant admiration for the British and French aviators.

In his reports on September 10th, Sir Douglas Haig stated that "the results of the heavy fighting during the past week had been that our line had been advanced on a front of six thousand yards to a depth varying from three hundred to three thousand yards, and that heavy losses had been inflicted on the enemy." "The spirit and dash of our troops," he added, "during this severe fighting, in face of frequent determined counter-attacks and constant intense artillery fire, have been magnificent." And, after paying tribute to the dashing gallantry of the Irish at Guillemont and Ginchy, he reported that splendid work had also been performed by " some of our rifle regiments and regiments from Warwickshire, Kent, Devonshire, Gloucestershire, Surrey, Cornwall, Wales and Scotland."

For several days after the capture of Ginchy hostilities were chiefly confined to the guns, the only infantry fighting of importance being an attack by the enemy on our trenches near Mouquet Farm on

Taking up medical stores.

the night of the 12th–13th, which was repulsed with considerable loss to the assailants. Two nights later we resumed the offensive south-east of Thiépval, and carried the German trenches on a front of 1,000 yards, including a strongly-defended locality known as the Wunder Werk.

This successful movement preceded by only a few hours the most important British advance since the beginning of the Great Push. For at 6.20 a.m. on the morning of the 15th our troops took the offensive along a front of six miles from the Pozières–Bapaume road to Leuze Wood, and with such brilliant success that by nightfall we had penetrated the German third line at some places to a depth of one and three quarter miles, captured most of the Bouleaux Wood, Flers, High Wood, Martinpuich and Courcelette, and over 2,300 prisoners, including sixty-five officers, of whom six were battalion commanders.

"The task that was set our troops yesterday," writes Mr Philip Gibbs, in his despatch of the 16th to the *Daily Chronicle*, "would have been formidable on the first day of a great offensive. Coming

Motor machine-guns taking cover in a sunken road.

A parade of the wounded walking cases.

after two and a half months, it was startling in its boldness, and showed that our generals had supreme confidence in the men, in their own powers of organization, and in the luck of battle that comes to those who have worked for it. The enemy believed that our offensive had petered out. There is much evidence for that. They did not believe it possible that an army of our size and strength could carry on the attack at the same fierce pace. They cherished the hope that our divisions were broken and spent, that our stores of ammunition were giving out, and that our men were overtired."

They were determined, however, to leave nothing to chance, determined that if the British still had the energy and the audacity to attempt a fresh important advance, they should have good cause to rue it. They had been digging furiously on dark nights to strengthen their third line of defence—the famous Flers line—which was, they thought, to be the boundary of our advancing tide. Their position was a most formidable one. It consisted, Sir Douglas Haig tells us, " of a treble line of entrenchments, con-

A light railway taking up its own rails to lay as we advance.

nected together by strong subsidiary trenches. In addition to this, the enemy was holding some advance positions with machine-guns, in trenches, works and shell-holes. Behind these fortifications, at a distance of some 7,000 yards from our front, he had recently constructed and wired a fourth line of trenches in front of the Le Transloy–Bapaume road."

These formidable defences were supported by more than one thousand guns of every calibre, and held in great force by some of the best troops in the German army. One part of High Wood alone was occupied by four companies of a Prussian regiment. A mine-crater, converted into a fortress, protected their left, a machine-gun redoubt their right, and wire and barricades their front. Eastwards by Ginchy, the Prussian Guards depended on a yet surer defence than either forts or wire. Between them and the British lay some half-mile of open country, and a little arsenal of machine-guns had been placed so as to sweep this area with a tornado of bullets.

Our brave fellows were well aware of the grim nature of the task which lay before them ; but they " went over " as dawn was breaking filled with the spirit of victory, and it was half the battle won.

Many of them "went over," too, in high good humour, laughing as they ran, being immensely encouraged by the sight of a new engine of war which was being tried with them for the first time.

"In this attack," wrote Sir Douglas Haig, "we employed for the first time a new type of heavily-armoured car, which has proved of considerable utility."

"Modern Germans," observes Mr. Garvin, "had been bred in the implicit conviction that they excelled all the world in technique, and, above all, in inventions applied to war. That was a cardinal dogma in the Teutonic cult of self-worship. The bottom was knocked out of it when the British mind, turning itself to war, produced a machine which, so far as effective war service on land is concerned, did more in one day than Zeppelins, poison-gas, flame-throwers, and all the devices of self-conscious and pretentious frightfulness have done in two years."

The secret of these moving fortresses mounted on caterpillar wheels had been most jealously guarded,

The church bells of Montauban.

and it was only a day or two before their services were to be requisitioned that it began to be whispered about. The official description of them, quoted above, is a dull one compared with all the rich and rare qualities that belonged to these extraordinary vehicles. In appearance they were monstrously comical, "like toads of vast size emerging from the primeval slime in the first twilight of the world's dawn," is the comparison of one special correspondent. "Those who inspected these saurians in their *al fresco* stalls beforehand," writes another, "or followed their lethargic course over impossible roads in the moonlight, gasped with humorous wonder at the prodigy. Munchausen never approached the stories imagined for them by the soldiers. Whales, boojums, dreadnoughts, slugs, snarks—never were creatures that so tempted the gift of nicknaming. But their pet name is Tanks, and they were chiefly regarded as a practical joke. They were said to live on trees and houses and to jump like grasshoppers or kangaroos."

They proved a most unpleasant kind of practical joke, so far as the Germans were concerned. With ludicrous serenity they wobbled across the gridiron fields, shrapnel, rifle and machine-gun bullets rebounding harmlessly from their iron sides like hailstones from the hide of an hippopotamus, for they

The military cemetery, showing the grave of Colonel Fuchs, of the Russian Imperial General Staff, who was killed recently while attached to the British armies in France.

Where the British line joins up with the French the two batteries have a tug-of-war.

were bomb-proof and bullet-proof, and could only be put out of action by the direct hit of a large shell. They trod down the barbed wire. They sat down on trenches and raked them right and left with their machine-guns. They pushed down walls and broken houses and barns, reared over the débris and crawled on. They went smashing through High Wood, the trees snapping like match-sticks before them, and knocked out nests and warrens of machine-guns in that quarter. They clanked through all obstruction into the main street of Flers, followed by cheering and laughing soldiers. And all the while they spat death amidst the enemy and created indescribable demoralization in their ranks. Indeed, until daylight revealed their true nature, many of the Germans appear to have regarded them with some sort of superstitious terror, and fled panic-stricken before them.

Space forbids us to recount more than one or two of the adventures of these monsters—adventures

A South African at home.

so amazing that they would seem hardly credible were they not vouched for by a score of witnesses. Two Tanks led the attack on Martinpuich, where, after the capture of the first line of trenches, our men were held up by machine-gun fire. The Tanks, however, recked nothing of bullets, and one, going on alone, went straight through the shells of broken barns and houses, straddled on top of a couple of German dug-outs and enfiladed the enemy mercilessly. From one of these dug-outs presently emerged a Bavarian lieutenant-colonel, with a white, frightened face, who held his hands very high in front of the Tank, shouting: "Kamerad! Kamerad!" "Well, come inside, then," said a voice in the belly of the beast, and from a hole, opening suddenly, a human hand came forth and grabbed the German officer, who for the rest of the day was carried about on the strangest journey ever man experienced.

A Tank also rendered splendid service at Courcelette. Just outside the south-east corner of the village stood the ruins of a sugar-factory, which the enemy had converted into a formidable redoubt with machine-gun emplacements. It was one of those deadly places which had cost the lives of so many of our men in other parts of the battle-ground now in our hands, and it seemed as if it would be impossible to capture it, except at the price of heavy casualties. But the Tank—" Crème de Menthe " was the name of this particular monster—came to the rescue. Forward it wobbled towards the factory, heedless of the stream of bullets which splashed its sides, and making for one of the broken walls, leaned up against it heavily, until it collapsed with a crash, when it mounted the bricks, passed over them and walked straight into the factory ruins. " From its sides," writes Mr. Philip Gibbs, " came flashes of fire and a hose of bullets, and then it trampled around over machine-gun emplacements, ' having a grand time,' as one of the men said with enthusiasm. It crushed the machine-guns under its heavy ribs, and killed

The mail arrives.

machine-gun teams with deadly fire. The infantry followed in, and then advanced again round the flanks of the monster."

Despite the assistance of the Tanks, the taking of Martinpuich and Courcelette, and of the approaches to them, was each in itself a great battle. The assault on Courcelette was hard and costly. Again and again our men came under withering machine-gun and rifle fire, for the Germans had dug new trenches, called the Fabeckgraben and the Zollerngraben, which had not been wiped out by our artillery, and they fought with courage and desperation. One machine-gun post was charged three times successively by three platoons. The first two were practically wiped out, but the third carried the position with an irresistible rush. It was not until six o'clock in the evening, after fighting had been in progress for twelve hours, that Courcelette was finally in our hands.

The struggle for Martinpuich was of a hardly less obstinate character. The outskirts of the village were carried early in the morning, but the storming of the main fortress was a most difficult undertaking, since the place was full of dug-outs and was manned by troops of the 2nd Bavarian Division, who had made a name for themselves long ago at the Hohenzollern Redoubt. They were in great force—probably

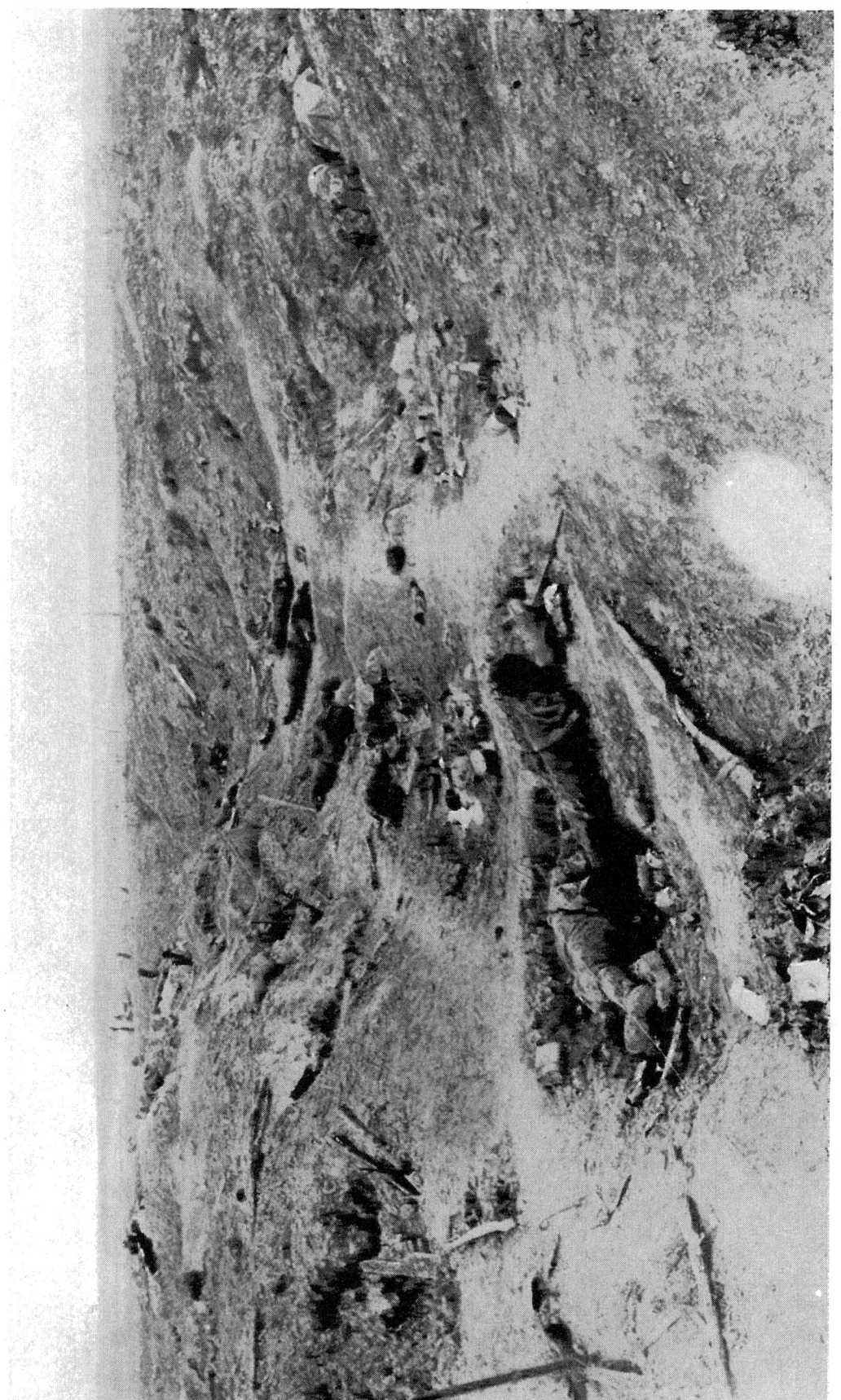

A scene in one of the German trenches in front of Guillemont, showing the havoc wrought by the British bombardment.

Wounded men waiting to be taken away to the clearing station.

preparing to attack—and they fought with a courage and obstinacy worthy of their reputation. It was late in the evening before the whole of Martinpuich was taken, and it was the crowning triumph of the day.

A young British soldier here had a most dreadful experience. A German crump killed a lance-corporal by his side and buried them both completely. Providentially, the steel helmet that the living man wore kept the earth from his face, and gave him a little air to breathe; and, after he had been in his terrible position for about half an hour, some of his comrades caught sight of the lance-corporal's leg sticking out of the earth and started to pull him out. The other managed to attract their attention, and they liberated him only just in time.

One of the finest feats of arms of that memorable day was performed by the Guards in the fighting

Cleaning a captured German machine-gun.

east of Flers, where they made the greatest attack even in their records. For the first time in the history of the Coldstreams three battalions of them charged in line, great solid waves of men, as fine a sight as the world could show. Behind them were the Grenadiers, and behind the Grenadiers the Irish Guards. They had to advance under the enfilading fire of massed machine-guns, but though many gaps were made in their ranks, they were speedily closed up, the wounded, instead of calling for help, cheering on those who swept past them, with shouts of " Go on, Lily Whites ! "—the old name of the Coldstreams—" Get at 'em, Lily Whites ! "

Through the scourge of bullets they dashed forward, carried two lines of trenches, though not until after some grim work with bomb and bayonet, and did not halt until they had advanced two thousand yards from their starting-point, and their right flank was " in the air," the troops on that side having been held up. Then they dug themselves in, or found what shelter they could in shell-craters, and held on doggedly to the ground they had won, despite a furious fire from the enemy's guns and repeated counter-attacks. Many of them had hairbreadth escapes during the terrible night which followed. One young officer of the Irish Guards lay in a shell-hole with two comrades, and then left them for a while to cheer up other men in surrounding craters. When he came back, he found his two friends dead, almost blown to pieces by a shell.

But whether Guards, Riflemen, or Linesmen, whether English, Irish, Scottish, or Welsh, or men from the Dominions, all alike did grand work and set an example of courage and endurance which the world can never excel. Transferred from the Ypres salient, Canadians had their chance at Courcelette and made splendid use of it. Australians and New Zealanders vied with the best of the Old Country's

Stretcher-bearers on their way out near Ginchy to bring back the wounded.

troops, as the South Africans had recently done, and the London battalions acquitted themselves right worthily. One of them, led most gallantly by their colonel, an old Territorial officer close upon sixty, carried two lines of the enemy's trenches with the bayonet, and held on to them with dogged tenacity under the fiercest shell-fire. Among ten machine-guns which these London lads captured was one the gunner in charge of which was "spotted" and shot dead by an officer, who was carrying a rifle, just as the German was beginning to sweep the ranks of our men. That rifle-shot must have saved many a Londoner's life.

The work of our artillery, both preceding and during the advance, was truly wonderful. In the intensity and accuracy of its fire it had never been surpassed. Every detail had been planned beforehand. Every "heavy" had its special objective and its own time-table, working exactly with the infantry, concentrating upon the enemy's trenches and *fortins*, throwing impenetrable curtains of fire

Scene near Guillemont: An armoured motor-car.

Scene on the battlefield near Courcelette.

across their lines of communication, following the progress of the Tanks, and, guided by our intrepid airmen, reaching out to distant targets. The field-batteries showed great dash and audacity in taking up new positions, and the gallantry and enterprise of the forward observing officers in making their way up to the high ground as soon as it had been occupied by our infantry, and registering their batteries for the new view-points, were beyond all praise.

Our airmen, too, were amazing, both in observation work and in attack. Throughout the day they kept up an active and successful co-operation with our artillery, and furnished frequent and accurate reports of the course of the battle. Fifteen hostile aeroplanes were destroyed and nine driven down in

Waiting their turn to advance.

a damaged condition; the enemy's artillery and infantry were frequently attacked by our aeroplanes with machine-gun fire and many bombing raids carried out against aerodromes and railway-stations.

"The battles in the air have never been equalled," writes Mr. Beach Thomas. "How many fights there were no one knows. . . . Village after village just behind the lines was bombed, and, to complete the work, the airmen came down low enough almost to stroke the backs of the Tanks, quite low enough to empty their bullet-drums at the enemy's infantry. The 'Archies' fired at them in vain, though, as it seemed to me, scores of our craft were perpetually rolling across the sky on ball-bearings of shrapnel cloud. From half an hour before dawn to sunset there was a continuous sky-patrol enemywards and a continuous chassé over our advancing troops and the enemy's batteries. Every headquarters that day rang with aircraft messages."

This splendid success was not achieved without heavy casualties; but if our losses were severe, those of the enemy were appalling. The whole field of our advance, over all its width and all its breadth, was simply littered with German dead. They lay everywhere—in the trenches, half buried in shell-holes, and in the open. One bit of trench, east of Ginchy, hardly forty yards long, contained forty bodies—a man to a yard. Outside Martinpuich, one hundred yards of trench had thirty or forty dead, and at a point on the Bapaume road the bodies of a platoon or more of Germans lay in the dust, half of them killed by the bayonet.

On the 16th we continued to make progress, and in the evening extended our gains in the vicinity of Courcelette on a front of about 1,000 yards, while the enemy's hold on Thiépval was further jeopardized by the capture of a fortified work known as the Wunder Werk on a front of half a mile. In his report that night Sir Douglas Haig announced that the number of prisoners captured during the past two days amounted to 4,000, of whom 116 were officers, while six guns and more than fifty machine-guns had been either taken or destroyed.

During the 17th the enemy launched several heavy counter-attacks against our new positions, all of which were repulsed. In two of these, one delivered from the direction of Lesbœufs and the other north of Flers, the advancing Germans were caught by our artillery barrage and suffered horribly. Between Flers and Martinpuich a German brigade, advancing to attack, was met by two of our battalions. A furious hand-to-hand fight ensued, which terminated in the victory of the British, the Huns being utterly

Waves of infantry going with a Tank.

routed and thrown back with heavy loss. Our "heavies" were very active, and a big conflagration occurred in the enemy's ammunition dump at Grandcourt, as the result of their attentions. During the night we slightly improved our position east of Courcelette and south of Thiépval. Under cover of heavy shell-fire, the enemy succeeded in entering our trenches to the west of Mouquet Farm, only to be driven out immediately with considerable loss.

On the 18th we made another important forward movement on our right, and wrested from the enemy the sinister maze of trenches between Bouleaux Wood and Ginchy, known as the Quadrilateral, which had hitherto resisted our efforts, and captured a number of prisoners. As a result of this successful operation, we advanced to a depth of 1,000 yards on a front of one mile. North of Flers several enemy counter-attacks were repulsed and some progress made, while between Lesbœufs and Morval German troops massed for attack were caught by our artillery fire and dispersed.

In his report that evening Sir Douglas Haig announced that the following additional pieces of artillery had been captured by us: five heavy howitzers, two field-guns, three heavy and three light trench-mortars and a number of machine-guns, and that the prisoners brought in during the past twenty-four hours numbered ten officers and five hundred other ranks.

German prisoners marching back past one of our Tanks.

A large German shell which did not explode. By the side of it is one of the smaller brand, commonly called a whizz-bang.

How bad water is guarded.

PART X. WILL BE READY ON TUESDAY, JAN. 30TH, 1917.

IT CONTAINS THE FOLLOWING ILLUSTRATIONS:—

How Tommy's food is cooked. The field kitchen works always in spite of wet weather.
Group of our gallant airmen in front of one of our machines.
A scene of the road.
Taking up a big gun with a 12-horse team and the help of the gun crew.
Mr. Massey coming out of a German dug-out.
Some of the German prisoners taken on September 15th.
New Zealanders on the rank to get things from the field canteen.
The Cavalry are very anxious to get to work.
Heavy trench mortar pit.
A rest on a shattered motor car.
Albert Church.

Worcesters returning from the trenches through the rain.
Rolling a big pile up for bridging purposes.
A wounded Tommy showing his helmet with a piece blown out.
A Cavalry patrol.
A few of our empties.
Returning from the trenches. "And everywhere that Tommy went, the goat was sure to go."
The French official kinematographer taking a close picture of one of our wounded.
Taking up ammunition along the very muddy roads.
Moving up the guns.
Carrying a wounded man down to an ambulance.

Middlesex returning from the trenches in the pouring rain.
Tommies arriving home at Mud Terrace.
In a captured German dug-out. The Germans have made some very fine dug-outs.
Inspection of the Guards by H.R.H. The Duke of Connaught:—
  H.R.H. the Duke of Connaught calls for three cheers for His Majesty The King.
  "I would like to borrow your coat, old chap!"
  Coldstreamers march past the Duke of Connaught after the Inspection.
  Duke of Connaught inspects Irish troops.
  H.R.H. The Duke of Connaught issued an order for the Police to allow the villagers up close to see the Inspection.
  Guards marching past H.R.H. The Duke of Connaught after the Inspection.
  The massed Drums and Pipes of the Guards at the Inspection.
  Passing down the Line.

ORDER FORM.

To M..
BOOKSELLER OR NEWSAGENT.

Please send me Part X. and the following Parts as published of "SIR DOUGLAS HAIG'S GREAT PUSH," for which I enclose..............................

Name..

Address..

SCALA THEATRE,
(Goodge Street Tube Station).   CHARLOTTE STREET, W.

AT THE FRONT
OFFICIAL WAR OFFICE FILMS.

Kut Relief Forces.   Salonika.   Russian Army.   French Army.   East Africa.
The King on the Somme Battle Field, &c.

THE BATTLE OF THE SOMME.

"There is no programme in London which gives so complete and vivid a description of the War on ALL FRONTS."—*Evening News.*

THE KING'S ADVICE:

SEE THE SOMME WAR FILM AND WHAT WAR MEANS.

"The public should see these pictures, that they may have some idea of what the Army is doing, and what war means."

This statement was made by the King after witnessing a programme of the Official War Office film, "The Battle of the Somme," which was shown by command to the King and Queen at Windsor Castle.—*Daily Express.*

Box Office, 10 to 10.   DAILY, 3 and 8.   'Phone: Gerr. 1444 & 1366.

SCALA THEATRE.

VOLUME I. with about 7,000 biographies and names of those who fell between 1914—1915, NOW READY, PRICE £2 2 0

IMPORTANT.

THE GREAT NATIONAL TRIBUTE.

The ROLL OF HONOUR

AN ILLUSTRATED BIOGRAPHICAL RECORD OF **ALL** OFFICERS, NON-COMMISSIONED OFFICERS AND MEN OF HIS MAJESTY'S FORCES WHO ARE KILLED OR DIE ON ACTIVE SERVICE

NOW BEING COMPILED BY

THE MARQUIS DE RUVIGNY

Author and Editor of "The Blood Royal of Britain," "The Titled Nobility of Europe," and other works.

THE debt which the Empire owes to those who have laid down their lives in the present War must, from the very nature of things, for ever remain unpaid.

There is, however, a universal desire to keep them in remembrance, and to ensure that their names and their glorious deeds shall not be forgotten.

For this purpose, "THE ROLL OF HONOUR" is now being prepared, to place on permanent record the name of every Officer, Non-Commissioned Officer and Man of His Majesty's Forces on land or sea who is killed in action, who dies of wounds, or whose death is otherwise caused in the present War.

It may here be briefly stated that it is proposed to give, whenever obtainable, the full name, place and date of birth, parentage, biographical sketch of career, and date and place of death, with extracts from letters of Commanding Officers or Comrades relating to the action in which the Officer or Man fell, or to the particular circumstances of his death.

Many a deed of heroism is covered by the bare announcement of a name in the daily long roll of casualties. To collect and record these is the purpose of the "ROLL OF HONOUR." The names of children will also be included, so that in the years to come they may themselves read, or teach their children to read, of the glorious way their fathers died; of those individual acts of bravery that are the chief redeeming feature of war.

Much valuable help is being given by the Authorities, by the Regiments, by Public Institutions, and the Heads of Schools, and the Publishers appeal with confidence to those who have lost relatives to assist them in the task they have undertaken by sending at once to the Editor the necessary particulars, extracts, from letters, etc.

The Editor and Publishers wish it to be distinctly understood that the insertion of any name is not in any way dependent upon the payment of any fee or of subscription to the book, and that no fee will be accepted for the insertion of any name.

A large number of portraits of Officers and Men will be included. With over 100,000 dead for the first year, it is clearly impossible to undertake that one will be given in every case, but when a portrait is supplied the Publishers will do their best to include it, and in the case of one supplied by a Subscriber, where there is no copyright fee, they guarantee that it will be reproduced.

SEND FOR A FORM to fill in particulars of your relation or friend who has been killed on active service. There is no charge, and his biography ought to be included. Unless you write probably only his name will be given,

To THE STANDARD ART BOOK CO. LTD.,

Publishers of "THE ROLL OF HONOUR,"

30-32, LUDGATE HILL, E.C.

EDITORIAL OFFICES:—
MARQUIS DE RUVIGNY.
"The Roll of Honour"
14-15, Hanover Chambers,
Buckingham St., Adelphi, W.C.

Please send me a form so that I may give you particulars concerning ....

.... who was killed on active service.

Name ....

Address ....

PRINTED AT THE CHAPEL RIVER PRESS, KINGSTON-ON-THAMES.

IN ABOUT 12 FORTNIGHTLY PARTS. HUTCHINSON'S NEW PART WORK Part XI. ready Feb. 13th. PART X. 8d. NET

SIR DOUGLAS HAIG'S
GREAT PUSH

THE BATTLE OF THE SOMME

A popular, pictorial and authoritative work on one of the Greatest Battles in History, illustrated by about **700** *wonderful* **OFFICIAL PHOTOGRAPHS AND CINEMATOGRAPH FILMS** *and other authentic pictures*

BY ARRANGEMENT WITH THE WAR OFFICE

GREAT VALUE FOR EIGHTPENCE

THIS PART CONTAINS **35 WONDERFUL REPRODUCTIONS** OF THE FAMOUS **WAR OFFICE CINEMATOGRAPH FILMS** AND **OFFICIAL PHOTOGRAPHS** OF THE BATTLE OF THE SOMME, BEAUTIFULLY PRINTED ON THE BEST ENGLISH ART PAPER.

LONDON : HUTCHINSON & Co.

NOW IN PREPARATION.
Both Edited by GENERAL SIR O. MOORE CREAGH, V.C., G.C.B., G.C.S.I., Secretary of the Military Department of the India Office, 1907-9; Commander-in-Chief in India, 1909-14; assisted by E. M. HUMPHRIS.

The V.C. and D.S.O.

"THE V.C. AND D.S.O." will be a complete and authentic record of the men and deeds that have earned these distinctions since their foundation. It is being compiled from the official records, as published in the *London Gazette* and in the dispatches, supplemented, wherever possible, by contemporary accounts in the Press, and from letters written by Commanding Officers or others who had cognisance of the acts for which the honours were awarded.

The need for such a publication is obvious. The deeds which have won such recognition are the finest episodes in British military history, and their perpetuation, in as complete a form as possible, is the aim of the editors. The assistance and co-operation of all those directly interested, the holders of the honours themselves, or their immediate relatives, are earnestly requested to that end.

"THE V.C. AND D.S.O." will be not only a record of the deeds themselves, but will be a who's who of those who performed them, military and brief biographical details being included.

Publication will take place as soon as possible after the issue of the final awards on the termination of the War.

It is proposed to include a Regimental Index in which will appear under each regiment the number of V.C.'s and D.S.O.'s awarded.

Many portraits will be given, and in the case of subscribers, where a portrait, upon which no fee is payable to the photographer is supplied, the publishers guarantee to include it.

The work will be complete in two large handsome volumes, of which Volume I. will be issued shortly, and Volume II. at the end of hostilities—as soon as possible after the final list of honours in connection with the War has been gazetted.

The price of the set of two volumes of the ordinary edition will be Two Guineas net. There will also be a special edition (limited to 200 copies numbered and signed) richly bound, price Five Guineas net. Copies of this special edition will, where desired, be stamped with the Regimental Crest.

The first edition published will be for subscribers only, and orders limited to the number of one thousand will now be accepted.

The EDITOR of "The V.C. and D.S.O.," THE STANDARD ART BOOK Co. Ltd., 30-32, Ludgate Hill, E.C.

The V.C. and M.C.

"THE V.C. AND M.C." will be a complete and authentic record of the men and deeds that have earned these distinctions since their foundation. It is being compiled from the official records, as published in the *London Gazette* and in the dispatches, supplemented, wherever possible, by contemporary accounts in the Press, and from letters written by Commanding Officers or others who had cognisance of the acts for which the honours were awarded.

The need for such a publication is obvious. The deeds which have won such recognition are the finest episodes in British military history, and their perpetuation, in as complete a form as possible, is the aim of the editors. The assistance and co-operation of all those directly interested, the holders of the honours themselves, or their immediate relatives, are earnestly requested to that end.

"THE V.C. AND M.C." will be not only a record of the deeds themselves, but will be a who's who of those who performed them, military and brief biographical details being included.

Publication will take place as soon as possible after the issue of the final awards on the termination of the War.

It is proposed to include a Regimental Index in which will appear under each regiment the number of V.C.'s and M.C.'s awarded.

Many portraits will be given, and in the case of subscribers, where a portrait, upon which no fee is payable to the photographer is supplied, the publishers guarantee to include it.

The work will be complete in two large handsome volumes, of which Volume I. will be issued shortly, and Volume II. at the end of hostilities—as soon as possible after the final list of honours in connection with the War has been gazetted.

The price of the set of two volumes of the ordinary edition will be Two Guineas net. There will also be a special edition (limited to 200 copies numbered and signed) richly bound, price Five Guineas net. Copies of this special edition will, where desired, be stamped with the Regimental Crest.

The first edition published will be for subscribers only, and orders limited to the number of one thousand will now be accepted.

The EDITOR of "The V.C. and M.C.," THE STANDARD ART BOOK Co. Ltd, 30-32, Ludgate Hill, E.C.

During the three following days heavy and continuous rain precluded any further important advance on our part. The bombardment on both sides continued, however, and the enemy delivered several determined, though unsuccessful, counter-attacks. Some of a particularly fierce character were launched on the night of the 20th-21st against the trenches held by the New Zealanders. But they were beaten off with severe loss to the enemy, who left a large number of dead in front of our lines. Despite the unfavourable weather, our airmen were active, and on the 21st destroyed two hostile machines and forced another to descend in a damaged condition.

During the night of the 21st-22nd we made another advance, and captured two lines of German trenches approximately between Flers and Martinpuich. This success had the important result of straightening out the British front between these two villages.

How Tommy's food is cooked. The field kitchen works always in spite of wet weather.

On the 22nd hostilities were chiefly confined to the artillery, but some isolated infantry actions took place, in the course of which we improved our positions and pushed forward detachments in several places.

Throughout the day great aerial activity prevailed. A highly successful raid was carried out by about fifty of our machines on an important railway junction, where much damage was done, two trains containing ammunition being destroyed and many violent explosions caused. A number of other successful attacks were also made on the enemy's aerodromes, railway-sidings and other points of military importance. In addition, many aerial combats took place, in the course of which three hostile machines were destroyed and five others driven to ground in a damaged condition.

Our heavy artillery maintained a very severe and astonishingly successful bombardment, with the result that ten hostile gun-pits were destroyed, fourteen severely damaged, five ammunition dumps blown up, and a big fire caused in a village much used by the enemy's transport for supply purposes.

During the night we made a further stride east of Courcelette on the Albert–Bapaume road, where a strongly-fortified system of German trenches was captured, and our line advanced over half a mile. West of Mouquet Farm, the enemy counter-attacked with great violence, but was repulsed with heavy loss.

On the 24th hostilities were again confined to the artillery, the British bombardment reaching a pitch of intensity which baffles all description. Hour after hour hundreds of great guns belched forth an unceasing stream of projectiles upon the enemy's positions. Beneath that tornado of shell the tortured earth spouted great geysers of smoke and soil, and for a dozen miles behind the battlefield, we are told, the earth trembled. Behind the German lines gun-pits were blown up and ammunition dumps sent sky-high; while the enemy in the trenches suffered unimaginable hell.

The Germans, fine soldiers though they are, do not possess the grit and stark unyielding tenacity which had enabled our men in past days, when we were utterly outgunned, to "stick it out" to the very death; and now that the tide had turned and they found themselves worsted in the war of material which they

Group of our gallant airmen in front of one of our machines.

had challenged, and exposed to horrors far worse even than those which they had once so pitilessly inflicted, they were becoming demoralized.

And so it happened that when, on the 25th, on the heels of this awful bombardment, our troops again assumed the offensive along the whole front between Combles and Martinpuich, the resistance encountered, though fierce enough in places, was, on the whole, far weaker than that which had been offered ten days earlier. Morval, which stands on the heights north of Combles and is the real key to that place—Morval, which, with its underground labyrinth and its maze of fortifications above, constituted a fortress second only in strength to Thiépval itself, was stormed with unexpected ease. Lesbœufs, to the north of it, was also carried, though not without some savage fighting, and with these two villages several lines of trenches, with the result that our line was advanced to a depth of more than a mile.

Meanwhile, to the north-east of Combles, the French, by a brilliant attack, had advanced to the southern outskirts of Frégicourt, so that Combles, though not yet occupied, was enveloped and doomed.

A scene on the road.

Engineers on the road.

The Battle of the Somme

CHAPTER IX

THE following day—Tuesday, September 26th—was perhaps the greatest in the whole Battle of the Somme. In the early dawn the French forced their way into the cemetery and the south-east part of Combles, while simultaneously the British broke over the last trenches into the village from the west. The garrison, though by this time reduced to about two battalions, offered a stout resistance, but by 10.30 a.m. the British and French advance-parties had come into touch near the railway-station, where they saluted one another and shook hands over " La Belle Alliance." A general assault was then concerted and delivered, and by noon the whole village was in the hands of the Allies, their losses being small.

" The capture of Combles in this inexpensive fashion," writes Sir Douglas Haig, " represented a not

Mr. Massey coming out of a German dug-out.

inconsiderable tactical success. Though lying in a hollow, the village was very strongly fortified, and possessed, in addition to the works which the enemy had constructed, exceptionally large cellars and galleries at a great depth underground, sufficient to give effectual shelter to troops and material under the heaviest bombardment. Great quantities of stores and ammunition of all sorts were found in these cellars when the village was taken."

Combles presented a truly appalling spectacle. " It is no longer a town—it is a charnel-house," observed a French officer to the correspondent of the *Liberté*. " One cannot take a step without treading upon a corpse. Among the heaps of brick and stone dead bodies are piled one upon another. Some had evidently fallen days ago. In the cellars and vaults dead and wounded are to be counted by hundreds. The prisoners we have taken are rags of humanity. They confess that they had been without supplies, and are dying of hunger."

According to the *Petit Parisien*, more than 1,500 corpses were counted in the streets, which explains the fact that only a comparatively small number of prisoners were taken.

Meantime, in the centre, the British had stormed the strongly fortified village of Gueudecourt, after the protecting trench to the west of it had been captured in a somewhat singular fashion.

The southern portion of this trench had been carried by our infantry, but two attacks upon the remaining part had been held up by a withering machine-gun fire. However, in the early morning a Tank came wobbling down the section still in possession of the enemy from the north-west, fire flashing from its flanks, and followed by bombers, who hurled their deadly missiles with great effect from behind the shelter of the monster. The Huns fled before this combined attack, but they could not escape, as we held the trench at the southern end. At the same time, one of our aeroplanes descended to within

Some of the German prisoners taken on September 15th.

400 feet to join in the sport, and flew down the length of the trench, raking the enemy with its Lewis gun. The affrighted Germans, attacked simultaneously from both sides and from earth and sky, started waving white handkerchiefs in token of surrender; and, on this being reported by the aeroplane, our infantry advanced and occupied the position. "By 8.30 a.m.," writes Sir Douglas Haig, "the whole trench had been cleared, great numbers of the enemy had been killed, and 8 officers and 362 other ranks made prisoners. Our total casualties amounted to five."

After rendering such splendid service in the capture of the trench, the Tank, apparently elated by its success, decided to go on alone in search of fresh adventures, and was on the point of wiping out another hostile trench, when on a sudden its machinery stopped. The Germans, with great pluck—for the Tank's machine-guns were still firing with deadly effect—rushed out, possessed by the frenzied notion of killing the beast, and, with shouts of triumph, closed about it, flinging bombs and firing volleys at it, belabouring it with the butt-ends of their rifles, and jabbing at it with their bayonets. As well might a swarm of

New Zealanders on the rank to get things from the field canteen.

The cavalry are very anxious to get to work.

wasps have attempted to kill a traction-engine! Behemoth continued to vomit death in all directions, and when our infantry came up and drove the enemy back, between 200 and 300 dead and wounded Germans lay around the monster, which presently, after a good deal of grinding and grunting, heaved itself up and wobbled away.

But the crowning triumph of the day was on the left, where Thiépval, the strongest of all the enemy's subterranean fortresses—Thiépval, which, though harrowed and ploughed and cratered under incessant storms of high explosive, had resisted our efforts for three long months—at last fell into British hands, with the exception of the north-west corner, which was captured early the following morning.

The success of our Fourth Army, on the right and in the centre, had now brought our advance to the stage at which the British Commander-in-Chief tells us that " he judged it advisable that Thiépval should

Heavy trench-mortar pit.

be taken, in order to bring our left flank into line and establish it on the main ridge above the village the possession of which would be of considerable tactical value in future operations."

Accordingly, at 12.25 p.m., before the enemy had had time to recover from the blow dealt them by the Fourth Army, and after a tremendous bombardment, rising to infernal heights of shell-fire, a general attack was launched against Thiépval and the Thiépval ridge. The objective consisted of the whole of the high ground still remaining in German hands, extending over a front of some 3,000 yards north and east of Thiépval, and including, in addition to that fortress, three redoubts—the Zollern, the Stuff and the Schwaben—with the connecting line of trenches.

On the right, our troops, advancing in three waves, carried the outer defences of Mouquet Farm, and, pushing on, penetrated into the Zollern Redoubt, which they stormed and proceeded to consolidate. These successes were achieved without great difficulty, but in the strong point formed by the buildings of the farm itself the enemy, securely posted in deep tunnels, maintained a stubborn resistance until six in the evening, when their last defences were forced by a working-party of a Pioneer battalion acting on its own initiative.

No sooner had our men advanced beyond the farm towards the Zollern Redoubt, than a number of Germans emerged from the tunnels of Mouquet and began firing machine-guns into the backs of the British. Fortunately, the young officer in charge of the working-party just mentioned had his wits about him, and, shouting to his men to throw down their shovels, rushed forward and attacked the Huns, who, after a short resistance, had recourse to the vanishing trick and disappeared into the bowels of the earth. Thither the pioneers followed them, and for six whole hours a savage struggle went on in the dark corridors. At the end, only 13 of the brave pioneers survived, but when they emerged into the

A rest on a shattered motor-car.

light of day again, they brought with them a German officer and 55 men as prisoners; and there was no living man left that evening in the tunnels of Mouquet.

Meanwhile, on the left, in Thiépval, an obstinate struggle was in progress. A brigade of Würtembergers had lived consecutively in Thiépval for two whole years. " It was their freehold," writes Mr. Beach Thomas. " They begged not to be relieved, for they had ' improved the property ' beyond recognition, till its cellars rivalled the Spanish cellars of Arras. They thought themselves almost impregnable, and it was a point of honour with them to hold the fortress to the end. When the shelling was bad, they could descend to corridors or galleries or cellars, where the explosions of 12-inch shells were no more than a rainstorm on a palace roof. One battalion or other of the 180th Würtembergers had garrisoned the fort continuously since July 1st, with alternate periods out of the line, near their depôt at Bapaume."

The Würtembergers—tough, stalwart veterans of the original German army—resisted with stubborn courage, and nowhere more stubbornly than in and around what remained of the château. The château —like an iceberg, nine-tenths below the surface—was the hub of the defence. It lay in the midst of the

Albert Church.

Worcesters returning from the trenches through the rain.

old German system of front trenches, and was strengthened by every device known to the new art of fortification. The part of it that was above ground was a mere heap of red rubbish; but from the cellars beneath came savage bursts of machine-gun fire, while from the left-hand top corner of the ground where the village had once stood other machine-guns effectively enfiladed our advancing troops.

Our men were astounded. " I didn't believe it possible," one of them remarked later in the day, " that any soul could be there after that shell-fire. But, as soon as it switched off, blessed if the Germans didn't come up like rabbits out of bunny-holes and fire most hellishly ! "

For a time it was impossible to get near the château or a trench dug in front of it. The machine-guns gabbled too fast for any infantry to face with reasonable odds.

But help was at hand. Lumbering and lurching along, crawling in and out of the shell-craters and

Rolling a big pile up for bridging purposes.

old German trenches, came a Tank. " It faced the ruins of the château," writes Mr. Philip Gibbs, " and stared at them very steadily for quite a long while, as though wondering whether it should eat them or crush them. Our men were hiding behind ridges of shell-craters, keeping low from the swirl of machine-gun bullets and imploring the Tank ' to get on with it.' Then it moved forward in a monstrous way, not swerving much to right or left, but heaving itself on jerkily, like a dragon with indigestion, but very fierce. Fire leaped from its nostrils. The German machine-guns splashed its sides with bullets, which ricocheted off. Not all those bullets kept it back. It got on top of the enemy's trench, and trundled down the length of it, laying its sandbags flat and sweeping it with fire. The machine-guns were silent, and when our men followed the Tank, shouting and cheering, they found a few German gunners standing with their hands held up as a sign of surrender to the monster who had come upon them. ' We couldn't have faced the château without the help of the old Tank,' said several men. ' It didn't care a damn for machine-guns. It did them in properly.' "

On the heels of this initial success the dash of our infantry rose beyond resistance, and Château Imprégnable fell. Nevertheless, much grim work still remained to be done, for our men had to fight an underground foe, who fired upon them from holes and crevices and all kinds of unexpected places, and, when cornered at last, often fought as fiercely as wolves at bay. However, by nightfall the place had been cleared, with the exception of the north-west corner, where a remnant of the garrison still maintained an obstinate resistance. Early on the morning of the 27th a gallant assault by South-Country troops swept this into our net also; and by 8.30 a.m. Thiépval was as firmly in our hands as was Combles, nine miles away on the right as the crow flies.

Some 1,300 prisoners were taken in Thiépval, together with a considerable quantity of war material.

A wounded Tommy showing his helmet with a piece blown out.

One batch of prisoners attempted to effect their escape, and wounded the two soldiers who were in charge of them, but they were speedily killed or recaptured.

Most excellent work was performed by our airmen, both in observation and attack, during the fighting of the 25th and 26th. On the first day, three hostile aeroplanes were destroyed and six driven down in a damaged condition; and on the second, two aeroplanes and two kite-balloons were accounted for.

During the night of the 26th-27th we made further progress, notably north of Flers, in the direction of Eaucourt l'Abbaye, a group of monastic buildings, now chiefly machine-gun emplacements; and our advance in this quarter was continued on the morrow, when we captured several enemy trenches on a front of 2,000 yards, which brought us level with the east side of the place.

Fierce fighting took place north-east of Thiépval, during which our troops stormed and held the southern and western sides of the work known as the Stuff Redoubt, 2,000 yards north-east of the village, together with the length of trench connecting that strong point with the Schwaben Redoubt to the west, and also the greater part of the enemy's defensive line eastwards along the northern slopes of the ridge.

A cavalry patrol.

A few of our empties.

The Schwaben Redoubt was assaulted in the course of the afternoon, and the whole of its southern face captured and held, notwithstanding counter-attacks delivered by strong reinforcements which the enemy had brought up. Subsequently, our patrols pushed forward to the northern face of the redoubt and in the direction of St. Pierre Divion.

In his reports that day Sir Douglas Haig announced that 1,800 rifles, four *flammenwerfers* and many thousands of rounds of artillery ammunition and grenades had been taken by the British at Combles, while our Allies had also made large captures of war material, and that the prisoners taken by us in the course of the past two days' fighting brought the total for the operations of the last fortnight to 10,000.

During the night our line was advanced at various points between Martinpuich and Gueudecourt, and posts were established west and south-west of Eaucourt l'Abbaye and within 800 yards of the village. On the left of our front our position was consolidated on the ridge north-east of Thiépval. A battalion

Returning from the trenches. "And everywhere that Tommy went, the goat was sure to go."

of German infantry with transport was caught on the march by our artillery and shelled with murderous effect.

It was an eloquent testimony to the complete domination established by our guns over the enemy's communications that the Germans were now obliged to move their troops and transport by night. Even then, as in the present instance, they suffered considerable losses, since all the roads were registered to a nicety.

On the 28th we again attacked the Schwaben Redoubt, and by the evening the greater part of it was in our hands. This redoubt occupies the crest of the ridge 500 yards north of Thiépval, and represents the highest ground in the Thiépval area, with a full view over the northern valley of the Ancre. Elsewhere on our front we consolidated our ground and advanced our line north and north-east of Courcelette.

Throughout the 27th and 28th our aircraft co-operated in brilliant style with the infantry. Much damage was done to the enemy's batteries, and there were many instances of our aeroplanes attacking troops and transport with machine-gun fire.

In his reports on the 28th, Sir Douglas Haig made the pleasing announcement that the fighting of the past few days had been " singularly economical." " Our losses," he continued, " are small, not only relatively to the importance of our gains, but absolutely. Our total casualties are not more than twice the number of enemy prisoners taken. One division, which had a specially difficult task allotted to it, took as many prisoners as it suffered casualties."

He also cited a captured report of the fighting on the Somme, issued by the commander of a German corps which took part in the battle, containing a tribute to the quality of our troops :

" The British infantry "—it says—" are smart in attack, largely because of their immense confidence in their great artillery superiority. One must admit the skill with which they consolidate themselves

The French official kinematographer taking a close picture of one of our wounded.

in newly-gained positions. They show tenacity in the defence. Small parties, when once established with machine-guns in a corner of a wood or a group of houses, are very difficult to dislodge."

Another sentence shows the devastating effects of our artillery fire :

" Hitherto our instructions, from experience gained in defence and attack, were based on a carefully constructed trench system. The troops on the Somme front found actually no trenches at all."

The night was quiet along the greater part of our front, though the positions we had recently won north of Thiépval were heavily shelled, and our bombing-parties were active in the neighbourhood of the Schwaben Redoubt and the Hessian trench, further east, parts of which were still held by the enemy.

Early on the following morning we captured Destremont Farm, a strongly-defended group of buildings 500 yards south-west of Le Sars. North of Ytres, which lies seven miles south-east of Bapaume, our aeroplanes observed a huge explosion, as if a large ammunition dump had blown up. The smoke ascended to a height of 9,000 feet.

Taking up ammunition along the very muddy roads.

Moving up the guns.

The Battle of the Somme

Rain fell heavily during the day, and, except for intermittent shelling, there was little activity in the centre or on the right of our battle-front. Some slight progress was made east of Lesbœufs, where we occupied 500 yards of hostile trenches, and in the Thiépval area there was heavy fighting around the Stuff Redoubt and the Hessian trench. Of the latter work we captured an important section, only to be subsequently forced out of it by a determined counter-attack. Later in the day, however, it was once more in our hands. In this sector our troops engaged—a division of the New Army—" showed," wrote Sir Douglas Haig, " great endurance and resolution."

The fighting on the north-east of Thiépval took place in a land of shell-craters, most of the trenches being just linked shell-holes, into which our men burrowed as soon as they had rushed the ground, to get a little cover in their depths from the barrage which searched them out.

Queer things happened in shell-crater land, particularly at night. Single combats over the rim of a shell-hole were of frequent occurrence. " Men knock up against each other in the dark," writes

Carrying a wounded man down to an ambulance.

a special correspondent, " and peer into each other's faces to know if it is friend or foe. If friend, they drop into a shell-hole together ; if foe, they fight till one is dead."

One night, in the Hessian trench or its vicinity, a British soldier encountered two German officers and a score of men. He fired and killed three of them, upon which the others took to their heels. The soldier pursued them, the chase leading him along a dirty ditch which had once been a trench, and, as he happened to be a dead shot and abandoned German rifles were lying all along the way, he managed to bring down the Huns one after another, until only a single man remained, who surrendered and was brought back as a prisoner.

Some of the shell-holes were open graves, half-filled with corpses ; in others lay wounded men, who had in some cases lain there for days, vainly endeavouring to attract attention. In one hole were found three Australians, one unhurt, the other two rotting with wounds. They had been there for nine days ; and the unwounded man, with splendid devotion, had remained with his comrades all that time, crawling out when darkness fell to rummage among the dead for rations and water-bottles, which he brought back and shared with them.

During the night there was considerable activity on the northern part of our line, no less than sixteen raids being made on the German trenches between Ypres and Neuve Chapelle, in which many prisoners were captured and heavy loss inflicted on the enemy. One of the most successful of these raids was that carried out by a London Territorial battalion south of Neuville St. Vaast.

Heavy counter-attacks were launched by the enemy against our lines in the neighbourhood of the Stuff Redoubt and the Hessian trench. But our New Army troops once more proved their quality, and the Germans were beaten back with heavy loss.

On the 30th the line of our new gains, Gueudecourt–Morval–Combles, was very heavily shelled, but no infantry attack developed.

Our airmen were in a very enterprising mood. Two hostile aerodromes were successfully bombed by them, and at least one machine destroyed. In the fighting over the front two German machines were

Inspection of the Guards by H.R.H. the Duke of Connaught : H.R.H. the Duke of Connaught calls for three cheers for His Majesty the King.

brought down, while our aeroplanes repeatedly attacked the enemy's troops and transport with machine-gun fire, and in one instance several hundred infantry were dispersed.

During the night some progress was made between Flers and Le Sars in the centre of our battle-front. There was heavy shelling in this neighbourhood and also around Gueudecourt. In the Thiépval area the enemy was driven out of the ground he still held near the Stuff Redoubt, and we increased our gains at the Schwaben Redoubt, only a minute portion of which now remained in German possession.

In the afternoon of October 1st our centre launched a successful attack against Eaucourt l'Abbaye and the German defences to the east and west of it, comprising a total front of about 3,000 yards. For the first time for two years we fought in cultivated fields, and near Eaucourt l'Abbaye our attacking troops charged through a crop of what our men described as red cabbages, but what was probably sugar-beet. " The men kicked them as they tramped on towards the enemy," writes Mr. Philip Gibbs, " using the roots as footballs. It was a queer kind of game to play on the way to a trench full of enemies, under

Middlesex Regiment returning from the trenches in the pouring rain.

Tommies arriving home at Mud Terrace.

showers of shrapnel and through the patter of machine-gun bullets. 'It kept us from worrying,' said one of the beetroot players. 'A little bit of sport helps one wonderfully.' "

To reach the first trench in front of Eaucourt l'Abbaye, which was part of the old German third line of defences, our men had to cross 800 yards of open country—a most perilous undertaking in ordinary circumstances. It was accomplished, however, within a few minutes and with very slight casualties, which was no doubt due to the intensity and accuracy of our artillery barrage. Our gunners went on pounding the enemy's trench until the infantry were close upon it, and some of our men actually saw Germans killed by the British shell-fire within twenty yards of them.

When the trench was reached, it was found choked with corpses, and a few machine-gunners, who continued to work their murderous weapons until the bayonets were almost touching them and then held

In a captured German dug-out. The Germans have made some very fine dug-outs.

up their hands, were its only living occupants. Most of the survivors had bolted for the second trench, 200 yards in the rear, and, thence, if they had the luck to get so far, into the ruins of the village behind it. Some of the fugitives were tall, burly fellows belonging to the 6th Bavarian Division, which had been holding Lille since September, 1914, and had only recently been brought into the fighting-line. But, big as they were, they appeared to have very little stomach for the business on hand, though, as 75 per cent. of them were afterwards asserted to have become casualties already, there may have been some excuse for them. "There was one big whopper," said a small English lad, "seven foot high, I should say, from the glance I had of him. Why, he could have eaten me for breakfast and then gone hungry! But he ran like a whippet on Bank Holiday. I didn't get a chance to close with him."

The second trench in front of Eaucourt l'Abbaye was also easily carried, as were the double line of trenches away on the left of the attack outside Le Sars, those Germans who had survived our bombardment refusing to face the bayonet. There was, however, a piece of ground on the right of the advance to Eaucourt, where machine-guns, skilfully placed and protected by a stretch of barbed wire which our artillery had failed to destroy, caused us not a few casualties, until two Tanks waddled up, flattened the entanglements, rolled down the sandbag defences, and wiped out machine-guns and gunners.

In the evening our patrols penetrated into Eaucourt and Le Sars; but subsequently the enemy brought up reserves and obliged them to retire.

Our aircraft again rendered valuable service during the day's operations. Several points of military importance behind the enemy's lines were successfully bombed, and in the course of a number of encounters in the air two hostile machines were destroyed and many others driven down. A German kite-balloon was also brought down in flames. We sustained no losses.

Our heavy artillery bombarded the village of Le Transloy, where an ammunition dump was blown up.

During the night the enemy delivered a determined counter-attack against our advanced positions east of Eaucourt l'Abbaye, but it was beaten back, and we succeeded in establishing our front in that area and in clearing the buildings of Eaucourt of the enemy.

Further west, we established our line from a point 1,200 yards

"I would like to borrow your coat, old chap."

north of Courcelette, in the direction of the Hessian trench. But an enemy counter attack forced us to relinquish a portion of the Regina trench which we had gained further to the north. Successful raids on the German trenches were carried out north of Neuville St. Vaast and east of Laventie.

On the 2nd heavy rain fell from early morning and interfered with operations. Severe fighting took place in and about Eaucourt l'Abbaye, where the enemy succeeded in regaining a footing in the buildings. South-west of Gueudecourt and north and east of Courcelette we improved our positions. Rain continued to fall heavily during the night and the earlier part of the following day. Fighting continued about Eaucourt l'Abbaye, where we made good progress. Elsewhere, except for intermittent shelling, our front was quiet.

During the night there was a good deal of artillery activity on both sides, but no infantry work of any importance except at Eaucourt l'Abbaye, which before midday on the 4th had been once more cleared of the enemy and was entirely in our hands. Later in the day, our trenches in the neighbourhood of the Zollern Redoubt and between Gueudecourt and Eaucourt l'Abbaye were heavily shelled. Half-way between the last-named points the enemy attempted a bombing attack, but were driven off, leaving a number of wounded outside our lines.

Coldstreamers march past the Duke of Connaught after the inspection.

At the inspection of the Guards by H.R.H. the Duke of Connaught.

Duke of Connaught inspects Irish troops.

The Battle of the Somme

Inspection of the Guards by H.R.H. the Duke of Connaught: H.R.H. the Duke of Connaught issued an order for the police to allow the villagers up close to see the inspection.

The night was marked by a good deal of artillery activity south of the Ancre, and north of the Schwaben Redoubt our gun-fire caused many casualties among enemy infantry on the move. In the Vimy area, north of Arras, a successful raid was carried out by a London Territorial battalion. East of St. Eloi the enemy made an unsuccessful attempt to enter our trenches.

On the 5th the German artillery shelled our trenches in the Gueudecourt neighbourhood, and in the Thiépval area the enemy delivered two counter-attacks, both of which were repulsed with heavy loss to the assailants.

Sir Douglas Haig reported that between July 1st and September 30th, besides large quantities of other war material, we had captured and recovered from the Somme battlefield: 28 heavy guns and heavy howitzers; 92 field-guns and field-howitzers; 103 trench artillery pieces and 379 machine-guns.

During the night we advanced our position north-east of Eaucourt l'Abbaye. On the northern part of our front we discharged gas at two points against the enemy's trenches, and carried out several successful raids.

On the 6th hostilities south of the Ancre were mainly confined to the guns. Several of the enemy's working-parties were shelled by our artillery and dispersed. At night the Germans delivered a bombing attack on our new positions north-east of Eaucourt l'Abbaye, which, however, was completely repulsed. In the Armentières and Loos areas our patrols raided the enemy's trenches with successful results.

At the end of September Sir Douglas Haig had handed over Morval to the French, in order to facilitate their attacks on Sailly-Saillisel; and on October 7th, after a postponement rendered necessary by the continuous rain of the past few days, our Allies made a considerable advance in the direction of the latter village. In the afternoon of the same day, in co-operation with the French, our Fourth Army attacked along the whole front from the Albert–Bapaume road to Lesbœufs.

The attack was attended with splendid success. The whole of the village of Le Sars was captured, together with the quarry to the north-west of it; while between Gueudecourt and Lesbœufs our line was advanced from 600 to 1,000 yards, and a footing gained on the crest of the long spur which screened the defences of Le Transloy from the south-west.

These successes were achieved under the most difficult conditions.

"To-day's attack," writes Mr. Beach Thomas, "was delivered in conditions of full winter. It was a marvel that either the Army or its air-scouts could

Inspection of the Guards by H.R.H. the Duke of Connaught :—

Inspection of the Guards by H.R.H. the Duke of Connaught :—

—Guards marching past H.R.H. the Duke of Connaught after the inspection.

—The massed drums and pipes of the Guards at the inspection.

Inspection of the Guards by H.R.H. the Duke of Connaught: Passing down the line.

push forward against an entrenched enemy and plentiful artillery. The wind blew half a gale from the south-west, and the ground, crumbled to a sort of dryness on the tops of the furrows, was a marsh in the pits and trenches.

"Nevertheless, our aircraft swarmed, blown about the windy and squally sky like rooks in a wind which must carry every winged bird into enemy country. They scouted over the barrage in unusual numbers, and then, after due interval, fought their way home, dropping messages which could be seen floating down on long streamers."

The most dramatic point of attack, though not altogether the most important tactically, was Le Sars, a village of considerable size, situated on a valuable minor elevation, and standing as a sort of keep along the principal road entrance to Bapaume. Our patrols, it will be remembered, had already penetrated this place on the evening of October 1st, and had then obtained valuable information concerning its defences.

Le Sars—or what was left of it, for our guns had already smashed the houses and barns to rubbish-heaps—was held by men drawn from two "Ersatz," or Reserve, regiments, who had been ordered to fight to the last gasp rather than surrender. They did not go quite so far as that in the majority of cases, but they offered a stubborn resistance, even sending out volunteers into No Man's Land to lie in the shell-holes waist-high in water to snipe our lads as they came across, which for middle-aged men with families, as most of them were, was a plucky thing to do. They fought their machine-guns well, too, particularly in a nasty quadrilateral redoubt called the Tangle, where our advance was held up for a while. Hereabouts it was that something happened to the internal organs of a Tank, and it committed hari-kari. But before it blew up it had rendered good service, and strewn the ground about it with dead and dying Huns.

Some trouble was also experienced in the taking of the Mill, another strongly-fortified place in the outskirts, and further back in a sunken road and in the hiding-places below ground there was grim and bitter fighting. But, on the whole, the village was captured and its dug-outs cleared with amazing rapidity; and before the attack was an hour old groups of prisoners had already reached our lines in front of Le Sars.

In the evening the enemy counter-attacked our new positions north of Lesbœufs and recovered a small portion of their lost trenches. At night they attempted to regain a footing in the Schwaben

Part XI. of "SIR DOUGLAS HAIG'S GREAT PUSH"

Will be ready on TUESDAY, FEBRUARY 13th, 1917.

READY TOWARDS THE END OF FEBRUARY.

PART I. of one of the most sumptuous and magnificently illustrated works ever published. The subject is

THE SPLENDOUR OF FRANCE

The story of a great and glorious nation, and a pictorial and authoritative record of a beautiful country, many of whose Towns and Architectural wonders have been ruthlessly ruined and destroyed by the unspeakable Prussian.

Fuller particulars will be given in the next Part.

VOLUME I. with about 7,000 biographies and names of those who fell between 1914—1915, NOW READY, PRICE £2 2 0

VOLUME II. with about 7,000 biographies and names of those who fell between 1915—1916, NOW IN PREPARATION, PRICE £2 2 0

VOLUME III. with about 7,000 biographies and names of those who fell between 1916—1917, NOW IN PREPARATION, PRICE £2 2 0

IMPORTANT.

THE GREAT NATIONAL TRIBUTE.

The ROLL OF HONOUR

AN ILLUSTRATED BIOGRAPHICAL RECORD OF **ALL** OFFICERS, NON-COMMISSIONED OFFICERS AND MEN OF HIS MAJESTY'S FORCES WHO ARE KILLED OR DIE ON ACTIVE SERVICE

NOW BEING COMPILED BY

THE MARQUIS DE RUVIGNY

Author and Editor of "The Blood Royal of Britain," "The Titled Nobility of Europe," and other works.

THE debt which the Empire owes to those who have laid down their lives in the present War must, from the very nature of things, for ever remain unpaid.

There is, however, a universal desire to keep them in remembrance, and to ensure that their names and their glorious deeds shall not be forgotten.

For this purpose, "THE ROLL OF HONOUR" is now being prepared, to place on permanent record the name of every Officer, Non-Commissioned Officer and Man of His Majesty's Forces on land or sea who is killed in action, who dies of wounds, or whose death is otherwise caused in the present War.

It may here be briefly stated that it is proposed to give, whenever obtainable, the full name, place and date of birth, parentage, biographical sketch of career, and date and place of death, with extracts from letters of Commanding Officers or Comrades relating to the action in which the Officer or Man fell, or to the particular circumstances of his death.

Many a deed of heroism is covered by the bare announcement of a name in the daily long roll of casualties. To collect and record these is the purpose of the "ROLL OF HONOUR." The names of children will also be included, so that in the years to come they may themselves read, or teach their children to read, of the glorious way their fathers died; of those individual acts of bravery that are the chief redeeming feature of war.

Much valuable help is being given by the Authorities, by the Regiments, by Public Institutions, and the Heads of Schools, and the Publishers appeal with confidence to those who have lost relatives to assist them in the task they have undertaken by sending at once to the Editor the necessary particulars, extracts, from letters, etc.

The Editor and Publishers wish it to be distinctly understood that the insertion of any name is not in any way dependent upon the payment of any fee or of subscription to the book, and that no fee will be accepted for the insertion of any name.

A large number of portraits of Officers and Men will be included. With over 100,000 dead for the first year, it is clearly impossible to undertake that one will be given in every case, but when a portrait is supplied the Publishers will do their best to include it, and in the case of one supplied by a Subscriber, where there is no copyright fee, they guarantee that it will be reproduced.

SEND FOR A FORM to fill in particulars of your relation or friend who has been killed on active service. There is no charge, and his biography ought to be included. Unless you write probably only his name will be given.

To **THE STANDARD ART BOOK CO. LTD.,**
Publishers of "THE ROLL OF HONOUR,"
30-32, LUDGATE HILL, E.C.

EDITORIAL OFFICES:—
Marquis de Ruvigny.
"The Roll of Honour"
14-15, Hanover Chambers,
Buckingham St., Adelphi, W.C.

Please send me a form so that I may give you particulars concerning ....

.... who was killed on active service.

Name ....

Address ....

PRINTED AT THE CHAPEL RIVER PRESS, KINGSTON-ON-THAMES.

IN ABOUT 12 FORTNIGHTLY PARTS. | HUTCHINSON'S NEW PART WORK | Part XII. ready March 6th. PART XI. 8d. NET

SIR DOUGLAS HAIG'S
GREAT PUSH

THE BATTLE OF THE SOMME

A popular, pictorial and authoritative work on one of the Greatest Battles in History, illustrated by about **700** *wonderful* **OFFICIAL PHOTOGRAPHS AND CINEMATOGRAPH FILMS** *and other authentic pictures*

BY ARRANGEMENT WITH THE WAR OFFICE

BRITISH v FRENCH

GREAT VALUE FOR EIGHTPENCE

THIS PART CONTAINS **32 WONDERFUL REPRODUCTIONS** OF THE FAMOUS **WAR OFFICE CINEMATOGRAPH FILMS** AND **OFFICIAL PHOTOGRAPHS** OF THE BATTLE OF THE SOMME. BEAUTIFULLY PRINTED ON THE BEST ENGLISH ART PAPER.

LONDON : HUTCHINSON & Co.

A

10s. 6d. PHOTOGRAVURE PLATE

IS GIVEN **FREE**

To the first 50,000 Subscribers of Part I., Price 8d.,

OF

The Splendour of France

HUTCHINSON'S NEW PART WORK.

READY MARCH 13th.

ORDER IMMEDIATELY FROM YOUR BOOKSELLER

In three months' time you could play this at sight.

Think what it means to be able to sit down at the piano, to open a difficult and hitherto unseen piece of music, and to play it off at once without hesitation, with absolute confidence and without a wrong note. As a rule this state of proficiency is only reached after years of patient practice and study. But the THELWALL System has been worked out so scientifically that the mind is trained along certain lines and its latent faculties are brought out. One half-hour's daily study under the THELWALL System will make you a rapid and infallible sight-reader in three months, even if you only have a small knowledge of music previously. The THELWALL System, moreover, is highly approved by the leading musicians of the country, including Mr. Landon Ronald and Dr. Borland. On receipt of a 1d. stamp to cover cost of postage we will send you a Booklet, "HOW EVERY PIANIST MAY BECOME A RAPID SIGHT READER." Send your application now.

WALTER THELWALL, Dept. D.1., 30-2, Ludgate Hill, LONDON, E.C.

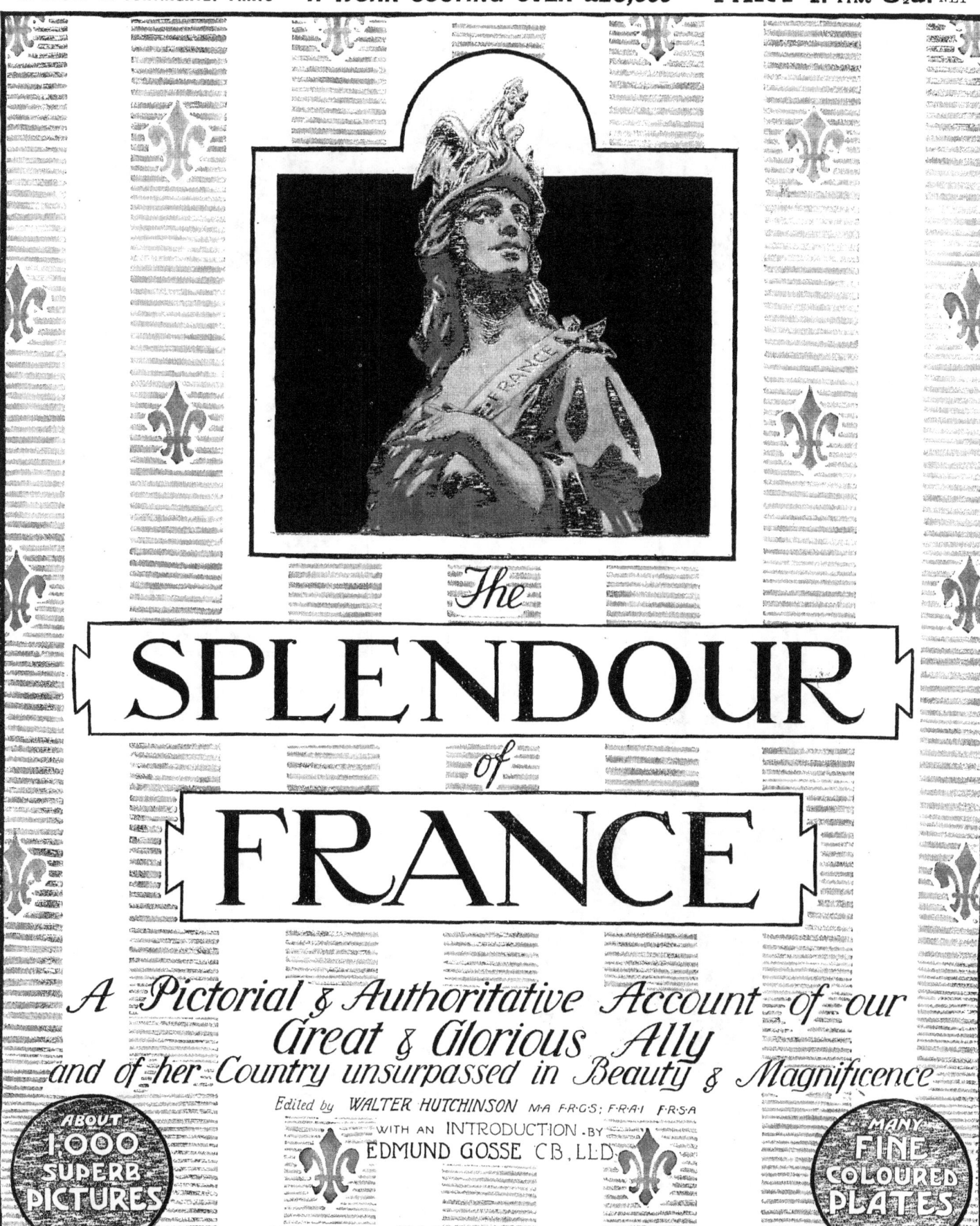

"The Splendour of France"

GENERAL VIEW OF THE OLD FRENCH TOWN OF AVIGNON
At the northern end of the city a precipitous rock, the Rocher des Doms, rises from the river and forms a plateau. To the south are the Cathedral of Notre Dame des Doms and the Palace of the Popes. The latter was begun by Pope John XXII in 1316, and it was continued by succeeding Popes till 1370. It has an appearance of great strength, and resembles a fortress rather than a palace. Avignon was the Papal Seat from 1309 till 1377, when the then Pope, Gregory XI, migrated to Rome.

WHEN we look back and see how near a large part of "La Belle France" was to being destroyed, and how, had it not been for her glorious army, our own country might have suffered invasion, our hearts are filled with lasting gratitude and friendship.

It is difficult for us to realise what it means to have a horde of barbarians advancing and pillaging everything as they pass, but our brave

---

PART 1—8½d.—Ready 13th March, contains:
79 Illustrations on ART PAPER,
A BEAUTIFUL COLOURED PLATE
and a MAP of FRANCE,
and a long Introduction by
EDMUND GOSSE, C.B., LL.D.,
Officer of the Legion of Honour, etc.
F. APPLEBY HOLT, B.A., LL.B.,
commences the romantic story of PARIS and its beautiful buildings.
A FREE GIFT of a SUPERB 10s. 6d. PHOTOGRAVURE PICTURE
will be made to each of the purchasers of the **FIRST**
50,000 Copies of Part I.

Ally experienced the pangs of this in the early days of th War, and many of her picturesque towns and villages, with the historic monuments, have been shamelessly ruined beyond repair.

Only by glancing through the pages of "THE SPLENDOU OF FRANCE" can it be realised what a loss it would hav been to the World had France been unable to keep back thes barbarians.

There is a corner of her country which contains the las resting place of over 100,000 of our gallant fellows, and a trac of land which has been graciously handed over to us by ou Ally as a national cemetery for our fallen heroes; this will fo ever be held in reverence by every British subject.

A fine pictorial work on this gallant Nation and her magnif cent country is therefore sure to be appreciated, and as nor exists in the English language, MESSRS. HUTCHINSON & Co. hav gone to the expense of £20,000 to issue "THE SPLENDOUR (FRANCE" at 8½d. a Part, a price well within the reach everyone.

AMIENS CATHEDRAL.
Amiens Cathedral, which was erected between 1220 and 1288, is, perhaps, the finest Gothic Church in France. The façade, here shown, is flanked by two square towers without spires. There are three portals decorated with a profusion of statuary, and above them are two galleries and a magnificent rose-window. The upper gallery and the three portals are decorated with a profusion of statuary. The nave rises to a height of 140 feet and above the crossing there is a slender spire.

This excellent publication will show *all* that is romantic and interesting in France—her picturesque towns ar villages, her quaint ceremonies and customs, her grand Cathedrals, her famous old Châteaux, her glorious scenery, ar her great paintings and other treasures of art.

(Continued on Page 4.)

"The Splendour of France"

A Beautiful 10/6 Photogravure Plate 22" × 16" of this picture Free to the first 50,000 purchasers of Part I 8½d

"LA MADELEINE" by the famous French Artist, J. J. HENNER.

"The Splendour of France"

"THE APPARITION," BY MOREAU, IN THE LUXEMBOURG MUSEUM, PARIS.
So pleased was Herod with the dancing of Salome, the daughter of Herodias, that he offered to reward her to the half of his kingdom. On seeking the advice of her mother, Salome was advised to ask for the head of John the Baptist in a charger. In his imagination the artist has depicted an incident supposed to have happened soon after the execution. While dancing before Herod, Salome is suddenly confronted by the accusing head of John the Baptist. The executioner, resting on his sword, is seen in the background.

Why you should Subscribe

1	It is the most sumptuous work on our great Ally, France, ever produced, and is entirely new
2	It gives all the most wonderful sights to be seen throughout France
3	The subject is one of the most fascinating in the world
4	It is a standard work for the library and the home
5	Written concisely and popularly by eminent authorities
6	Every page teems with romance
7	Famous paintings by the greatest artists are given
8	There are some 1,000 magnificent pictures
9	Exquisitely printed on finest English art paper
10	Many maps and plans
11	Many beautiful coloured plates
12	It combines pleasure with instruction
13	It is wonderful value
14	It has cost over £20,000 to produce
15	It costs you only EightPENCE-Halfpenny per Part

(Continued from Page 2.)

There will be about 1,000 illustrations, beautifully reproduced on most expensive art paper, and many fine coloured plates specially painted for the work by L. BURLEIGH BRUHL and other famous artists.

The letterpress is being written by eminent authorities, and as the work will be dealt with geographically, the last Parts will be just as interesting as the first.

When bound it will make two sumptuous volumes, which, though costing but a few shillings, will remain a lasting treasure in thousands of British homes—a fitting compliment to our great Ally-in-arms. "THE SPLENDOUR OF FRANCE" has also a special interest to our Soldiers, for it is on French soil that, side by side with our Ally, they are fighting for freedom and humanity; it is accordingly anticipated that copies of the Parts will be posted to them regularly by relatives at home.

THE BOMBARDMENT OF RHEIMS CATHEDRAL.
The systematic destruction of Rheims Cathedral which began about September 14th, 1914, after the Battle of the Marne, has filled Europe with horror. Rheims was the Westminster Abbey of France for nearly every King of France was crowned there. The church was founded in 1211 and the larger part of it was completed by the beginning of the 14th Century. The west front was regarded as perhaps the finest production of mediaeval art.

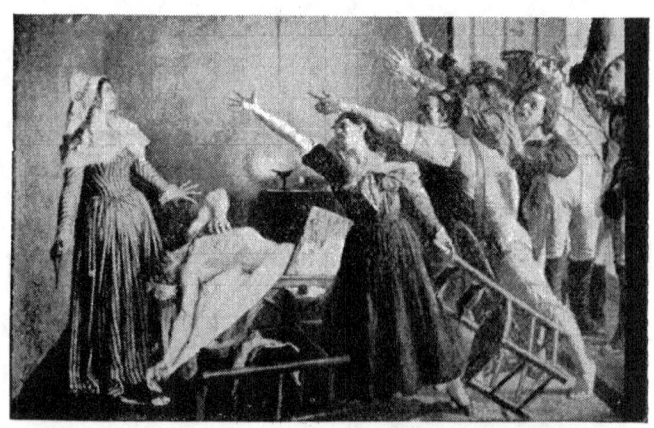

ASSASSINATION OF MARAT BY CHARLOTTE CORDAY, 1793.
Excited by the downfall of the Girondists, with whose ideas she sympathized, Charlotte Corday set out from Caen for Paris with the determination to avenge them. Marat appeared to her the most ferocious and uncompromising opponent of the Girondists, and gaining admittance to his house she stabbed him as he lay in his bath. Referring to the indictment before the Revolutionary Tribunal, she said that she had nothing to say except that she had succeeded.

To avoid disappointment and to secure a copy of the first Edition of Part I. with the beautiful 10/6 photogravure plate, intending subscribers should order from their Bookseller or Newsagent NOW. The Free Plate CANNOT be reprinted, and it is obvious that the demand will be great. See also the easy £70 prize rules Competition

Redoubt, but failed to reach our lines. North and north-east of Courcelette we made a considerable advance.

At five o'clock on the morning of the 8th the Germans launched another counter-attack against the Schwaben Redoubt, and small parties of them succeeded in penetrating our trenches, only, however, to be made prisoners. Severe fighting took place north of the Courcelette–Warlencourt road, where we gained some ground.

During the day our front south of the Ancre was heavily shelled, especially in the neighbourhood of Le Sars and Gueudecourt. South-west of the latter place we advanced our lines. Sir Douglas Haig reported that during the last two days we had taken 13 officers and 866 other ranks prisoners.

British soldiers' graves in France.

During the night our troops made progress and established posts east of Le Sars, in the direction of the Butte de Warlencourt, three miles south-west of Bapaume. At different points along our front north of the Ancre gas was discharged with good effect, after which our patrols penetrated the enemy's trenches and brought back prisoners. In the neighbourhood of Neuville St. Vaast and Loos several successful raids were carried out, many casualties being inflicted on the enemy, a number of prisoners taken, and considerable damage done to their trenches. South-east of Souchez, a strong party of Germans rushed a crater in front of our lines, from which, however, they were speedily ejected, sustaining heavy casualties in the process.

On the 9th, as the result of a local operation, we gained ground to the north of the Stuff Redoubt, inflicting serious losses on the enemy and taking over 200 prisoners, including 6 officers. In the neighbourhood of Le Transloy a party of the enemy was caught by our artillery in the open and dispersed. Now that we had reached the crest of the spur overlooking Le Transloy the Germans in that quarter could not move a step except at peril of their lives.

During the night a successful raid was carried out south-west of Givenchy, where, notwithstanding that the enemy's trenches at this point were held in considerable strength, our men succeeded in effecting an entry, bombing two dug-outs and inflicting many casualties.

At dawn on the 10th a party of German infantry, moving across open ground in the neighbourhood of Grandcourt, was "spotted" by our artillery and badly cut up. South of the Ancre the day was employed by us in further strengthening our new positions.

Our aircraft were very aggressive and successful. Our bombing aeroplanes, penetrating well behind the German lines, attacked railway-stations, trains and billets with excellent results. Two enemy battery positions were destroyed and many others damaged.

Aerial encounters were numerous, and in one instance two of our machines engaged seven hostile aeroplanes and drove down or dispersed them all. One of these enemy machines was seen to be destroyed

Wiring parties going up to the front line after heavy rain.

and two others severely damaged. Our aerial successes that day were not, however, gained without some loss, as four British machines were reported missing.

At night the enemy's artillery was unusually active on the greater part of the battle-front, and during the following day our positions south of the Ancre were heavily shelled, more particularly north of Courcelette, at the Hessian Trench, around the Stuff Redoubt, and in the neighbourhood of Flers and Gueudecourt. North of Courcelette the Germans attempted a counter-attack, but we were prepared for them, and no sooner did they show themselves above their parapets than they were caught by our barrage and so severely mauled that they were only too glad to get under cover again.

At Neuville St. Vaast the enemy attacked a crater occupied by us, but were repulsed, after suffering considerable losses from our machine-gun fire. A similar attempt near the Hohenzollern Redoubt was equally unsuccessful. During the night no incident of any importance occurred south of the Ancre. On our Flanders front the German trenches were raided at five points, in each instance with good results, a number of prisoners being captured and numerous casualties inflicted on the enemy.

About 2 p.m. in the afternoon of the 12th we delivered an attack on the low heights which intervened between our front and the Albert–Bapaume road and advanced more than 1,000 yards on a front of about a mile and a quarter west and north of Gueudecourt.

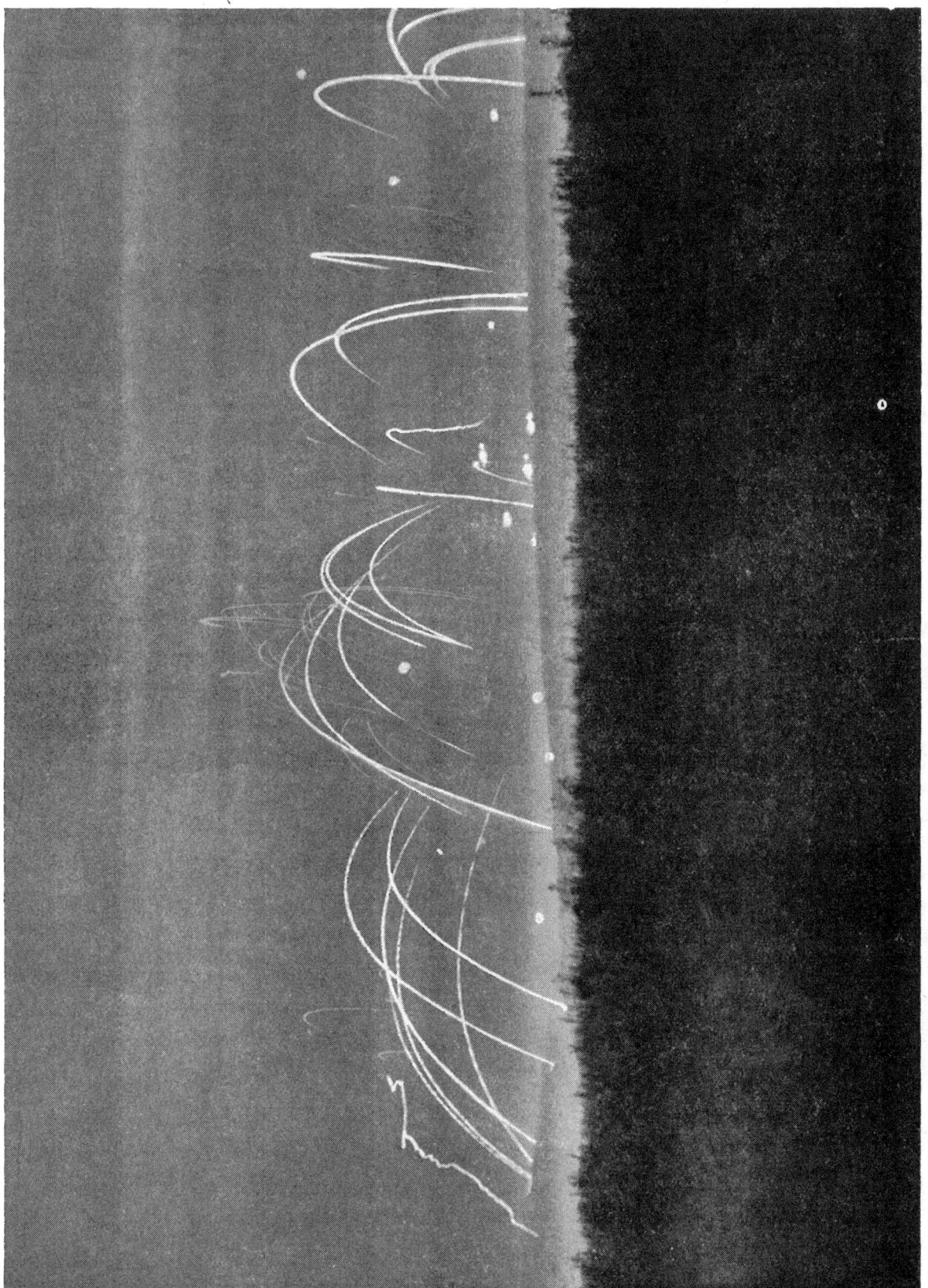

An early morning scene on the battlefield before the assault on the 15th September.

"Woodman, spare the tree." Highlanders in a wood.

Though the infantry fighting was on a comparatively small scale, the day was a colossal artillery duel.

"The size as well as the quantity of guns," writes Mr. Beach Thomas, "leaves one aghast. The biggest I have seen is a howitzer of 18-inch calibre, throwing nearly a ton of metal. A mobile gun of 12-inch calibre—itself big beyond the previous imagination of soldiers—hit a target eleven miles away. Lesser monsters, especially 9.2-inch and 8-inch, crouched here, there and everywhere.

"In front of them guns filled the slope in diminishing scale. So close were they in places, you could scarcely pass between them. . . .

"The German guns, too, multiply. They silt down from other parts of the line, and new ones come up to supply the wastage. But always we out-multiply their multiplication, and all the while our gun birth-rate exceeds our death-rate by great figures. Guns seem to spawn guns. The result is that after five minutes or less of the bombardment which precedes attack little is anywhere visible of the battle itself. The only thing that penetrates the smoke and dust is the flame of the gun and the flash of the burst."

CHAPTER X

Mr. Henry Wood, the special correspondent of the United Press of America with the French Armies, in a despatch to the Exchange Telegraph Company, estimated that the German artillery concentration on the Somme front now consisted of 850 guns facing the British, 650 facing the French north of the Somme, and 600 facing them south of the river

In a new trench.

—a total of 2,100 guns, in comparison with the 2,500 guns which were concentrated against Verdun. "Following the capture by the French and English of 500 guns since the beginning of the Somme offensive," he continues, "Allied airmen have been able to establish the fact that the Germans have adopted a systematic policy of placing their artillery at a greater distance than formerly behind the lines, for the purpose of preventing the capture of guns by surprise attacks. Their heavy guns are now placed from one to five miles behind the lines, while the average distance used to be two and a half miles. The Germans now place only one or two guns on each emplacement, instead of an entire battery, so as to reduce the losses of guns when an emplacement is captured."

The German losses during the fighting of the 12th were very heavy, and in many places, notably along the front of the Rainbow Trench, the ground is described as being "absolutely littered" with their dead. Our own casualties were comparatively light.

During the night the enemy attacked our lines north of the Stuff Redoubt, but were driven back. In the Ypres and Armentières areas we successfully raided the German trenches at more than a dozen points, taking a number of prisoners and inflicting considerable casualties.

Early on the morning of the 13th the enemy, after a bombardment, attempted a raid upon our trenches north-east of Wulverghem, but were driven back by our fire. In the course of the day there was a good deal of hostile shelling south of the Ancre, particularly in the Gueudecourt and Martinpuich areas and north of Courcelette. Otherwise, nothing of importance occurred.

On the 14th we achieved a double and highly-gratifying success north and north-east of Thiépval, where the enemy were deeply ensconced in two warrens.

Cigarette firms send the different batteries cigarettes, and the sergeant is seen receiving a packet.

The westernmost of these, the Schwaben Redoubt, was, with perhaps two exceptions, the most formidable of all the fortresses on our front, and was regarded as the innermost stronghold of the Thiépval citadel, and of that web of trenches and *fortins* woven hereabouts in and behind the old German front line. The enemy had made every sort of arrangement to strengthen the redoubt, which possessed all the complicated cellarage imaginable for storing and saving men, and to supply the garrison, who were fed by way of alleys running up the hill, from the marshes along the Ancre. Since the capture of Thiépval, the Schwaben Redoubt had been the scene of much bitter fighting, and we had been obliged to force our way almost by inches past this traverse and that block. For it was lustily defended by detachments of the 110th and 111th Regiments, and great enterprise was shown by the feeders of the garrison, notwithstanding the severe losses they frequently sustained from our artillery barrage, while making their way up the hill. The defenders fought bravely enough on this occasion, too, but our men, pushing forward

Highlanders working on the roads.

in determined fashion, close behind an intense and admirably-timed barrage, which quite cut off the enemy's reinforcements, succeeded in advancing our line well to the north and west of the redoubt and in capturing the crown of the hill. Heavy casualties were inflicted on the enemy, while our own were comparatively slight.

The assault on the Stuff Redoubt, further east, a place of less tactical importance, but also a difficult nut to crack, was another splendid piece of work, and the single company to whom the task was entrusted have to their credit as notable an individual feat as any in the war. For not only did they capture the redoubt, but cleared two lines of hostile communication trenches to the north of it for a distance of nearly 200 yards, and made prisoners of an officer and 100 other ranks. They did all this cheaply, too—more

Free soup for our Tommies. There are a lot of these around the Somme and other districts.

cheaply than anyone had imagined possible—since their total casualties were scarcely a third of the number of their prisoners. The total number of prisoners captured in both operations was just over 300.

During the night we successfully raided the German trenches west of Serre and at three points on the northern part of our front, capturing prisoners and inflicting considerable damage on the enemy's defences.

On the 15th, as a result of a successful local operation, we advanced our line slightly north-east of Gueudecourt. Between Lesbœufs and Courcellette, and also in the neighbourhood of the Schwaben Redoubt and the Ancre Valley, our lines were heavily shelled. Much successful work was carried out by our aeroplanes in conjunction with our artillery. One hostile battery position was completely destroyed and many others severely damaged; while our airmen dropped bombs upon a railway-station and upon transport moving behind the enemy's lines with excellent effect. The shelling of our positions south of the Ancre continued at intervals during the night, and the enemy also attempted a small bombing attack upon our trenches north of Courcelette, which, however, was easily repulsed.

At the Schwaben Redoubt a more important attack, delivered after heavy artillery preparation and assisted by flame-throwers, was likewise repulsed. The enemy's losses were exceedingly heavy, and nearly seventy prisoners remained in our hands. Our own losses were slight. At three points on our Flanders front the German trenches were successfully raided, a number of the enemy being killed and prisoners taken.

No infantry fighting of any importance took place on the 16th, but there was considerable artillery activity, and in the neighbourhood of Neuville St. Vaast our heavy artillery and trench-mortars carried out an organized bombardment of the enemy's lines. Good results were seen to be obtained.

The weather being fine and clear, there was great aerial activity. Our aeroplanes carried out a large number of successful reconnaissances and bombed enemy railway-lines, stations, billets, factories and depôts. Numerous fights in the air took place, in the course of which three hostile machines were destroyed, another driven to earth and many dispersed. Two enemy kite-balloons were attacked and forced down, one being afterwards seen in flames. These successes were, however, not achieved

Working on the roads.

without loss, as one British machine was brought down by anti-aircraft gunfire and six others were reported missing.

During the night we successfully raided the enemy's trenches west of Serre; otherwise, nothing of importance occurred.

On the 17th our artillery continued its bombardment of the German lines in the Neuville St. Vaast area, and also devoted considerable attention to the enemy's defences in the neighbourhood of Wytschaete and north-east of Ypres. South of the Ancre the gunners on both sides indulged in some heavy bouts of shelling. There was again a great deal of aerial activity, our aircraft carrying out three bombing raids against enemy communications, in which railway stock and buildings were damaged and a train hit and derailed. In the course of many fights in the air, four hostile machines were driven down in a damaged condition and another fell into a lake. Four of our machines failed to return to the British lines.

Rain fell heavily during the night and the early morning of the 18th, but, notwithstanding this, we made progress at various points between the Albert–Bapaume road and Lesbœufs (a front of about four miles), and extended our line north of Gueudecourt and towards the Butte de Warlencourt.

Our success was greatly facilitated by the terrific pounding to which the German positions were subjected by our artillery, which wrought such appalling havoc among the defenders of one trench that when our troops reached it there was not a man in it capable of offering the least resistance.

"Not even the troops who fought through Delville and High Woods," writes Mr. Beach Thomas, in his despatch of October 18th to the *Daily Mail*, " saw grimmer examples of the deadliness of a modern battle than the men who charged, or waded, up to a certain German trench north of Eaucourt l'Abbaye. In an earlier phase of the fight this particular ditch had been missed by our artillery, owing to a kink in the ground, and the attack against it was easily repelled. The oversight was more than made good in the early hours of this morning.

"Without warning, without the firing of so much as a registering shot, the heavy howitzers and field-guns turned their 'ghastly hail' on to this devoted line, which was strongly held, perhaps because the enemy trusted in its continued immunity. The accuracy of the fire was supreme. When the company to whom the attack was allotted reached the place where they expected to meet showers of

Some men of a navvy battalion at work on the Ancre.

bombs, and perhaps to engage in hand-to-hand fighting, they found nothing but dead bodies. They had no fighting, and they found no hale prisoners. The enemy were all dead or wounded men.

"The battle at this spot began and ended with artillery. The infantry had only—though this is much —to dig and defend, and later to bury."

Rain fell heavily during the night of the 18th–19th. Near Loos and south of Arras we successfully raided the enemy's trenches. On the rest of our front no incident of importance occurred.

On the 19th we slightly advanced our line at the Butte de Warlencourt, and an enemy counter-attack in that neighbourhood was stopped by our artillery barrage. In the evening our new positions at the Stuff and Schwaben Redoubts were heavily shelled by the enemy; while during the night we carried out two small raids against the German trenches in the Loos neighbourhood.

On the morning of the 20th, after a bombardment of our trenches, to the west of the Schwaben Redoubt, the enemy delivered a counter-attack, which, however, was repulsed with considerable loss before reaching our trenches.

Wood is used for making up the roads on the Somme. Scene in a wood.

The cook saves a large one for himself.

The Battle of the Somme

The weather being clear, much successful work was done by our aircraft. Our bombing aeroplanes raided the enemy's communications, attacking, among other points, an important railway junction and an ammunition depôt and derailing four coaches of a train. There was continuous fighting in the air, in the course of which three hostile machines were destroyed and many others driven down in a damaged condition. Two British machines were reported missing.

No incident of importance occurred during the night, but shortly before 5 a.m. the following morning, the Bavarians of the 28th Reserve Division made a determined attack in considerable force upon the Schwaben Redoubt. At all points, except two in the north-east corner, they were repulsed with loss before reaching our trenches. At these they succeeded in gaining a momentary footing; but, in the words of a Staff officer, "They were no sooner in than they were sorry for it." and a rush of our bombers up the trench cleared them out. The enemy left 5 officers and 79 men prisoners in our hands and a large number of dead in front of our lines.

About midday our troops took the offensive and advanced against the line of Regina Trench and Stuff Trench (which runs northward from the Stuff Redoubt), from the Courcelette–Pys road westward to the Schwaben Redoubt, a front of some 5,000 yards. Assisted by an excellent artillery preparation and barrage, our infantry—Canadians and troops of the New Army—carried the whole of their objectives very quickly and with remarkably little loss, and advanced our line from 300 to 500 yards, capturing the Stuff and Regina Trenches, as well as advanced posts to the north and north-east of the Schwaben Redoubt. Over 1,000 prisoners were taken in the course of the day's fighting, a figure only slightly exceeded by our casualties, which would have been much smaller, but for the resistance offered by one *fortin* garrisoned by 70 men with machine-guns. The prisoners, who were of the 28th Bavarians—the division which had suffered so heavily in counter-attacks on the Schwaben Redoubt—and the 5th Ersatz—contained an unusually large proportion of non-commissioned officers, which meant that the men had surrendered easily. Some groups of the enemy, indeed, rushed a long way out of their trenches to meet our first storming wave, shouting for mercy, with hands aloft and fingers spread. Neither party paused, our infantry pushing on to their objective without a check, while the

The snob and the cook are opponents at this game, while Tommy looks on. The man on the left made this board and chessmen himself.

Germans careered even more quickly in the opposite direction, seeking the safe harbourage of the British lines. A more bizarre scene has probably never been witnessed in modern warfare!

The night was quiet, the enemy making no attempt to recover the ground that they had lost, and the following day passed without any infantry fighting calling for mention. There was, however, considerable aerial activity. Our aeroplanes bombed two railway-stations, hitting a train in motion and doing much damage to buildings and rolling-stock. Seven hostile machines were brought down, and many others forced to land in a damaged condition. Eight of our machines failed to return to the British lines.

During the night two German raids were attempted against our trenches in the Gommecourt neighbourhood. One was stopped by our fire, from which the enemy suffered severe losses. The second succeeded in penetrating our outpost lines, but was promptly driven back by a counter-attack. South of the Ancre, our front between Le Sars and Gueudecourt was somewhat heavily shelled.

Returning from leave and nearing the old spot again.

In the afternoon of the 23rd, after waiting all through a foggy morning, in the hope of better weather, we made another successful advance on the right of our front south of the Ancre, and pushed forward our line east of Gueudecourt and Lesbœufs, capturing over 1,000 yards of hostile trenches, including one known as the "Hazy Trench," which had now changed hands five times.

There was a need to amend and simplify our own line at these points, as the stresses of the fighting had twisted and complicated it till it had grown unhandy; and there was likewise a need to amend the enemy's arrangements among the shell-holes which pitted the earth between Lesbœufs and Le Transloy, where their machine-gun positions were causing us a good deal of annoyance, and their trenches spreading from crater to crater in a way that threatened to present a most serious obstacle to our further progress in that quarter.

The difficulties with which our attacking infantry had to contend were very great, as the advance lay over ground which, blasted as it had been for weeks by gun-fire, was one mass of shell-holes, round which our men had to thread their way like persons walking on a rocky shore, and so slippery that a foothold was scarcely to be had. It was the gun positions which offered the chief problem. They were pits, groups of old shell-craters joined into one, almost impossible to see from above by scoutin airmen,

Tommy at home in his winter quarters.

Big shells for one of our guns.

and from them came a regular hailstorm of lead. But they were captured in gallant style, and the trenches as well, though not without much grim work at close quarters, particularly at a point some 400 yards beyond the north-western edge of Lesbœufs, where the 2nd Regiment of Bavarians, who had formerly defended Delville Wood so stoutly against us, faced bayonet and bomb courageously enough and littered the ground with their dead.

During the day our front in the neighbourhood of Le Sars was heavily shelled. In the afternoon the enemy massed for an attack on our trenches south of Grandcourt, but, owing to the well-directed fire of our artillery, it did not develop.

The night was quiet, with the exception of some intermittent shelling by the artillery on both sides.

Cleaning up German trenches at St. Pierre Divion.

In the early morning a strong party of the enemy raided our trenches east of Loos, apparently with the intention of destroying mine-shafts. But they were at once ejected.

During the day, which was one of drenching rain, hostilities were mainly confined to the guns, there being some heavy shelling by both sides south of Armentières, and a good deal of intermittent activity by the German artillery south of the Ancre, which continued throughout the night, particularly north-east of Courcelette and along the Pozières–Bapaume road.

Rain fell again during the greater part of the 25th, and no infantry operations were undertaken by either side, though there was a good deal of shelling, the German gunners devoting particular attention to our positions in the neighbourhood of Le Sars and Eaucourt l'Abbaye. In spite of the unfavourable weather, our aeroplanes co-operated very successfully with our artillery, and bombed many enemy billets and depôts. Three of our machines did not return to our lines.

During the night the enemy heavily bombarded our front between Eaucourt l'Abbaye and Lesbœufs and in the neighbourhood of the Stuff and Zollern Redoubts. Near Monchy, and also north-east of Arras, we successfully raided the German trenches, doing considerable damage and taking some prisoners.

On the morning of the 26th, after a bombardment, the enemy launched an attack against the Stuff Redoubt; but they were repulsed with considerable loss, our artillery proving very effective. Forty-one prisoners remained in our hands. During the day there was a good deal of hostile shelling south of the Ancre, and also in the neighbourhood of Loos and Fouquevilliers.

The German aeroplanes showed unusual activity, and an aerial engagement took place between large numbers of machines on both sides. Five machines were reported to have fallen during this fight, three German and two of our own. On another part of our front a very gallant action was performed by one of our pilots, who, encountering a formation of ten hostile aeroplanes, attacked them single-handed and dispersed them far beyond their own lines.

Bringing up big shells for our guns.

Rain fell heavily during the night. South of the Ancre the German artillery showed considerable activity, while at one point in the same area we successfully raided the enemy's trenches.

Heavy rain continued throughout the 27th, and hostilities were again confined to the guns, the German artillery operating against our positions in the neighbourhood of Beaumont-Hamel and between La Bassée and Hulluch, while our own bombarded the enemy's trenches south of Armentières. Nothing occurred during the night, with the exception of some hostile shelling in the Lesbœufs area.

On the morning of the 28th our troops advanced once more against the bewildering system of shell-craters, machine-gun emplacements and trenches to the north-east of Lesbœufs, and succeeded in carrying several important trenches; while 2 officers and 138 other ranks fell into their hands. Our artillery bombardment which preceded the attack was very effective, and the enemy, when driven from their position, were caught by our rifle-fire and suffered heavily.

This operation reflected the highest credit on the troops taking part in it, as the conditions under which it was undertaken were terrible. " If they did not ' fight upon their stumps ' as at Chevy Chase," writes Mr. Beach Thomas, " on occasion they waded in mud much beyond their knees, and not a few were

A wintry scene on the Western Front.

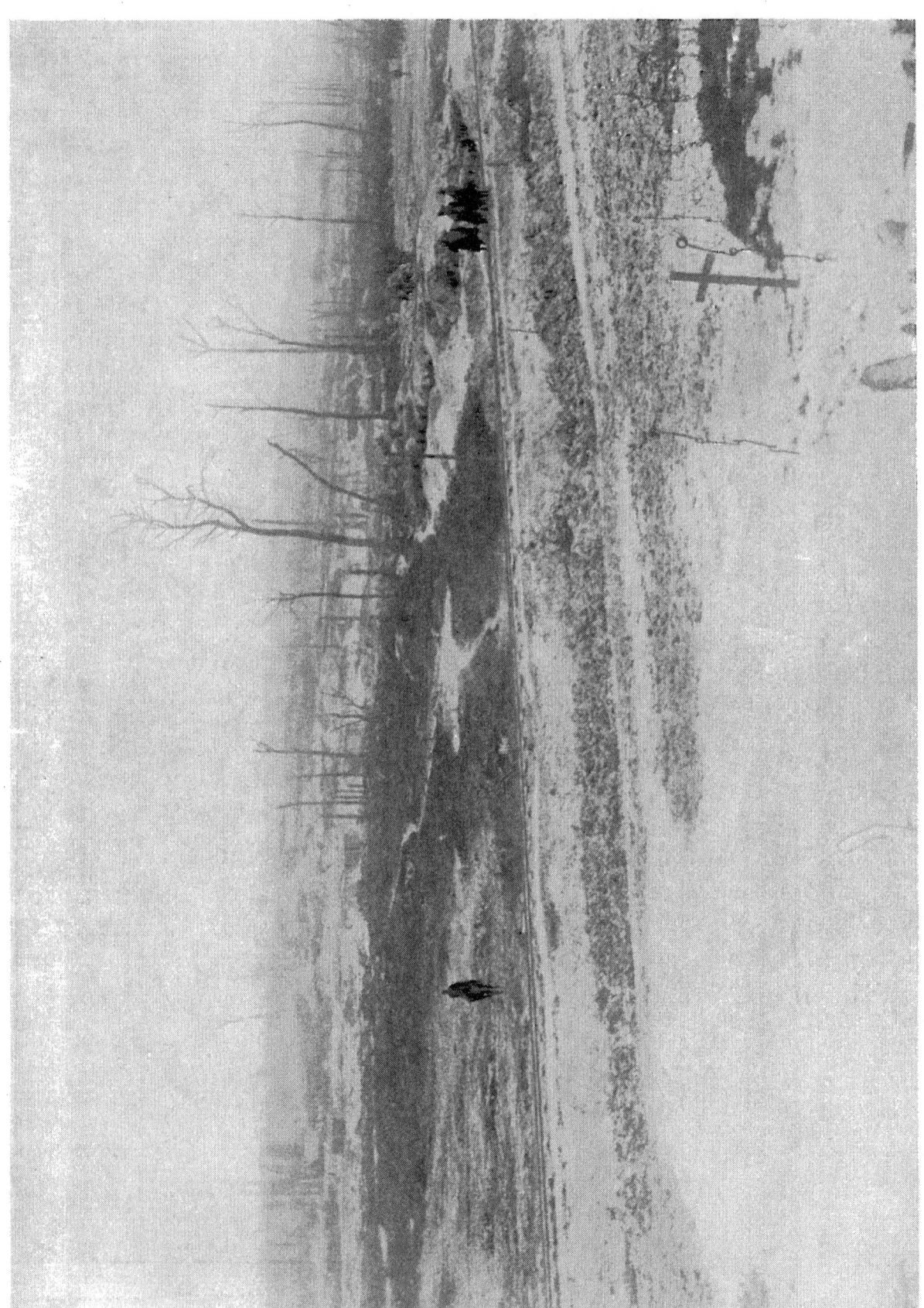

A scene on the Somme in the recent snowstorm.

only salved from foundering by their companions tugging them to firmer berths. . . . The hundred or so prisoners who waded back this afternoon were armoured with mud, and every man who returned after the walk, whether wounded or not, fell into deep sleep the instant opportunity offered, so weary were they all."

The same correspondent relates an amusing story:

" In one of these local struggles, carried through during the very foulest of the foul days, the storming party found at their goal as welcome a reward as the hot tea that greets the walking wounded at the clearing hospital. They arrived at the German trench a few minutes after the enemy's parcel-post, which was a full one. Nearly all the parcels contained food, and many of them rum. Never was an alfresco meal more thoroughly seasoned with ' Spartan sauce ' or better enjoyed. It is, after all, no bad thing that, as a means towards the maintenance of *moral*, the Germans have spent extra trouble in perfecting their postal arrangements."

During the 28th the enemy shelled the neighbourhood of Eaucourt l'Abbaye and Martinpuich, while

Boche machine-guns captured at Beaucourt-sur-Ancre.

our own artillery were active against the German front in the Gommecourt area and in several sectors further north. In spite of a strong adverse wind, much useful reconnaissance work was accomplished by our aeroplanes. One of our machines was reported missing.

Nothing of importance occurred during the night, but on the following morning we resumed the offensive north-east of Lesbœufs and captured another hostile trench. Portions of our front south of the Ancre were heavily shelled. Owing to the inclement weather, there was little aerial activity, but a German machine was seen to fall in flames.

During the night we carried out two successful raids on the enemy's trenches on our Flanders front, one west of Wytschaete, the other east of Boesinghe, taking prisoners and inflicting considerable damage. In the neighbourhood of the La Bassée Canal enemy working-parties were attacked by our bombers and suffered many casualties.

Heavy rain fell during the 30th, and no infantry operations were attempted. Our artillery bombarded Beaumont-Hamel, and there was considerable shelling in the Hébuterne and Auchy areas. The night was quiet, save for intermittent artillery activity on both sides.

On the 31st the enemy's artillery was very aggressive south of the Ancre, notably round the Stuff and Schwaben Redoubts and Regina Trench. Portions of our front in the Ypres area and at Hébuterne also came in for a good deal of attention. Our own artillery and trench-mortars bombarded the enemy's line in the neighbourhood of the Hohenzollern Redoubt and the La Bassée Canal. Our aircraft accomplished some useful work in reconnaissance and in bombing hostile batteries. One German machine was driven down in a damaged condition, and one of ours was reported missing. During the night we successfully raided the enemy's trenches north-east of Festubert and in the neighbourhood of Messines.

In the afternoon of November 1st, in conjunction with the French, we made a local attack east of Lesbœufs, where some ground was gained. Our front between Le Sars and Gueudecourt and in the neighbourhood of the Schwaben Redoubt was heavily shelled. South of Hulluch we bombarded the enemy's line with good results. West of Angres the Germans attempted a raid, but they were easily repulsed. A number of enemy batteries were successfully bombed by our aircraft. A German machine

A smashed-up mill near St. Pierre Divion.

was driven to ground in a damaged condition, and one of our own machines was reported missing. Heavy rain fell during the night, which was uneventful.

Nothing of importance occurred during the daylight hours of the 2nd, with the exception of some shelling by the artillery of either side in certain northern sectors, and the destruction of two hostile machines by our aircraft. In the evening, by a surprise attack, we captured a trench east of Gueudecourt, and consolidated our position during the night, while near Arras the German lines were successfully raided.

In the afternoon of the 3rd the enemy delivered a counter-attack against the trench east of Gueudecourt which we had captured the previous day, but it was completely repulsed. During the day our artillery and trench-mortars bombarded the German lines east of Fauquissart and in the neighbourhood of Blairville.

Our aircraft were very active throughout the day, and successfully bombed many of the enemy's billets. One of our machines attacked and destroyed a hostile aeroplane, but was, in turn, attacked and fell inside the German lines. Four others failed to return. In his reports of the 4th Sir Douglas Haig stated that: "The strong westerly winds of the past three weeks have made our aerial operations difficult, since they drift our machines far over the enemy front and compel them to return against a head wind." In

Prince Arthur of Connaught decorating a French sergeant. With him is General Fayolle, commanding 6th Army.

Prince Arthur of Connaught decorating a French General.

the same reports he announced that the German counter-attack east of Gueudecourt had suffered very heavy losses in proportion to its strength, over 100 dead having been counted, while 30 prisoners and 4 machine-guns had been captured by us.

During the night we carried out a successful raid on the enemy's lines north-east of Armentières. A strong party of Germans succeeded in entering our trenches near Cuinchy, but was at once driven out.

On the 4th there was no infantry fighting calling for mention, but a good deal of artillery activity, the German gunners directing their attention to the Lesbœufs area, Destremont Farm and Le Sars, south of the Ancre, and, on the Flanders front, to the vicinity of Ypres; while ours bombarded the enemy's lines north of the La Bassée Canal and in the neighbourhood of Bois Grenier and Messines. Heavy rain fell most of the night, during which nothing of importance occurred.

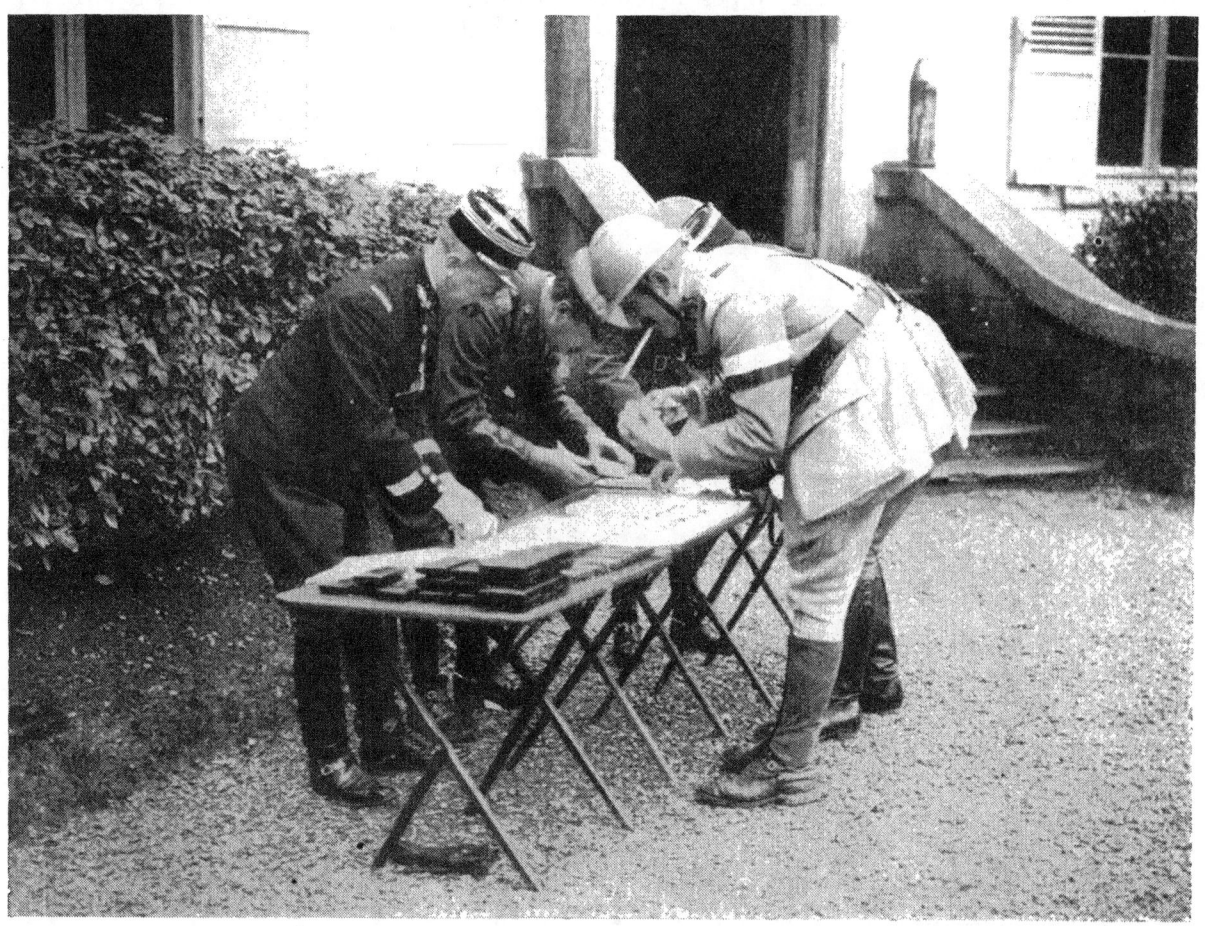

Officers laying out the decorations.

On the morning of the 5th, during a spell of fine weather, our attacks on the enemy's positions east of Lesbœufs and Gueudecourt were renewed, in conjunction with the French operations against the Sailly-Saillisel heights and St. Pierre Vaast Wood. Considerable further progress was achieved. Our footing at the crest of the Le Transloy spur was extended and secured, and the much-contested tangle of trenches at our junction with the French left at last passed definitely into our possession.

Upon the left, and thence to the Butte de Warlencourt, our fortune was not so good. The centre of the opposing line was very strongly held by troops who had recently returned to it, and were therefore comparatively fresh, and to reach it our men had to flounder across a desert of mud and shell-craters, in the face of very heavy shell and machine-gun fire. However, struggling along behind their own barrage, they reached it at last, and, after some murderous fighting, carried the position—a crumbling, zigzag ditch—with the bayonet. But a sunken road running back from the enemy's position gave the Germans the means of pouring down reinforcements under cover from observation, and our men were eventually obliged to fall back, bringing with them a number of prisoners, not a few of whom were killed on the way by the German shell-fire which was loosed upon the retiring British.

In the morning we gained a footing on the western face of the Butte de Warlencourt, a mound some 100 yards square at its foot, and perhaps 40 feet high, which the enemy had equipped with a bristling armoury of machine-guns, many in concrete emplacements; and by the middle of the afternoon, after fierce and obstinate fighting, always at the closest of quarters, we held all the western and southern sides of the Butte, and had posts in shell-holes running south-east from the south-eastern corner. But here, too, was a sunken road leading back to the German support positions; and about 4 p.m. reinforcements came pouring down this road, and our advance-posts were driven in. When darkness fell, heavy and repeated counter-attacks were launched against our positions on the Butte, which eventually obliged us to abandon the ground we had won, though not until the enemy had been made to pay a bitter price for its recovery.

Returning for more ammunition.

During the day, notwithstanding that a strong south-westerly gale was blowing, our aircraft accomplished much useful work in observing for our artillery. One machine was in the air for three hours.

At night we carried out three successful raids in the Armentières areas.

On the 6th our front between the Ancre and the Somme was heavily shelled, particularly in the neighbourhood of Lesbœufs and Le Sars. On our right we consolidated the ground we had won the previous day. Our heavies and trench-mortars successfully bombarded the German lines south of Armentières.

During the night we improved our position east of the Butte de Warlencourt, and successfully raided the enemy's trenches between Gommecourt and Serre, taking some prisoners and inflicting considerable casualties. An enemy patrol south of Monchy was dispersed by our fire.

Heavy rain fell during the 7th. South of the Ancre our front in the Lesbœufs area was somewhat heavily shelled, while our artillery bombarded the enemy's support and communication trenches in the neighbourhood of Armentières and Wytschaete. There was no infantry action.

During the night the enemy heavily bombarded our front west of Beaumont-Hamel, where an unsuccessful attempt was made to raid our trenches. On the 8th the enemy's artillery was active against our whole front south of the Ancre. Otherwise, the day was uneventful.

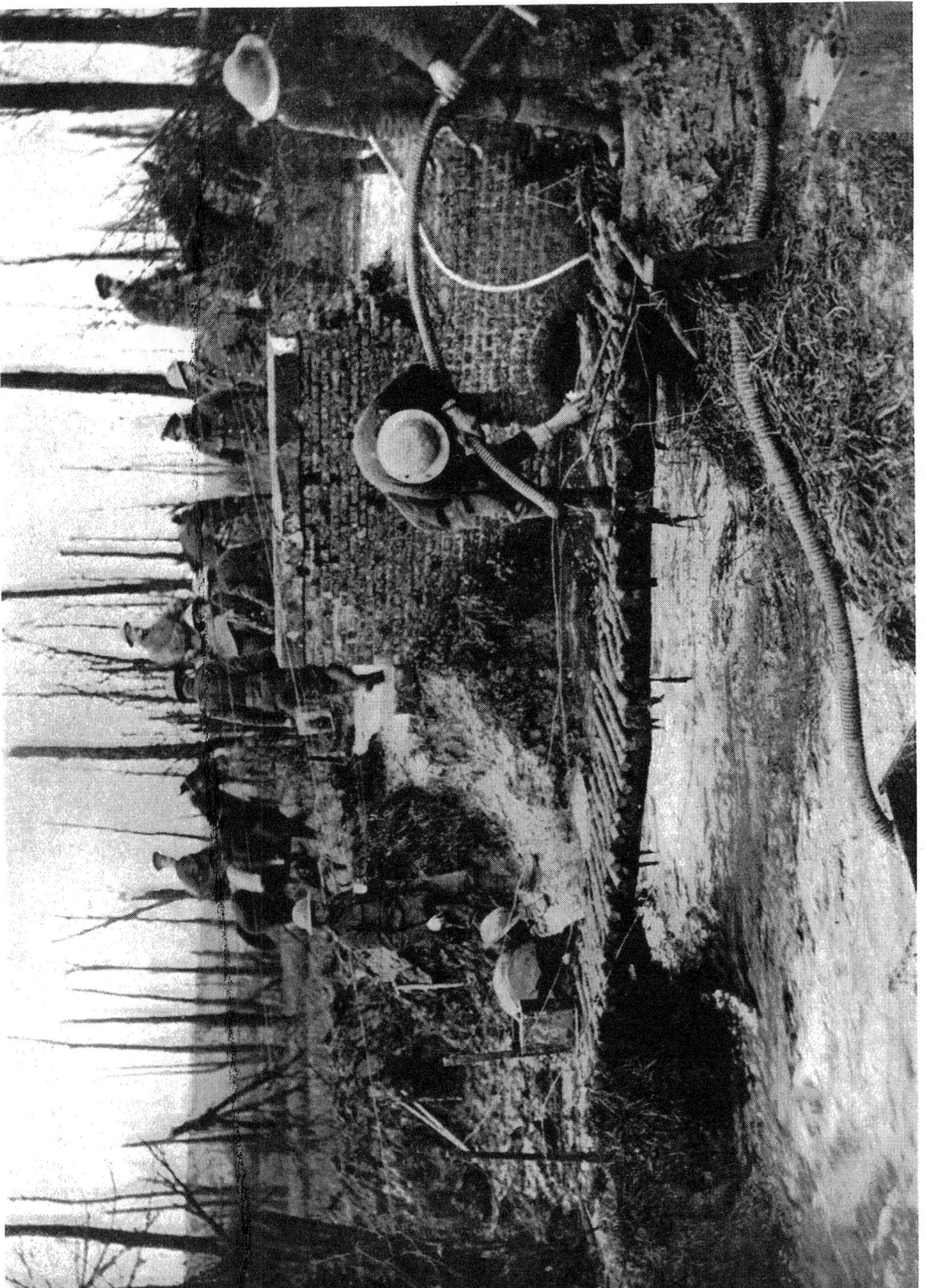

A water refilling point.

On the road to the trenches.

In the early morning of the 9th we discharged gas east of Armentières and bombed the enemy's trench-line. There were no infantry operations during the day; but, as the result of an improvement in the weather, great aerial activity prevailed and much useful work was accomplished. Our bombing aeroplanes carried out a number of raids on the enemy's communications, billets and stores, inflicting a considerable amount of damage. Air fighting was almost continuous. One of our squadrons of 30 aeroplanes encountered a hostile squadron of from 30 to 40 machines, and a regular pitched battle ensued, from an aerial point of view one of the most thrilling spectacles that has been witnessed during the War. The conflict ended in the enemy's squadron being broken up and dispersed. Six of their machines were seen to be beginning to fall out of control, but, owing to the severity of the fighting, it was not possible to watch them to the ground. As the result of other combats, nine more hostile machines were driven down in a damaged condition, of which three are known to have been destroyed.

Returning from the trenches.

A German kite-balloon was also attacked and sent down in flames. Seven British machines failed to return to our lines. During the night our artillery and trench-mortars bombarded the German front line north-east of Festubert and silenced a number of the enemy's trench-mortars which had been causing us some annoyance. There was considerable artillery activity on both banks of the Ancre, where the enemy discharged a large number of gas-shells.

We may here observe that for some time past the German gunners had been far more active by night than during the daytime. "They fear to fire by day," writes Mr. Beach Thomas, "in face of our Argus airmen, in planes or kite-balloons, and our artillery observers on the ridge. A considerable number of batteries are exclusively night-birds in certain sections of the line, and these use all manner of shells. Of course, the day shelling is considerable in places and at times, and high velocity naval shells are fired promiscuously at ranges up to fifteen miles; but where our observation is good, the lulls are wide and long by day, and our batteries often thunder unanswered. At night the duel is more equal, and the owls play their part with smaller risk, if with less effect."

The 10th was a quiet day, and, save for the usual amount of shelling by both sides, unmarked by any event of importance.

It will be remembered that in our successful advance on October 21st we had captured the western portion of the Regina Trench; but the part of it lying to the eastward of the Courcelette–Pys road still remained in the enemy's hands, and it was important to get possession of it for several reasons, one of which was that it had become a veritable hot-bed of skilful snipers, who took an unceasing toll from our positions.

Accordingly, a few minutes after midnight on the 11th our troops advanced to the attack, in the wake of a barrage which a Staff officer subsequently described as " the best barrage that we had ever put over," adding that, " as a spectacle, there was never anything like it."

" That," writes Mr. Percival Gibbon, the special correspondent of the *Daily Chronicle*, " was because it was done by night, at an hour of perfect moonshine, under a sky of black-blue, upon which the stars

Muddy mules.

were glinting needle-pricks, and the burst of the shells beyond the ridge which runs north and east from Thiépval showed white and diamond-like in that glamour of moonlight. If one could imagine some great decoration of jewels turned and shifted in the air above a thousand yards of broken, blackened ground, with the narrow, mud-clogged trench writhing through it, and the moonlight flashing back from its moving facets, winking redly or whitely upon a thousand points and edges—and all this orchestrated in the key of great gun-tones—that was the barrage!

" Of its precision, the split-second timing of it, the rigid exactitude of the lifts as it hoisted its death-zone forward in strides, those who are responsible for it speak delightedly. ' The best barrage we have ever put over, and that is saying a lot!' "

Our men, advancing behind this wonderful barrage, found the " going " bad, as might have been expected, but not nearly so difficult as it would have been had the attack been delivered a week earlier, for the winds of the last few days had somewhat dried the ground, and the brilliant moonlight made it easier for them to pick their way among the shell-holes. A heavy hostile barrage was sweeping No Man's

Moving up the guns.

Land, but, on the other hand, the enemy's machine-gun fire was much less intense than that which we had lately encountered, and the trench was reached with very few casualties. Most of its garrison had already " executed a strategic movement to the rear," or been put out of action, and those that remained offered but a tame resistance, the greater number surrendering in the approved Hun fashion as soon as our bombers began their drive along the trench. One of the prisoners remarked afterwards in an ingenuous, child-like way : " When I threw up my hands and called out, ' Good, kind enemy ; mercy, mercy ! ' your men stopped throwing bombs, and one of them patted me on the shoulder and told me to go home to your lines." A semi-official verdict given later in telegraphese contained the phrase : " Prisoners much fed up." It did not mean that they had been banqueting too freely upon delicacies sent them by their friends in the Fatherland, but merely that they had had more than their fill of the

An army chaplain helping along a Boche prisoner taken on the 23rd.

delights of trench warfare. Fifty unwounded captives who were brought into our lines in one group were quite frankly delighted at their fate.

Taking advantage of the moonlight, our airmen were very active during the attack, some of them descending to 300 feet and using their machine-guns on the enemy's troops and transport.

The enemy subsequently indulged in some pretty smart shelling of the position which they had failed to hold, and on more than one occasion our artillery had to go to work to silence the hostile batteries, which it did in every effective fashion ; and by midday the new trench had been joined up with our old line and the position secured. The remainder of the day was uneventful.

During the night gas was successfully released by us against the German salient south of Ypres. Beyond the usual artillery activity nothing of any importance occurred along the rest of our front.

The German guns were active on the 12th, particularly in the neighbourhood of Lesbœufs and Eaucourt l'Abbaye, where our positions were somewhat heavily shelled. Early in the morning and

Part XII. of "SIR DOUGLAS HAIG'S GREAT PUSH"
Will be ready on TUESDAY, MARCH 6th, 1917.

READY ON 13th MARCH.

PART I. of one of the most sumptuous and magnificently illustrated works ever published. The subject is

THE SPLENDOUR OF FRANCE

With an Introduction by EDMUND GOSSE, C.B., LL.D., Officer of the Legion of Honour, etc.

The story of a great and glorious nation, and a pictorial and authoritative record of a beautiful country, many of whose Towns and Architectural wonders have been ruthlessly ruined and destroyed by the unspeakable Prussian.

Fuller particulars will be given in the next Part.

THE WORK IS COMPLETE WITH PART XII.
Bind your Parts now, before they become damaged.

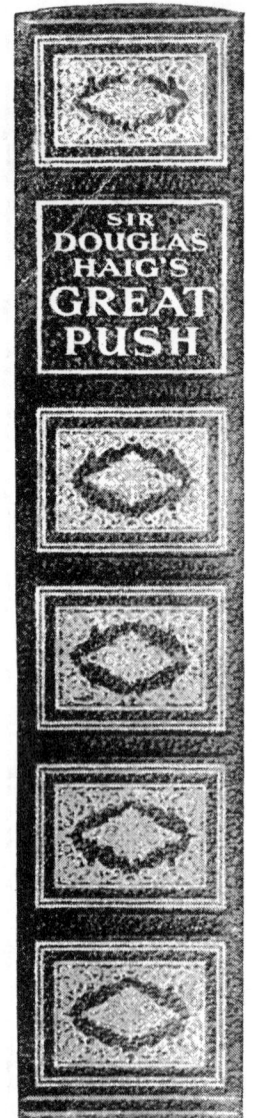

Back of Leather Cases Embossed in 22-carat English Gold.

This Design is on the Publishers' cloth case only, and is beautifully Embossed in 22-carat English Gold and will not tarnish.

A BEAUTIFULLY DESIGNED TITLE-PAGE AND LIST OF CONTENTS AND ILLUSTRATIONS WILL BE PRESENTED FREE only to those who purchase THE AUTHORISED COVERS, so remember to tell your binder to use the Publishers' Cases only.

USE THIS ORDER FORM (and be sure of securing the Beautifully Designed Title-page, etc., Free).

To...(*Bookseller* or *Newsagent*)

BINDING CASES	With 8-page Title & Contents.		
	s. d.	THESE PRICES DO NOT INCLUDE COST OF BINDING.	*Please* **bind my Parts in** the **Publishers' Cases** as marked, for which I enclose
....Red Cloth, handsomely embossed in Gold	2 0 net		
....Half Green French Morocco, lettering and ornaments in Gold ..	3 0 net		Name..
....*Half rich Red Persian Morocco, lettering and ornaments in Gold..	3 3 net		
....Full rich Red Persian Morocco, lettering and ornaments in Gold..	6 3 net		Address...
	If by Post 4d. Extra.		

Specially recommended for its handsome appearance and durability.

LONDON: HUTCHINSON & CO., PATERNOSTER ROW, E.C.

PRINTED AT THE CHAPEL RIVER PRESS, KINGSTON-ON-THAMES

ORDER PART I. (8½d.) OF "THE SPLENDOUR OF FRANCE" TO-DAY.

IN 12 FORTNIGHTLY PARTS.   PART XII. 8d. NET

SIR DOUGLAS HAIG'S
GREAT PUSH

THE BATTLE OF THE SOMME

A Beautiful 10/6 Photogravure Plate 22" × 16½" of this Picture Free to the first 50,000 purchasers of Part I 8½d

"LA MADELEINE," by J. J. HENNER.

LONDON : HUTCHINSON & Co.

HUTCHINSON'S NEW PART WORK

THE SPLENDOUR OF FRANCE

PART I.—8½d.—Now Ready, contains:
76 Illustrations on ART PAPER,
A BEAUTIFUL COLOURED PLATE and
A MAP OF FRANCE,
and a long Introduction by
EDMUND GOSSE, C.B., LL.D.,
Officer of the Legion of Honour, etc., and
F. APPLEBY HOLT, B.A., LL.B.,
commences the romantic story of PARIS
and its beautiful buildings.
**A Free Gift of a Superb 10s. 6d.
Photogravure Picture**
will be made to each of the purchasers of the
First 50,000 Copies of Part I.

Ready March 29th.

ORDER TO-DAY TO AVOID DIS- APPOINT- MENT.

Why you should Subscribe—

1	It is the most sumptuous work on our great Ally, France, ever published, and is entirely new
2	It gives all the most wonderful sights to be seen throughout France
3	The subject is the most fascinating in the world
4	Written concisely and popularly by eminent authorities
5	It is a standard work for the library and the home
6	Every page teems with romance
7	Famous paintings by the greatest artists are given
8	There are some 1,000 magnificent pictures
9	Exquisitely printed on finest English art paper
10	Many maps and plans
11	Many beautiful coloured plates
12	It is wonderful value

In three months' time you could play this at sight.

Think what it means to be able to sit down at the piano, to open a difficult and hitherto unseen piece of music, and to play it off at once without hesitation, with absolute confidence and without a wrong note. As a rule this state of proficiency is only reached after years of patient practice and study. But the THELWALL System has been worked out so scientifically that the mind is trained along certain lines and its latent faculties are brought out. One half-hour's daily study under the THELWALL System will make you a rapid and infallible sight-reader in three months, even if you only have a small knowledge of music previously. The THELWALL System, moreover, is highly approved by the leading musicians of the country, including Mr. Landon Ronald and Dr. Borland. On receipt of a 1d. stamp to cover cost of postage we will send you a Booklet, "HOW EVERY PIANIST MAY BECOME A RAPID SIGHT READER." Send your application now.

The THELWALL RAPID SYSTEM OF SIGHTREADING, Dept. 1, 30-2, Ludgate Hill, LONDON, E.C.

Those who have taken the above famous course (many thousands have), and others who can read any music by sight should not fail to take my "KEYBOARD CONTROL SYSTEM." It will give you complete mastery of the Keyboard.

My "KEYBOARD CONTROL SYSTEM" is as easy and pleasant as my famous Rapid System of Sightreading, and will teach you by your sense of touch to know exactly where every note is without looking at the Keyboard at all, and you will be able to pass from any one note to any other, no matter how far apart and whether crossing hands or not. You will be able to concentrate your eyes on the music and be sure of not striking wrong notes. Send to-day a 1d. stamp for further particulars and fees. Your whole playing will be immensely improved and you will be delighted.

The THELWALL KEYBOARD CONTROL SYSTEM

Dept. H 2, 30-32, LUDGATE HILL, LONDON, E.C.

The Battle of the Somme

again during the afternoon we discharged gas with good results against the enemy's trenches north of the Ancre.

Meanwhile, the welcome change in the weather which had set in on the 9th had encouraged us to push on our final preparations for attacking the enemy's positions on the Ancre, the only part of the original German front line of defences which still remained intact, though, as the ground was still very bad in places, Sir Douglas Haig deemed it "necessary to limit the operations to what it would be reasonably possible to consolidate and hold under the existing conditions."

"The enemy's defences in this area," he continues, "were already extremely formidable when they resisted our assault on July 1st, and the succeeding period of four months had been spent in improving and adding to them in the light of the experience he had gained in the course of our attacks further south.

Muddy wheels of an ammunition-cart.

The hamlet of St. Pierre Divion and the villages of Beaucourt-sur-Ancre and Beaumont-Hamel, like the rest of the villages forming part of the enemy's original front in this district, were evidently intended by him to form a permanent line of fortifications, while he developed his offensive elsewhere. Realizing that his position in them had become a dangerous one, the enemy had multiplied the number of his guns covering this part of his line, and at the end of October introduced an additional division on his front between Grandcourt and Hébuterne."

CHAPTER XI

At 5 a.m. on November 11th the bombardment which was to prepare the way for the attack began. It continued with bursts of terrific intensity for forty-eight hours, and then at 5.30 a.m. on the 13th came the most terrific burst of all, when along five miles of front, from east of the Schwaben Redoubt to north of Serre, a veritable tempest of shells swept the German positions, smashing their parapets—or what remained of them—to atoms, blowing up their machine-gun emplacements, and levelling with the ground the great barrier of wire entanglements that rose in front of their trenches. Eight feet high stood that barrier and 40 to 50 feet wide, made of finger-thick strands of spiky wire; and the bombardment mowed it down like grass.

For a quarter of an hour the hurricane raged, when it momentarily subsided, as the muzzles of the guns moved upwards for the barrage which was to cover our assaulting infantry, who just before six o'clock swarmed out of their trenches and advanced to the attack.

The advance began at an hour when it ought to have been light, but when, in point of fact, it was still dark. "An autumn mist, almost a sea fog," writes Mr. Beach Thomas, "swamped the dead earth.

Clearing away mud on the Somme.

The flashes of the guns were broadened to the likeness of furnace flares. The most forward observers could see no more than a second, denser, more turbid fog, where the tawny explosions of our shells broke along the German trenches. When the curtain lifted and fell farther back, nothing definite at all could be seen."

The fog served to complicate operations which were already difficult, for we were attacking both north-east and due east, and the two lines of advance had to be very nicely adjusted and timed. Tactically, the junction of the forces moving at a tangent south of the Ancre with those moving east to the north of the river was a triumph of accurate organization.

The objective positions varied in their distance from our line. The ground to be won was widest in the centre, just north of Beaumont-Hamel, and narrowest in the north; and over each sector our advancing troops, as they pushed forward through the mist, were preceded by a wall of shells, which moved deliberately over the ground in giant strides and turned it into a flaming Gehenna where nothing could live.

Feeding the guns and upsetting the Huns.

Thrashing for their own straw for the men.

The battle naturally divided itself into two parts, separated by the Ancre. South of the river, where our assault was directed north-eastwards against the northern slopes of the Thiépval ridge, it met with a success altogether remarkable for rapidity of execution and lightness of cost. " By 7.20 a.m.," writes Sir Douglas Haig, " our objectives east of St. Pierre Divion had been captured, and the Germans in and about that hamlet were hemmed in between our troops and the river. Many of the enemy were driven into their dug-outs and surrendered, and at 9 a.m. the number of prisoners was actually greater than the attacking force. St. Pierre Divion soon fell, and in this area nearly 1,400 prisoners were taken by a single division at the expense of less than 600 casualties. The rest of our forces operating south of the Ancre attained their objectives with equal completeness and success."

It is doubtful whether any engagement in the war had gained us more solid advantages at less cost.

After being rescued from the mud.

For this success we were largely indebted to the thoroughness of our previous observations of the enemy's dispositions, strength and communications. The river road—their only practicable avenue for supplies and reliefs—was peppered with shrapnel by day and night; their bridges and culverts across the Ancre were shelled continually; their machine-gun emplacements were located and treated to doses of intense fire, with the result that many of them were destroyed, and the casualties which our advancing troops suffered from the Huns' favourite weapon were very slight. And the day of the attack happened to be that on which the newly-formed 223rd Division was relieving the 38th, which had already been fifteen days in the firing-line, so that both divisions were caught on the ground and held there by our barrage; and the bombs, which our men used in great quantity, fell into crowded trenches and wrought terrible execution.

Barrage and bombs between them had knocked so much fight out of the enemy that they had no fortitude left wherewith to encounter the bayonet, and long before the cold steel was within striking distance of their ribs, their hands, to borrow the simile of a special correspondent, were going up " as freely as oars at a regatta salute." Nearly thirty officers and over 1,800 other ranks were counted in the collecting-station reserved for this part of the field before the battle was many hours old.

Even more remarkable than the attack was its sequel. On ordinary occasions, as soon as a hostile position is carried our men have to crouch down in the trench and toil in desperate haste to transfer the parapet, the while the enemy's artillery shells them more or less fiercely, and their infantry prepare to counter-attack. But nothing of the kind happened now; there was no shelling and no sign of a counter-attack developing, and, instead of toiling and sweating to strengthen the ground they had won, our men were able to consolidate at leisure, and stroll about in the open in the intervals of digging in perfect security, picking up souvenirs of the fight, and smoking German cigars from a store of full boxes which

Collecting Boche rifles left at St. Pierre Divion.

some of them had found. The explanation of this unprecedented serenity appears to have been that the country had been cleared of Germans up to the south bank of the Ancre, and that the enemy's artillery was either on the move or in ignorance that the ground had been captured.

St. Pierre Divion, from the nature of its fortifications and its situation as outflanking a series of positions on the northern bank of the river, was an important position in itself; and between it and our line lay a maze of new and old trenches, some of which were strongly held. It was here that the most strenuous fighting occurred south of the river, in which a Tank, which had preceded by some distance the advance of our infantry, rendered excellent service. The monster came to a halt on the rim of a shell-crater, and the Germans, believing it to be stuck or helpless, swarmed out of their trenches and endeavoured to destroy or capture it. But the bombs with which they attacked it made no impression on the beast's impenetrable hide, and its machine-guns had already taken a heavy toll of the assailants, when our infantry came up, drove them off, and carried the trenches from which they had emerged.

A kite-balloon about to ascend.

Cleaning up his rifle. The only way is to wash the woodwork.

Tommies going up to the trenches.

The Battle of the Somme

The struggle north of the river was more severe. Here we had to cross a two-year-old system of trenches, and the operations were more adversely affected by the fog than those on the southern bank. Keeping direction and making junction were harder manœuvres, and the ground was so pitted with shell-holes and so undermined by hiding-places, that the triumphant advance of one wave of men did not necessarily involve the success of the waves which followed it, and battalions pushing forward side by side met with very different fortunes.

Nevertheless, highly satisfactory results were achieved. Beaumont-Hamel, which, even before the Great Push began, a foreign military critic had declared we should never succeed in taking, and where our gallant troops had suffered so costly a repulse on July 1st—the "impregnable" Beaumont-Hamel—

Resting in their cage. Boche prisoners taken on the 13th in St. Pierre Divion.

was carried almost at a single rush, a rush that took our troops across the village and out to the sloping ground beyond, where the road to Beaucourt winds downwards to the Ancre. Then, pushing forward up the broad swell of hill that rises between Beaucourt and Serre, they stormed all the German positions, until they had established themselves well up on the side, where they dug themselves in, in the face of some heavy shelling.

At these points the attacks appear to have had all the success of a surprise. The German front-line trenches, pulped into shapelessness by our fire, were very weakly held, and, indeed, the attacking troops met with no very serious opposition until they reached the fourth line of defence, where the Germans who had hurriedly retreated from the advanced positions along the communication trenches had gathered to reinforce its original occupants. But a gallant rush by our bombers, who slammed their deadly missiles down into the overcrowded trenches with murderous effect, took much of the heart out of the Huns, and in a few minutes they were surrendering on all sides. Among the captives was a Prussian *unter-offizier*, who had been one of the first to appeal for mercy, but who, as soon as he had satisfied himself that there was no intention of killing him—a matter about which he would appear to have been more than a little doubtful—set to work to organize his men into stretcher parties to carry back the wounded to our lines. They accomplished their journey without loss, for happily the enemy's shelling was not severe, and the machine-guns in this quarter were mostly silent.

Of the unfortunate little village of Beaumont-Hamel, which for five months had been the target of our vast artillery, not so much as a house, or even the remains of one, was left standing; the very bricks had been pounded to dust by the frightful shelling to which the place had been subjected. But under it, twenty or thirty feet below the surface, a new village had come into being. Here, as at Ovillers, Thiépval and other places along the German front, was a labyrinth of dug-outs, where men could shelter safe from

Once a trench, but now a small river.

the greatest shell that ever stabbed the earth into a crater, and emerge at the right moment to man the trenches against our advancing infantry. Some 600 prisoners were collected out of these vaults and sent to join their captive comrades above. On the north—opposite Serre—the ground was so heavy that it became necessary to abandon the attack at an early stage, although, in spite of all difficulties, our men had succeeded in places in reaching the German trenches.

The troops attacking close to the right bank of the Ancre met with better fortune, and reached their second objective during the morning, where they held on for the remainder of the day and night, though practically isolated from the rest of our attacking force. "Their tenacity," wrote Sir Douglas Haig, "was of the utmost value and contributed very largely to the success of the operations."

The troops of whom Sir Douglas Haig speaks so highly formed part of the Naval Division, which had already greatly distinguished itself at Antwerp and in Gallipoli.

The line the sailors held, and from which they advanced to the attack, extended from the Ancre northwards to just below Beaucourt, and their objectives included the sprawling maze of trenches

A corner of the great heap of bombs and stores left by the Germans when they were driven out of St. Pierre Divion.

Field kitchens on the Western Front.

and communications and machine-gun redoubts which the Germans had constructed in this sector, and the village of Beaucourt itself. The ground over which and towards which they had to advance rose in the centre to a ridge, which was steepest on the river side, and on the slope of this, and actually behind the German first line, stood a redoubt bristling with machine-guns, commanding the forward and northern slope of the ridge.

"Accounts vary," writes Mr. Perceval Gibbon, "as to how many machine-guns this one redoubt alone turned loose upon the attackers. Their fire swayed to and fro like searchlight beams. Nothing could live within the focus of it."

On the left, our men were held up by a driving sleet of bullets, but the troops on the right pushed forward, with an exposed flank, under the lee of the steeper slope. Their leader, a colonel commanding

A message for the Hun.

one of the battalions, already known for an adventurous career of his own choosing, had been wounded in the first rush over the parapet and again not long afterwards. But he had seen many battles in many different parts of the world, and he had no intention of missing the great adventure for the sake of a couple of wounds, more painful than serious. And so he held the attack together and pushed steadily on across more than a mile of ground swept by shell and machine-gun fire and barred by a maze of defences, until he found himself with some 400 or 500 men occupying a line of trenches and shell-holes at least a thousand yards in front of the troops who had been held up by the redoubt and within striking distance of Beaucourt village.

Our position at nightfall on the northern bank of the Ancre is thus described by Sir Douglas Haig:

"Our troops were established on the northern outskirts of Beaucourt, in touch with our forces south of the river, and held a line along the station road from the Ancre towards Beaumont-Hamel, where we occupied the village. Further north the enemy's first-line system for a distance of about half a mile beyond Beaumont-Hamel was also in our hands."

In the course of the day's operations some 4,000 prisoners had been taken. Mr. Beach Thomas, who met a thousand or so of them on their way to the "cages" in rear of our lines, was struck with their comparative cleanliness and with the curious pallor of their faces, which appeared to indicate that they had seen little sunshine or even daylight. "It is, indeed, I believe, literally true," he writes, "that dug-out existence, coupled with the fear of movement by day, has bleached a great part of the German Army."

Throughout the day's fighting our infantry displayed the most splendid dash and resolution. As was the case on July 1st, the battle was almost wholly confined to home troops, and the English county regiments had a large share in the triumph. The artillery, too, was admirable, in spite of the exceeding

The mill at Beaucourt-sur-Ancre.

difficulty of firing without observation. For, owing to the misty weather, no aeroplanes or kite-balloons could be employed and the artillery-observers were nearly useless. The co-operation with the infantry was excellent, nevertheless, and though here and there the latter found themselves dangerously close to the barrage, this was attributable rather to excess of eagerness on their part than to any miscalculation on that of our gunners.

The battlefield was one of the strangest and most novel in history. "Fiction," writes the special correspondent of the *Daily Mail*, "is quite baffled by fact at every turn. The men who stormed the positions north of the river and along it might have been advancing over roofs in a street fight. Underneath them were rooms upon rooms containing hidden and unsuspected groups, and down in the street-trenches below—some nearly empty, some crowded—the enemy lifted their hands and shouted for mercy or occasionally fired into the air. The battlefield is still unsearched or unplumbed. Pockets of men, dumps of stores, reserves of weapons lie hidden here, there and everywhere. . . . The scale of these hiding-places

The observer of a kite-balloon testing the telephone before ascending.

A scene on the Ancre.

is on that of a town of many streets and well-cellared houses. Seven hundred prisoners, all together in one row, were clean passed by in our first advance."

But the crowning marvel of the German subterranean defences lay on the south side of the Ancre, at St. Pierre Divion, which was the site of a remarkable underground labyrinth which our Intelligence officers christened "The Tunnel."

A very interesting description of this extraordinary place is given by Mr. Perceval Gibbon, in his despatch of November 14th to the *Daily Chronicle*:

"The village stands—or stood when it was yet a village—upon a shelf of upland above the little brook Ancre; and below it the ground broke towards the stream in 'the short, dry cough of a cliff.'

"A perpendicular bank of clay, some twenty feet high, showed towards the water-meadows on the

Sending a message to the Hun.

riverside, and into this the industrious German had burrowed wonderfully. His trenches were on the lip of the bank, and under them he had burrowed a vast refuge, whose plan resembles, roughly, a capital T.

"The stem of the T is a gallery 300 yards long, fully eight feet high and four feet wide, neatly timbered in, traversed in methodical zigzags, in order to increase its proportions without adding to its strength, from end to end.

"From the main galleries there branch minor passages, leading to the chambers, where beds and bunks are fitted, and where an enormous deposit of various stores has been discovered. Some of these chambers aim so close to luxury that the walls are even papered. Along the main galleries are innumerable shelves, crowded with stores and provisions, and hooks with bundles hanging from them.

"The labyrinth is connected with the trenches above by broad flights of steps. The whole is so deep that it is not only proof to the impact of the largest shell, but the very barrage is inaudible from its chambers.

"Hither, when the squall of shelling burst over the trenches, the garrison could be hurried below, to sit under a roof of twenty feet of earth, like deep-buried corpses; then, when the barrage had jumped, and the attack was coming forward, they could be resurrected and hustled up the broad stairways to man their parapets.

"And here, when the Intelligence officers came to explore, was the chief treasure. The electric light system had been disconnected when our exploring party arrived; the search and examination had to be carried out with torches.

"They searched the length of the stem of the T, marking its many exits to the river bank, where men, driven back from the water's edge, could duck into holes in the bank like water-rats, to emerge still whole and dangerous a couple of hundred yards away.

Watering Canadian artillery horses at the front

"A noisome smell pervaded the place that was not at first to be accounted for. It proved to be from quantities of *kriegsbrot*, the war-bread, which the Germans make out of potato and flour and other matters.

"The electric pocket-torches of the explorers flashed here and there, till at length they found what they had been looking for. Here, twenty feet deep and scores of yards in, was the stuff—the gallery was a mine of machine-guns.

"They had been driven from their squatting places in the open by the thrash of our shells, and carried hither for safety. It is probable that the plan was to bring them up at the critical moment and fling back the attack with them, but our barrage prevented that."

The night of the 13th–14th was employed by our troops in consolidating the ground won without any interference from the enemy in the way of counter-attacks, though the sailors who lay before Beaucourt had to endure some sharp shelling, in the course of which their intrepid commander received two further

A scene on the roadside.

One of our armoured petrol engines.

wounds, though happily they were only slight. Under cover of the darkness, small detachments pushed up on the right to reinforce them, while three machine-guns were also sent to their aid. Even so, they formed but a slender force; while many of them were wounded and the majority worn out by their exertions of the previous day. Nevertheless early on the following morning, in the cold and darkness of the hour before dawn, their commander, carrying his four wounds, led them forward to the assault of the village.

The Germans who occupied the ruins of the place stood their ground with stubborn courage, and a desperate hand-to-hand fight ensued—so desperate that, after it was over, Briton and German were found in more than one instance lying side by side, each transfixed by the other's bayonet. But the sailors and their comrades were not to be denied, and Beaucourt was stormed and occupied throughout its length and breadth in less than twenty minutes.

Meanwhile, on the left, a Tank had advanced against the redoubt which was holding up the advance in that quarter. Closer and closer it crawled, the enemy's bullets rebounding harmlessly from its steel

A busy scene at a watering-point for horses.

sides, while the Germans watched its approach with astonishment and dismay. At last, when it was within a hundred yards of the fortress and was preparing to rake it with its machine-guns, they prudently decided that further resistance to the monster would only be to court destruction, and a pole with a white rag attached to it was thrust out of a loophole in the redoubt, in token of surrender.

This obstacle to their advance removed, the Naval battalions on the left pushed resolutely forward, and by the evening our line had been extended in a north-westerly direction along the Beaucourt road across the southern end of the spur just north of Beaumont-Hamel.

By that time the number of prisoners had risen to over 5,000. They were from the 12th, 38th, 58th, the newly-formed 223rd and the 2nd Guards Reserve Division, and included men from all parts of Germany: Prussians, Westphalians, Würtembergers, Saxons, Bavarians and Silesians. "Pocketfuls" were coming in all day, marshalled along the roads by cavalry scouts, who rode to and fro until their horses were tired out, following a leisurely infantryman, or riding in ramshackle wagons, with bound-up heads and slung arms. The biggest haul came from "Y" ravine south of Beaumont-Hamel, where the 700 warriors who had been overlooked by our men in their first advance, and had been waiting patiently ever since for some one to come and fetch them, gave themselves up in the course of the afternoon.

Some of the material collected by parties detailed to clear up the battlefield.

A singular incident occurred at a spot north of the Ancre. Some 400 Germans surrendered to a party of less than a score of our men, the officer in command of them being at that time in ignorance of the small number of his captors. When he discovered it, he shouted to his men to pick up the rifles they had thrown down; but a well-aimed bullet dropped him stone-dead, and the "mutiny" was promptly quelled.

Among the enemy's stores captured by us were some suggestive discoveries. In one lot of machine-gun belts every twentieth bullet was explosive—a real explosive bullet, like a miniature shell. A machine-gunner who was found in possession of this diabolical pattern of ammunition explained that it was only intended for use against aeroplanes; but there can be no doubt that, in times of stress, if not always in infantry fighting, the belts would be run through the guns just the same.

Our losses during the two days' fighting were, on the whole, slight—very slight, indeed, in comparison with the important results achieved. They varied inversely with the depth of the "going." South of the river quite two-thirds of the total casualties, which were inconsiderable, were light wounds, "stretcher-cases" being few. North of the river they were heavier, some few units, who met machine-gun fire and had to compass the mud, suffering severely.

In the course of the 14th there was sharp fighting east of the Butte de Warlencourt, where we advanced our front some distance and captured 80 prisoners.

After dark ten of our machines carried out a bombing raid upon enemy stations and rolling stock, in the course of which two bombs were dropped upon a moving train, which was brought to a standstill.

The night and the following day were employed by our troops north of the Ancre in consolidating the ground they had won, the enemy making no attempt to counter-attack either here or south of the river. The weather being now more favourable for aerial work, our bombing aeroplanes carried out several successful raids behind the German lines, and there was also some fighting over the front, in the course of which a hostile machine was driven down in a damaged condition. During the night of the 15th–16th our positions both north and south of the Ancre were somewhat heavily shelled.

On the 16th we resumed the offensive north of the Ancre and extended our line eastwards from Beaucourt towards Grandcourt, on the opposite bank of the stream. Our new positions on both sides of the Ancre received a good deal of attention from the German artillery, particularly in the vicinity of Beaucourt, while our front between Le Sars and Gueudecourt was also smartly shelled. Our own artillery responded vigorously and caused several explosions behind the German lines, while their positions in the Armentières and Souchez areas were also effectively bombarded.

East of the Butte de Warlencourt a strong enemy counter-attack, pressed home with real courage and determination by the Prussian Guard, obliged us, after some fierce fighting, to relinquish part of the ground we had won on the 14th.

Much successful work was carried out by our aeroplanes. Two important railway junctions were attacked with bombs, at one of which six coaches were blown off the line and two of the station buildings destroyed; and bombs were also dropped on railways, billets and aerodromes. The enemy's aeroplanes showed more enterprise than usual, and suffered heavily for it, 3 of their machines being brought down behind our lines and 2 behind the German front, while at least 5 others were driven to ground in a damaged condition. Three British machines were reported missing.

During the night there was heavy hostile shelling against Beaucourt and Beaumont-Hamel.

On the 17th nothing occurred along our new front on the Ancre, except intermittent hostile shelling, which was heaviest in the neighbourhood of Beaucourt. Our own guns heavily bombarded the German positions on both sides of the river, and aerial observers reported that our fire had caused great damage. The enemy's lines in the Loos and Hulluch areas were also severely shelled.

Smoke-bomb just exploded.

The weather is very bitter in France. Note the frost on the trees

A great deal of fighting took place in the air. In one particular combat between 5 of our aeroplanes and 8 of the enemy, a German machine was destroyed and the rest dispersed. In other encounters 7 hostile machines were driven down damaged. Three of our machines failed to return to our lines.

In his reports that day Sir Douglas Haig announced that the prisoners taken since the 13th had now reached a total of 6,190.

During the night we successfully raided an enemy redoubt north of Ypres, taking 20 prisoners and a machine-gun.

About 6 a.m. on the 18th—a snowy, dark, miserable morning—we resumed our offensive on both banks of the Ancre. The attack was preceded by a fierce burst of shelling from our artillery. But, as these bursts frequently occurred without being followed by any infantry advance, the Germans along

General Gourard visits a school of instruction for officers.

a great part of their line hardly appeared to have realized that an attack was in progress, until parties of British and Canadian bombers had sprinted across the open and were hurling their deadly missiles amongst them. The result was that success came quickly—more quickly, perhaps, than in any attack on a large scale that we had yet made.

On the southern bank of the Ancre our troops, attacking from the base of Regina and Stuff trenches, on a line more or less parallel with the river, penetrated into the western outskirts of Grandcourt village; while on the extreme right we captured the high ground due south of Miraumont, which lies on the northern bank of the stream, from which point patrols pushed forward towards the village and returned with prisoners.

A simultaneous and yet separate attack on a smaller scale was made north of the river, where, on the northern cliff and along the road in the valley, we succeeded in forcing our way right up against what may be called the second German system of defence.

The enemy fought stubbornly on the outskirts of Grandcourt and on the north of the northern advance, and here we sustained a good many casualties; but where our success was quickest it was singularly bloodless.

The prisoners taken amounted to 20 officers and 752 other ranks. They were, for the most part, Hessians and Saxons; the former fine, well-built men, the latter of poor physical quality.

Thus, in six days' fighting, just at the moment when the Germans had convinced themselves that the weather had rendered a fresh offensive out of the question and that the British advance was over for the year, our indomitable troops had stormed the huge fortress system of Beaumont-Hamel, Beaucaire and St. Pierre Divion, had gained a firm footing in the outskirts of the strongly-fortified village of Grandcourt, and had carried the height dominating Miraumont, the largest of all the villages in this quarter.

A scene on the Ancre.

The ground captured was more formidably fortified and larger in extent than that secured in the first week of the Somme offensive and over 7,000 prisoners had fallen into our hands.

Winter, which interrupts Victory and gives Defeat a respite, was now at hand, and during the rest of the year no further forward movement was attempted by us. Our guns, however, were proof against the arresting power of Nature, and day and night they still thundered across the wintry wastes, never resting, and never allowing the Germans to rest. Whenever the weather permitted, our aircraft co-operated with the artillery in their usual effective manner, and carried out successful bombing raids behind the German lines. A particularly successful raid took place on the night of November 20th–21st, when enemy railway stations, billets and transport were attacked with bombs and machine-gun fire, and much damage done. One of our aeroplanes dropped three bombs from a height of 500 feet upon a number of German lorries, which missed their mark. Whereupon the machine turned, flew over the lorries again, and dropped three

A scene on the Ancre.

A scene on the Ancre.

more bombs, this time right into the middle of them; after which, turning again, it swooped down to within 150 feet of the enemy and fired upon them with its machine-gun. A month later (December 20th), a number of successful raids were carried out, in the course of which a ton of explosives is officially stated to have been dropped on points of military importance behind the German lines.

At times a good deal of fighting took place in the air, in which our aviators continued to show a great superiority over the enemy. On November 22nd a number of German aeroplanes ventured to cross our line, but were at once attacked and chased home again, three being captured, while a fourth was driven to ground behind the enemy line. The following day, 12 of our machines encountered a hostile squadron

Bringing in a wounded Canadian through the mud.

of 20 aeroplanes, which they routed and dispersed. One German machine was destroyed and several others driven down in a damaged condition. All our own machines returned safely.

From the Ancre to beyond Ypres raids upon the German trenches, of which some 360 had been carried out between the beginning of July and the middle of November, continued to be of almost daily—or rather nightly—occurrence, and besides inflicting many casualties upon the enemy and causing much damage to their defences, contributed to keep them in a constant state of alarm.

The most successful of these enterprises appears to have been a daylight raid carried out by the Canadians on the German trenches north of Arras on December 20th. The Canadian Official gives the following account of this dashing affair:

" The raid was made in the early afternoon, while the low winter sun was still shining. Kinematograph films were obtained within a short distance of the attack. At the appointed hour our artillery barrage opened with a sudden crash. Dense clouds of smoke were also liberated, isolating the area of attack. Little resistance was met with in crossing No Man's Land. The German garrison were seeking shelter from our avalanche of shells in their deep dug-outs. A number of bombers at one point attempted resistance, but these were quickly disposed of, and the survivors sent back as prisoners.

"Swiftly our men went about their allotted tasks. Special attention was paid to the dug-outs, from which many Germans came out to surrender. Bombs and igniting explosives were thrown inside, destroying and setting on fire the wooden supports. Many of the enemy were killed, and fifty-eight prisoners, including two officers, were captured and taken back to our lines. Our own casualties were remarkably slight. We remained in possession of the German trenches for over two hours before withdrawing."

A German gun after our artillery got through with it. On ground captured by the Canadians.

Another very effective raid was carried out by a party of New Zealanders a couple of nights later, in which over 50 of the enemy were killed and wounded and nine prisoners taken. Engineers who accompanied the raiders blew up a powerful pump, with which the enemy had been endeavouring to drain their trenches, at this point waist-deep in water, and also destroyed a section of tramway behind the German lines.

Although the heavy autumn rains had prevented full advantage from being taken of the favourable situation created by our advance, at a time when we had good grounds for hoping that we were on the eve of securing yet more important successes, by the third week in November the three main objects with which we had commenced our offensive had already been achieved: Verdun had been relieved; the main German forces had been held on the Western Front; and the enemy's strength had been very considerably worn down.

Serviceable winter clothing for our troops.

"Any one of these three results," writes Sir Douglas Haig, "is in itself sufficient to justify the Somme battle. The attainment of all three of them affords ample compensation for the splendid efforts of our troops and for the sacrifices made by ourselves and our Allies. They have brought us a long step forward towards the final victory of the Allied cause. . . .

"The total number of prisoners taken by us in the Somme battle between the 1st of July and the 18th of November is just over 38,000, including over 800 officers. During the same period we captured 29 heavy guns, 96 field-guns and field-howitzers, 136 trench-mortars and 514 machine-guns.

"So far as these results are due to the action of the British forces, they have been obtained by troops

Two smiling Canadians at their rest billets with German helmets.

the vast majority of whom had been raised and trained during the war. Many of them, especially amongst the drafts sent to replace wastage, counted their service by months, and gained in the Somme battle their first experience of war. We were compelled either to use hastily-trained and inexperienced officers and men, or else to defer the offensive until we had trained them. In the latter case, we should have failed our Allies. That these troops should have accomplished so much under such conditions, and against an army and a nation whose chief concern for so many years had been preparation for war, constitutes a feat to which the history of our nation records no equal. The difficulties and hardships cheerfully overcome, and the endurance, determination and invincible courage shown in meeting them, can hardly be imagined by those who have not had personal experience of the battle, even though they have themselves seen something of war."

THE END

SEE PAGE 4 OF THIS COVER

POSTPONED OWING TO THE HEAVY DEMAND UNTIL
THURSDAY, 29th MARCH.

PART I. of one of the most sumptuous and magnificently illustrated works ever published. The title is

THE SPLENDOUR OF FRANCE

With an Introduction by EDMUND GOSSE, C.B., LL.D.,
Officer of the Legion of Honour, etc.

The story of a great and glorious nation, and a pictorial and authoritative record of a beautiful country, many of whose Towns and Architectural wonders have been ruthlessly ruined and destroyed by the unspeakable Prussian.

P.T.O.

The WORK IS COMPLETE WITH THIS PART
Bind your Parts now, before they become damaged.

Back of Leather Cases Embossed in 22-carat English Gold.

This Design is on the Publishers' cloth case only, and is beautifully Embossed in 22-carat English Gold and will not tarnish.

A BEAUTIFULLY DESIGNED TITLE-PAGE AND LIST OF CONTENTS AND ILLUSTRATIONS WILL BE PRESENTED FREE only to those who purchase THE AUTHORISED COVERS, so remember to tell your binder to use the Publishers' Cases only.

USE THIS ORDER FORM (and be sure of securing the Beautifully Designed Title-page, etc., Free).

To..(Bookseller or Newsagent)

BINDING CASES	With 8-page Title & Contents. s. d.	THESE PRICES DO NOT INCLUDE COST OF BINDING.
....Red Cloth, handsomely embossed in Gold	2 0 net	
....Half Green French Morocco, lettering and ornaments in Gold	3 0 net	
....*Half rich Red Persian Morocco, lettering and ornaments in Gold..	3 3 net	
....Full rich Red Persian Morocco, lettering and ornaments in Gold..	6 3 net	
If by Post 4d. Extra.		

Specially recommended for its handsome appearance and durability.

Please **bind my Parts in the Publishers' Cases** as marked, for which I enclose

Name..

Address..

....

LONDON : HUTCHINSON & CO., PATERNOSTER ROW, E.C.

INDEX

HISTORICAL INTRODUCTION

The War by Land

	PAGE
AFRICA	9
Africa, German East	9
Africa, German South-West	9, 14
Africa, South	10
Africa, Western	16
Aisne, The	9
Antwerp	9
Artois, The	13, 14
Asia Minor	16
Auberive	15
Aubers ridge, The	10
Augustovo	6
Austria	14
BÉTHUNE-LA BASSÉE canal	9
Bialystok	14
Binche	3
Bois Grenier	13, 15
Boulogne	9
Brussels	3, 5
Bukovina	16
Bulgaria	15, 16
CALAIS	9
Cameroons, The	9, 16
Champagne	15
Charleroi	3, 5
Condé	3
Czernowitz	16
DUAL MONARCHY, The	16
EGYPT	10, 13
Erzerum	16
FESTUBERT	13
Frankenau	6
Frezenberg ridge, The	13
GALICIA	6
Gallipoli Peninsula	13
George, Mr. Lloyd	14
Germany	3
Givenchy	15
Great Britain	3, 14
Greece	16
Grodno	14
Gumbinnen	6
HAVRE	9
Hill 60	10
ISONZO, The	14
Italy	14
Ivangorod	14
KAISER, The	3
Khedive Abbas II.	10
Kiao-chau	9
Kovel	14
Kovno	14
Kum Kale	13
Kut-el-Amara	16
LA BASSÉE	9, 15
Landrecies	6
Le Cateau	6
Lemberg	6, 14
Liége	3
Loos	15
MARNE	6, 9
Maroilles	6
Mesopotamia	16
Mons	3, 5
Munitions, Ministry of	14
NAMUR	3, 5
Narev	6
Neuve Chapelle	10, 15, 16
New Pomerania	9
PERSIAN GULF	10
Poland	6, 10
Prussia, East	6
Przemysl	14
RUSSIA	3, 15, 16
SALONIKA	16
Sambre, The	3, 5
Samoa	9
San, The	14
Serbia	15, 16
Serbia, King of	16
Suez Canal, The	13
TAHURE	15
Tannenberg	6
Togoland	9
Tsingtau	9, 10
Turkey	10
VERDUN	16
Vimy heights, The	15
WARSAW	10, 14
Windhoek	14
YPRES	9, 13, 14, 15, 16

Troops Engaged and Generals in Command

	PAGE
ALLENBY, MAJOR-GENERAL	3
Allies, The	6, 9, 14, 16
Australians, The	9
Austria, Armies of	6
BELGIAN Army	5
Beyers (South African rebel leader)	10
Blues, The	13
Botha, General Louis	10, 14
British Expeditionary Force, The first (two army corps and one cavalry division)	3, 5, 6, 9
2nd Corps	6
6th Division	9
8th Brigade	13
1st Army	15
Buelow, General von	5
CANADIANS, The	13, 16
Central Powers, The	10, 15, 16
DE WET (South African rebel leader)	10
Essex Yeomanry, The	13
FRENCH Army, The:	
5th	3, 5, 6
10th	15
French, Field-Marshal Sir John	3, 5
GERMANS, The	9, 10, 16
HAIG, SIR DOUGLAS	3
Hamilton, Sir Ian	13
Hansen, General von	5
Hindenburg, Field-Marshal General von	6, 10
Hussars, 10th	13
INDIA, Force from	10
Italians, The	14
KEIR, MAJOR-GENERAL	9
Kluck, General von	5, 6, 9
MACKENSEN, FIELD-MARSHAL GENERAL VON	14
Maritz (South African rebel leader)	10
NEW ZEALANDERS, The	9
Nicholas of Russia, The Grand Duke	14
RUSSIANS, The	6, 14, 16
Russian mobilization	10
SERBIANS, The	16
Smith-Dorrien, General Sir Horace	3, 6
South African rebellion	10
TOWNSHEND, GENERAL	16
Turks, The	13, 16

The War by Sea

	PAGE
Coronel	10
Falkland Islands	10
Heligoland Bight	6
Kitchener, Lord, Death of	16
Jutland	16
Orkneys, The	16

Names of Ships and Admirals in Command of Fleets Engaged

	PAGE
British naval force (Dardanelles)	13
Cradock, Admiral	10
Dardanelles, The	13, 14
French naval force (Dardanelles)	13
Good Hope, H.M.S.	10
Hampshire (cruiser)	16
Köln, The (German cruiser)	6
Lusitania, The	13
Mainz, The (German cruiser)	6
Monmouth, H.M.S.	10
Narrows, The	13
Spee, Admiral von	10
Sturdee, Admiral	10

Index

THE BATTLE OF THE SOMME

Place Names and Descriptions of Actions

Acid Drop Copse . . 90
Albert Cathedral . . 41
Albert-Bapaume road 125, 213, 298, 325, 330, 337
Amiens 24
Ancre, The 39, 53, 66, 73, 74, 77, 81, 98, 158, 177, 193, 197, 200, 225, 241, 246, 249, 250, 253, 266, 313, 325, 329, 330, 334, 336, 337, 342, 345, 346, 349, 350, 353, 354, 357, 361, 362, 365, 366, 369, 370, 373, 377, 382, 383, 385, 389
Ancre Valley, The . 50, 336
Angle Wood . . . 253
Angres . . . 31, 350
Antwerp 370
Anzac 145
Armentières 28, 74, 141, 142, 185, 205, 206, 249, 266, 325, 334, 345, 346, 353, 354, 357, 383
Arras 39, 185, 193, 201, 206, 249, 265, 306, 325, 338, 346, 350, 389
Artois 19
Auchy . 80, 186, 245, 349
Authuille . . 53, 54, 58

Bailiff Wood . . . 106
Bapaume 39, 158, 246, 306, 314, 328, 329
Bapaume road 136, 149, 161, 190, 194, 201, 294
Bazentin-le-Grand 36, 85, 106, 118, 125, 130, 162, 250
Bazentin-le-Petit 118, 125, 162, 181, 185, 210, 226, 230, 233, 245, 250
Bazentin-le-Petit Wood 125, 126, 130, 133, 185, 202
Bazentin-Longueval line . 145
Bean, Capt. (Australian Press representative) 141, 149
Beaucaire . . . 386
Beaucourt-sur-Ancre 361, 369, 370, 373, 378, 381, 383
Beaumont-Hamel 53, 54, 346, 349, 354, 361, 362, 369, 370, 373, 374, 381, 383, 386
Bécourt Wood . . . 185
Bellewaarde Lake . . 200
Bernafay Wood . 77, 94, 118
Béthune . . . 198, 246
Blairville 350
Boesinghe . . . 349
Bois des Foureaux (High Wood) 125, 130, 145, 154, 170, 177, 182, 194, 200, 202, 209, 210, 213, 218, 225, 226, 230, 246, 249, 250, 266, 278, 281, 285, 338

Bois des Trônes 94, 97, 101, 102, 105, 110, 114, 117, 118, 129, 149, 178, 182, 198, 201, 262
Bois Grenier . . 197, 353
Bouleaux Wood . 278, 294
Bray-sur-Somme . 36, 39
Butte de Warlencourt 329, 337, 338, 353, 354, 382, 383

Cabaret Rouge . . 205
Calais 24
Calonne 205
Cambrai . . . 64, 93
Carency . . . 24, 197
Caterpillar Wood . . 185
Champagne . . . 19
Combles 94, 265, 298, 301, 310, 313, 318
Contalmaison 53, 70, 77, 81, 85, 86, 89, 90, 101, 106, 109, 110, 114, 117, 161, 162, 217, 226, 234
Cordonnerie . . . 206
Courcelette 177, 182, 193, 209, 229, 230, 265, 266, 278, 285, 286, 290, 294, 298, 313, 322, 329, 330, 334, 336, 345
Courcelette-Pys road . 341, 358
Courcelette-Thiépval road . 245
Courcelette - Warlencourt road 329
Crucifix trench . . 46
Cuinchy . . . 137, 353

"Danzig Avenue" (German trench) . . . 44
Delville Wood (Devil's Wood) 125, 126, 129, 137, 138, 145, 149, 165, 166, 170, 173, 174, 178, 182, 185, 206, 213, 218, 238, 245, 246, 270, 338, 345
Destremont Farm . 314, 353
Douai 64

Eaucourt l'Abbaye 310, 313, 318, 321, 322, 325, 338, 345, 346, 349, 360

Fabeckgraben trench (Courcelette) . . . 286
Falfemont Farm 261, 262, 265
Fauquissart . . . 350
Festubert . . 77, 350, 357
Flanders 36, 246, 330, 337, 349, 353
Flanders front, The . . 101
Flers 278, 285, 289, 294, 297, 310, 318, 330,
Flers line, The . . 281
Fouquevilliers . . 346
Frégicourt Wood . . 298
Fricourt 23, 36, 41, 44, 45, 46, 64, 65, 66, 70, 81, 85, 217
Fricourt ridge . . . 117
Fricourt Wood . 65, 185

Gallipoli . 145, 274, 370
Gibbon, Percival (*Daily Chronicle*) . 358, 373, 377
Gibbs, Philip (*Daily Chronicle*) 40, 57, 69, 118, 149, 166, 190, 209, 217, 226, 237, 262, 273, 278, 286, 309, 318
Ginchy 213, 246, 249, 253, 261, 265, 266, 269, 270, 273, 274, 277, 278, 281, 294
Givenchy 98, 185, 226, 265, 266, 330
Givenchy-en-Gohelle . . 23
Gommecourt 23, 50, 54, 94, 342, 349, 354
Grandcourt 294, 330, 345, 361, 383, 385, 386
Gueudecourt 302, 313, 318, 322, 325, 329, 330, 334, 336, 337, 342, 350, 353, 383
Guillemont 36, 129, 138, 149, 154, 178, 198, 200, 205, 209, 210, 218, 221, 229, 241, 246, 249, 253, 254, 257, 258, 261, 262, 265, 269, 274, 278
Guillemont quarry . . 230
Guillemont station . . 230

Hairpin Crater . . 177
Hamel 226
Hardecourt . . . 137
"Hazy Trench" . . 342
Hébuterne 50, 117, 349, 350, 361
Hessian trench 314, 317, 318, 322, 330
High Wood. See Bois des Foureaux.
Hill 160 (Pozières plateau) 161, 186, 194
Hohenzollern Redoubt 74, 93, 114, 178, 205, 233, 265, 286, 330, 350
Hooge . . . 101, 193
Hulluch 77, 80, 93, 185, 200, 201, 205, 206, 226, 346, 350, 383

"Intermediate Trench" (Martinpuich), The . 249

La Bassée . . 233, 346
La Bassée Canal 77, 117, 198, 265, 266, 349, 350, 353
La Boiselle 23, 41, 42, 53, 66, 69, 70, 73, 77, 81, 85, 134
La Boiselle Wood . . 69
La Folie Farm (Vimy ridge) 205, 206
La Targette . . . 24
Laventie 322
Le Plantin . . . 226
Le Sars 314, 318, 321, 322, 325, 328, 329, 342, 345, 350, 353, 354, 383
Le Sars Mill . . . 328

Le Transloy 322, 325, 329, 342, 353
Le Transloy-Bapaume road 281
Leipzig Redoubt 81, 145, 146, 190, 198, 213
Leipzig salient . . 229, 233
Lesbœufs 294, 298, 317, 325, 328, 336, 337, 342, 345, 346, 349, 350, 353, 354, 360
Leuze Wood 262, 265, 266, 278
Liberté, The 24, 102, 110, 161, 301
Ligny 230
Lille . . . 50, 321
Lille-Paris trunk line . . 73
Longueval 23, 36, 118, 122, 125, 129, 130, 133, 137, 138, 145, 154, 162, 165, 166, 170, 173, 174, 185, 200, 213, 246
Loos 23, 36, 74, 77, 80, 85, 114, 186, 193, 197, 198, 200, 201, 209, 226, 325, 329, 338, 345, 346, 383
Loos salient . . 177, 185

"Machine - gun House" (Longueval) . . . 170
Mailly 226
Maltzorn Farm . . 178, 185
Mametz 36, 39, 41, 44, 58, 64, 77, 200, 217
Mametz Wood 66, 90, 97, 101, 105, 106, 114, 117, 129, 185, 186, 206, 245, 250
Marne, The . . 81, 85
Martinpuich 39, 194, 202, 210, 214, 217, 229, 249, 278, 285, 286, 289, 294, 297, 298, 313, 334, 349
Maurepas . . 209, 241
Messines . . . 350, 353
Miraumont 193, 246, 385, 386
Monchy . . . 346, 354
Mons 274
Montauban 23, 36, 46, 48, 49, 64, 77, 81, 101
Montauban-Guillemont road 241
Montauban ridge . 117, 145
Morval . 294, 298, 318, 325
Mouquet 306
Mouquet Farm 206, 209, 213, 226, 229, 245, 246, 249, 253, 262, 265, 266, 278, 294, 298, 305
Mouquet stream . . 190
Mounault Farm . . 205

Neuve Chapelle 24, 170, 205, 265, 318
Neuville-St. Vaast 23, 93, 177, 197, 202, 249, 318, 322, 329, 330, 337

Ovillers 53, 54, 73, 81, 82, 97, 98, 130, 133, 136, 137, 149, 182, 209, 213, 370

Index

	PAGE
Paris	24
Pearl Wood	118
Pendant Copse	50
Péronne	49, 94
Petit Parisien, The	302
Picardy	97, 166, 229
Plevna	54
Polygon Wood	265
Pozières	23, 36, 106, 130, 137, 149, 154, 157, 158, 161, 162, 165, 174, 177, 181, 182, 185, 193, 194, 197, 198, 200, 201, 202, 205, 206, 209, 213, 214, 217, 221, 222, 226, 229, 234, 246, 265, 266
Pozières-Bapaume road	222, 278, 345
Pozières-Bazentin-le-Petit line	165
Pozières-Guillemont section	129
Pozières mill	194, 217, 222
Pozières-Miraumont road	229
Pozières ridge, The	89, 200, 202, 217, 229
Puits 14 bis	177
Pys	230
Quadrilateral, The (trenches)	294
Rainbow trench	333
Regina trench	322, 341, 350, 358, 385
Richebourg l'Avoué	265, 266
Rochincourt	93, 198
Roye	50
Sailly-Saillisel	325, 353
Schwaben Redoubt	305, 310, 313, 314, 318, 325, 328, 329, 334, 336, 337, 338, 341, 350, 361
Serre	50, 336, 337, 354, 361, 369, 370
Shelter Wood	46, 89
Somme, The	23, 35, 36, 66, 73, 74, 77, 98, 162, 177, 178, 193, 197, 200, 225, 249, 250, 266, 333, 354
Somme Valley, The	89
Souchez	173, 185, 193, 198, 266, 329, 383
St. Eloi	186, 193, 197, 325
St. Pierre Divion	313, 361, 365, 366, 377, 386
St. Pierre Vaast Wood	353
Stuff Redoubt	305, 310, 317, 318, 329, 330, 334, 336, 338, 341, 346, 350
Stuff trench	341, 385
Suvla Bay	274
Tangle Redoubt	328
Thiépval	23, 36, 41, 54, 57, 74, 77, 80, 81, 117, 145, 154, 161, 185, 190, 209, 210, 213, 222, 226, 229, 230, 233, 234, 241, 246, 250, 265, 278, 294, 298,

	PAGE
Thiépval—continued. 305, 306, 310, 313, 314, 317, 318, 325, 334, 370
Thiépval ridge	305, 310, 313, 358, 365
Thiépval Wood	246
Thomas, Beach (Daily Mail) 80, 157, 174, 197, 221, 233, 238, 258, 293, 306, 325, 333, 338, 346, 357, 362, 374
Vailly	23
Valenciennes	85, 93
Verdun	27, 36, 154, 229, 333, 390
Vermelles-La Bassée road	31
Verstraat-Wytschaete road	206
Vimy	209, 325
Warlencourt	230
Warren, The	46, 48
Wartelot Farm	133, 138, 178
Wedge Wood	261, 262
Wieltje	23
Wood, Henry (United Press of America)	333
Wulverghem	334
Wunder Werk (Thiépval)	278, 294
Wytschaete	23, 117, 137, 337, 349, 354
"Y" ravine	381
Ypres	24, 85, 117, 177, 202, 206, 265, 290, 318, 334, 337, 350, 353, 360, 385, 389
Ypres-Commines canal	206
Ypres-Commines road	186
Ypres-Menin road	23
Ypres-Pilkem road	158
Ypres salient	200, 245, 250
Yser Canal, The	200
Yser, The	23
Ytres	314
Zollern Redoubt	305, 306, 322, 346
Zollerngraben trench (Courcelette)	286
Zwartelen	198

Troops Engaged and Officers Specially Mentioned

	PAGE
Anzacs (Australians—Gallipoli campaigners)	28, 30, 98, 149, 150, 153, 158
Australians	141, 142, 149, 150, 153, 154, 157, 158, 189, 190, 194, 201, 214, 217, 249, 253, 254, 262, 290, 317
Baden, Men of	58, 65
Batten-Pooll, Lieut. A. H., V.C.	30
Bavarians	58, 130, 153, 158, 194, 205, 249, 266, 270, 285

	PAGE
Bavarian Divisions:	
2nd	286
6th	321
Bavarian Reserve Divisions:	
2nd	381
28th	341
Bavarian Regiments:	
2nd	345
6th	145
16th	136
16th, 2nd-3rd Battalion	137
16th, 3rd Battalion	136
122nd	109
190th	145
Bedfords	39, 46
Below, General von	194
Borderers	54
Brandenburgers	173
5th Brandenburg Division	170
Buffs	39
British Corps and Divisions:	
Fourth Army	305, 325
Canadians	177, 290, 341, 389
Bombers	385
Coldstream Guards	289
Cornish regiments	278
Deccan Horse	126
Devonshire regiments	278
Dorsets	54, 58
Dragoon Guards	126
Dublins	254, 269, 270, 273
East Yorkshires	39
Engineers, Royal	42
English county regiments	374
English troops	105, 214, 218, 229, 238, 253, 254, 257
French, The	27, 89, 178, 209, 210, 217, 241, 253, 261, 298, 301, 325, 350, 353
Fusiliers, Royal	39
German Corps, Divisions and Regiments:	
Army, 2nd	86
Reserve Corps:	
9th, 17th and 18th Divisions	190
14th	65
Divisions:	
5th Ersatz	341
12th	381
19th	270
38th	365, 381
58th	381
223rd	365, 381
Battalions, Ersatz, or Reserve	190
Regiments:	
110th	334
111th	334
133rd	229
Regiments, Ersatz, or Reserve	328

	PAGE
German General Staff	86
Gloucestershire regiments	278
Gordon Highlanders	44, 58
Grenadier Guards	289
Haig, Sir Douglas	20, 23, 31, 42, 74, 98, 110, 118, 133, 136, 138, 145, 182, 246, 278, 281, 282, 294, 301, 302, 313, 314, 317, 325, 329, 350, 361, 365, 370, 373, 385, 392
Hampshires	39
Hessians	386
Highland Light Infantry	31, 54, 77
Highland troops	138
Home County battalions	46
Irish, The	254, 257, 269, 270, 273, 274, 278
Irish Brigade	270
Irish Fusiliers, Royal	114, 254
Irish Guards	289, 290
Irish Rifles	269
Kent battalion (New Army)	189, 190, 278
Kumme, Lieut.-Col.	137
Lancashire Fusiliers	39
Lancashire troops	46, 50, 53, 85
Lincolns	53
London Scottish	39
London Territorial battalions	149, 153, 158, 290, 318, 325
Manchesters	39, 44, 54
Marine Artillery, Royal	40
Munster Fusiliers, Royal	30, 31, 177, 254, 269, 273, 274
Naval Division	370, 378, 381
New Army (British)	341
New Zealanders, The	98, 290, 297, 390
North-country troops	85, 134
Prussians	28, 58, 122, 254, 369, 381
Prussian Guards	237, 241, 242, 262, 281, 383
3rd Division	85, 86, 89, 93, 134, 161
1st Regiment Reserve	253
2nd Regiment, 2nd Battalion	86
2nd Regiment, 3rd Battalion	86
9th Regiment, 10th Battalion	86
Prussian Regiments:	
29th	221
123rd	221
127th	221
186th	70
Rifle Brigade	74

	PAGE		PAGE		PAGE		PAGE
Saxon troops 28, 194, 381, 386		Westphalians . . , 381		Aeroplanes (German)—cont.		Douai aerodrome . . 93	
Scots, Royal . . . 54		Wiltshires 234, 237, 241, 242, 245		245, 246, 261, 265, 266, 277,			
Scottish regiments . . 278		Worcesters 40, 234, 237, 241, 242		293, 297, 310, 318, 322, 330,		Ginchy 222	
Scottish troops 122, 214, 229, 238		Würtembergers . 306, 381		337, 341, 342, 346, 349, 350,		Grandcourt . . . 182	
Seaforth Highlanders . . 114		180th Würtembergers . 306		357, 383, 385, 389			
Sherwood Foresters . . 74				Fokkers . 35, 64, 129, 146		High Wood. See Bois des Foureaux.	
Silesians . . . 381		Yorkshire troops . 46, 181		Airmen (British) 35, 64, 66, 93,			
South Africans 129, 138, 290				129, 146, 174, 177, 193, 205,			
South-country troops . 310		**Aerial Operations**		250, 261, 265, 266, 277, 293,		Kite-balloons (British) . 23,	
South Midland troops . 218				297, 310, 318, 325, 336, 342,		64, 97, 357	
Suffolks 39		Aeroplanes (British) 23, 32, 35,		346, 357, 360, 389		Kite-balloons (German) 35, 174,	
Surrey battalion (New Army)		41, 61, 64, 66, 73, 77, 93, 97,		Airmen (German) 66, 157, 198,		261, 310, 322, 337, 357	
189, 190, 278		98, 101, 117, 126, 129, 145,		250, 261, 277			
Sussex, The . . . 118		146, 165, 170, 181, 185, 186,		Albert 73		Lille-Paris trunk line . 73	
Sussex battalion (New Army)		193, 197, 198, 201, 206, 210,					
189, 190, 200		222, 226, 230, 241, 245, 246,		Balloons (German) 23, 64, 157,			
		261, 265, 266, 293, 297, 302,		226		Mons 202	
Ulster battalions . . 53		313, 314, 318, 322, 328, 330,		Bapaume . . . 77, 170			
		336, 337, 341, 342, 345, 346,		Bois des Foureaux (High		Namur 202	
Warwicks . . 213, 214		349, 350, 354, 357, 382, 383,		Wood) . . . 218, 221			
Warwickshire regiments . 278		385, 386, 389		Brussels, Zeppelin sheds at . 202		Royal Flying Corps 101, 162,	
Welsh Fusiliers, Royal 39, 77		Aeroplanes (German) 23, 35, 64,		Busigny railway station . 202		181, 182, 202, 206, 265	
Welsh regiments . . 278		66, 73, 98, 101, 117, 129, 145,					
Welsh troops . 102, 105		146, 157, 170, 174, 177, 181,		Combles 73		St. Quentin . . . 73	
West-country troops . . 265		182, 185, 186, 193, 198, 201,		Courtrai railway station . 202			
West Kent Regiment . . 120		206, 210, 218, 226, 230, 241,		Cumines 73		Ypres 73	

ERRATA

Page 15.—Legend: for " the battlefield," read " parade."

,, 21.—Legends: top left-hand, for " stretcher-bearers," read " Lewis gun team drawing Lewis gun carts." Top right-hand, for " baggage," read " ammunition." Bottom left-hand, after " motor-cyclist," read " carrying a basket of carrier pigeons."

,, 31.—Second Legend: for " Army Medical Corps," read " regimental stretcher-bearers."

,, 218.—Legend: for " Captured German howitzer," read " German attraction gun."

,, 230.—First line of text: for " Warlincourt," read " Warlencourt."

www.ingramcontent.com/pod-product-compliance
Lightning Source LLC
Chambersburg PA
CBHW082005220426
43670CB00014B/2557